THE ONLY WAY OUT

The Racial and Sexual Performance of Escape

KATHERINE BREWER BALL

Duke University Press   Durham and London   2024

© 2024 Duke University Press
All rights reserved

Project Editor: Bird Williams
Designed by Aimee C. Harrison
Typeset in Portrait Text and Ouroboras (designed by
Ariel Martín Pérez) by Copperline Book Services

Library of Congress Cataloging-in-Publication Data
Names: Brewer Ball, Katherine, author.
Title: The only way out : the racial & sexual performance of
escape / Katherine Brewer Ball.
Other titles: Only way out : the racial and sexual performance
of escape
Description: Durham : Duke University Press, 2024. | Includes
bibliographical references and index.
Identifiers: LCCN 2023037212 (print)
LCCN 2023037213 (ebook)
ISBN 9781478030270 (paperback)
ISBN 9781478026044 (hardcover)
ISBN 9781478059271 (ebook)
Subjects: LCSH: Escape in literature. | Race in literature. |
American fiction—History and criticism. | Escape (Psychology)—
United States. | African American arts. | Performing arts—Social
aspects—United States. | Queer theory. | BISAC: PERFORMING
ARTS / Theater / History & Criticism | LITERARY CRITICISM /
Semiotics & Theory
Classification: LCC PS374.E8 B74 2024 (print)
LCC PS374.E8 (ebook)
DDC 813/.6—dc23/eng/20231205
LC record available at https://lccn.loc.gov/2023037212
LC ebook record available at https://lccn.loc.gov/2023037213

Cover art: Suzanne Wright, detail from *Galactic Gloryhole Series*.
Courtesy of the artist.

Contents

vii		Acknowledgments
1		*Escape is Such a Thankful Word*: An Introduction
31	1	The Repetitions of Henry "Box" Brown
67	2	Feeling Out of This World: *That's What I Guess These Stories Are About*
96	3	The Optics of Escape: Patty Hearst through the Mouth of Sharon Hayes
129	4	*This Face Is Not for Us*: Grounding Pleasure
157		Coda: Less of a Theater Audience
169		Notes
187		Bibliography
201		Index

Acknowledgments

Thank you goes first to José Esteban Muñoz. The ideas for this book were born under your tutelage, in the spaces of fantasy and deep care for the worlds of performance and pleasure. This is not the last thing I will write for you. And to Ann Pellegrini, I am grateful to you for introducing me to the world of Tony Kushner and showing me how to cruise the Sappho section of the bookshop. You taught me how to read queerly, in detail, and with great panache. Thank you to Tavia Nyong'o, Karen Shimakawa, Barbara Browning, and Heather Love for your guidance and brilliance during my time as a graduate student in the halls of New York University. The generosity of my colleagues at Wesleyan University has been consistantly heart-warming. I am lucky to have had the pleasure of workshopping parts of this book with Margot Weiss, J. Kēhaulani Kauanui, Mary-Jane Rubenstein, Demertius Eudell, Ronald Jenkins, Marcela Oteíza, Nicole Stanton, Matthew Garrett, Lisa Cohen, Axelle Karera, Abbie Boggs, Douglas Martin, Christina Crosby, Benjamin Haber, Ren Ellis Neyra, and Victoria Pitts-Taylor. Thanks go also to Wesleyan University's Center for the Humanities, especially the fellowship of Natasha Korda, Ethan Kleinberg, Ulrich Plass, Rashida Shaw McMahon, Catherine Quan Damman, Roger Matthew Grant, and Heather Vermeulen. Thank you to my comrades at New York University, Joshua Lubin-Levy, Joshua Chambers-Letson, Julia

Steinmetz, Daniel Dinero, Summer Kim Lee, Jonathan Mulliins, anna watkins fisher, Fisher, Alex Pittman, Sujay Pandit, Aniko Szucs, Sandra Ruiz, and James Brashear. Having brilliant artist scholars as fellow graduate students kept me on my toes and taught me how to always keep one foot in the world of practice. This book also greatly benefited over the years from friendly encouragement and readings by the Sexual Politics/Sexual Poetics Collective: Damon Young, Amber Jamilla Musser, Ramzi Fawaz, Zakiyyah Iman Jackson, Uri McMillan, Jennifer Row, Kadji Amin, Roy Pérez, Shanté Paradigm Smalls, and Jordan Stein. Your support and challenges in the early stages of this project were invaluable.

I am grateful to my kind and generous editor, Courtney Berger, and the folks at Duke University Press. And many thanks to my friends and family at home: Svetlana Kitto, Morgan Bassichis, Jordy Rosenberg, Sacha Yanow, Asher Pandjiris, R. J. Messineo, Jaime Shearn Coan, Ethan Philbrick, Amelia Bande, K-Sue Park, Cass Peterson, Jibz Cameron, Hedia Maron, Gwen Bialic, Linda Y. Brewer, Joel Ball, Sophie Robinson, Ella Leith, Will Rawls, Tourmaline, Nicholas Weist, Dori Midnight, Britt Rusert, Vick Quezada, and Noémie Solomon. Your artistic provocations inspire me daily. And finally, all the gratitude and love I could possibly speak into this world and the next goes to my forever collaborator and coconspirator: Fancy Fizzgig Pyewacket.

> We like a Hairbreadth 'scape / It tingles in the Mind / Far after Act or Accident / Like paragraphs of Wind // If we had ventured less / The Breeze were not so fine / That reaches to our utmost Hair / Its Tentacles divine.
>
> —**Emily Dickinson**

> But his imagination is wild and extravagant, escapes incessantly from every restraint of reason and taste, and, in the course of its vagaries, leaves a tract of thought as incoherent and eccentric, as is the course of a meteor through the sky.
>
> —**Thomas Jefferson**

ESCAPE IS SUCH A THANKFUL WORD

An Introduction

The word *escape* is wide open, "its tentacles divine," as Emily Dickinson writes. Seductive and sensorial, the promise of escape reaches out its many fingers and holds tight to its audience. A northern white woman at the end of the nineteenth century longing for elsewhere, Dickinson describes the sensual story of escape, the story of a narrow passage out of danger. Invoking her beloved Shakespeare's *Othello*, she recounts escape as that which lingers, "tingles" erotic. The promise of escape's death-defying run-in with capture drifts on the wind and flows through Dickinson's hair far after the tale graces the lips of Othello himself. In her poem, she ventriloquizes Othello's account to an enthralled Desdemona. "Wherein I spoke of most disastrous chances, / Of moving accidents by flood and field, / Of hair-breadth 'scapes i' th' imminent deadly breach, / Of being taken by the insolent foe / And sold to slavery, of my redemption thence."[1] Dickinson repeats Othello's "hair-breadth 'scapes" in her breathy rhyme. Dickinson's "we" invokes a collective Desdemona mouthing in echo of the words of Othello. Her repetition of these two words, as Páraic Finnerty observes, "invokes an entire scene and mood" borrowed from Othello.[2] And while the slavery in Shakespeare's verse does not reflect a nineteenth-century American understanding of racial slavery, the Amherst, Massachusetts, of 1872 in which Dickinson writes was not far from its reach.

I begin with Dickinson's poem on the "hairbreadth 'scape" to consider the fantasy that escape holds for its white readers. Dickinson writes during the Civil War, from within the white literary appeal of Elizabethans, and in proximal reach of the nearby abolitionist legacies by Sojourner Truth, William Lloyd Garrison, and Frederick Douglass. Dickinson did not speak out on the topic of slavery; in fact, as Benjamin Friedlander notes, in some of her work it "appears to have served, perversely, as her inspiration."[3] Dickinson is not alone among white writers in her "perverse" move to use slavery and Blackness as a mode of thinking creatively or naming desire. This "perverse" erotic desire is in fact quite typical of whiteness in the United States. And while I am not particularly interested in lingering in the words of Dickinson or Thomas Jefferson here—to whose escape fantasies I shall return—Dickinson provides a starting point to trace the American narrative of escape, the white tentacles that hold the term and the Black narrative work which, "overwhelmed by the persistence of the specter of captivity," to quote poet Dionne Brand, continue to imagine escape and freedom's (im)possibility.[4]

The Only Way Out is interested in the stories of escape, the white fantasies built into its spectacular retelling, as well as the always already alternate ways in which Black queer artists and thinkers mobilize the work of escape. My intentions are not to tell you something about Black life or radicality, nor to theorize or render comprehensive a Black world for the reader, but instead to consider the ways in which narratives of liberation, resistance, and change have been and might be told. I pay particular attention to the ways in which these narratives are always already racialized and sexualized. To that end, this book seeks to center queer of color critique and decolonial Black thought, experience, and philosophy as a model for abolishing white commonsense experience as the universal norm. As I am a reader and student of Black studies, it is worth noting the ways in which I benefit from whiteness and risk reproducing a possessive and determinative reading of Black aesthetics and thought. For the purpose of this book, I understand Black studies as both the centering of Black life and thought as well as a critique of the Eurocentric tenets which undergird knowledge production and the university itself. Through an exploration of escape, I primarily engage queer artists, both Black and non-Black, who employ performative strategies in their exploration of the pathways toward freedom. Consequently, Black Study provides concepts and practices to imagine livable lives for everyone by centering a critique of property and the human. I turn to Black studies and Black feminist theory in an effort to parse the emergence of racialization in the modern world. I do this also to foreground that in the United States the word *escape*, as Dickinson so clearly illustrates, cannot be fully untethered from the history of racial slavery. As there are a number of ways in which escape might be taken up as an object of analysis, this is not an exhaustive account of escape as a genre. Rather, this book serves as a highly idiosyncratic account of narratives of escape sewn together by my own associative logics and questions. I can see some of the drives that fuel my thought journeys, and some I admittedly cannot. Born out of queer studies and queer of color critique, it is my hope that by drawing together both Black and non-Black artists I might provide a stepping stone for other thinkers and makers to imagine change.

As I write this introduction, the United States is in a series of unending uprisings against the anti-Black brutality that is woven into the fabric of this country. In this moment, I hear collective calls for Black queer and trans liberation, and calls to center Black thought, creative production, and scholarship. I read Saidiya Hartman imagining the "wayward lives" of "too fast black girls trying to make a way out of no way."[5] I hear artist and activist Morgan Bassichis explain Palestinian liberation and prison abolition by telling a group of students that "the only way out is through." I hear the artist Tourmaline ask, "In a moment of heightened violence and increased visibility, which could also be called increased surveillance of our communities, how do we sustain ourselves? How do we make a way out of no way?"[6]

What is the way out from global anti-Blackness, from relational logics predicated on white supremacy? How do we in the university and in the art world find our way out of the pervasive logics of individualism, private property, and extractive land ownership? Escape signifies both a directionality and a temporality; the telos of escape is freedom, it is a way out of captivity and confinement, a way out of the ongoing violence of settler colonialism and anti-Blackness. Finding, making, imaging, and sensing a way out resonates more with an abolitionist logic than it does with a reformist one. In early (anti)slave narratives, escape is theorized and taken up by white readers and editors as proof of humanity and literacy. And yet, as I argue, such stories do the work of imagining beyond what Hortense Spillers has named the "grammar of capture," imagining beyond the walls, the floors, the material relational and psychic frames of a settler, capitalist, and anti-Black state.[7] I take up the work of escape not as an individual narrative project, but as an open and site-specific term that names one genre of change. Escape, I argue, is most powerful when it involves the crowd.

I begin with Dickinson's white framing desire for escape as it illuminates the anti-Black culture which produces the circumstances and demand for Black narratives of escape—from enslavement to incarceration. Moving from white fantasies of escape, I also explore the Black and queer narratives that play on the generic form of escape to produce continued forms of critique and survival, opacity and flamboyant fantasy in service of dismantling an anti-Black world. Part of my argument is also that stories of escape tend to concretize around certain object-concepts such as freedom, fantasy, captivity, and enclosure. Such ideas form genres, creating the avenues through which exit and defection emerge as a story. These are modes of describing change, of imagining a shift, an alteration, a refusal, or a rejection in service of what could or will be.

Following Spillers, I argue that narratives of escape are always sexualized narratives of possession, where race and sex are co-constituted in the schemas of the Enlightenment individual. Consequently, as part of this project I am interested in how sexuality—which I often shorthand as queerness to mark, in part, that sexuality is never "straight"—is taken up by both the Black and non-Black artists and writers. Here, queer marks both an affective and relational attachment, a "not-yet," in the words of Ernst Bloch and José Esteban Muñoz, or a reparative gesture, following Melanie Klein and Eve Kosofsky Sedgwick.[8] While sexual modernities have formed in relation to anti-Black and settler colonial policies that regulate the sexuality of Black and Indigenous peoples, I wish to retain an understanding of queerness as a utopian mode that exceeds conceptions of settler sexuality. Instead of simply claiming that escape is a queer strategy disentangled from colonial and anti-Black disciplinary logics, I argue that escape is taken up in both modernist and utopian queer ways—as a marker of gay cis white male exceptionalism, as a mode of white desire for titillation and proximity to Blackness, and as an unexpected form of what Ashon T. Crawley calls "a desire for otherwise."[9] Queer here works as neither simply radical nor as only an extension of settler and white supremacist logics, but it instead brings together sexuality and desire in service of imagining a way out. It likewise helps me pay particular attention to the excessive, the spectacular, the aesthetic, the glamorous, and the sensual.

The Only Way Out argues that the American public has historically sought out escape stories in national productions of identification, belonging, and liberation. Consequently, the lure of escape plays a unique role in American public life and identity. Tracking the racialized and sexualized story of escape, this book is a meditation on the structure of the escape story and how we understand this common word today. More specifically, I advance the idea of escape as a genre of change, where escape is in turns radical and ambivalent.

The Story

Escape is first and foremost a story recounted in retrospect by the escapee. The act can be grand, spectacular, quiet, or undercover. One escapes when the simple act of walking out is impossible. There is an enclosure, a gate that must be broken, a boundary that must be defied. When one escapes there is a great risk involved. Originating in the fourteenth century, escape describes a movement to "free oneself from confinement," to "extricate oneself from trouble," "to get away safely by flight (from battle, enemy, etc.)," or "to get out or keep out of a person's grasp."[10] Escape begins as a solitary act and verb written about in the works of Chaucer and other Middle English poets. The exit in question could be from either a grievous injustice or accountability before the law. The etymology of the term returns us to the Latin *excappare*, "to leave the pursuer with one's cape."[11] The cap of *excappare* is a protective woman's head covering, a hooded cape, a costumed second skin. The pursuit is not gentle; the threat of violence trails the escapee. A hand reaches out, a branch pulls on her costume as she runs through the woods. Not vigilant or quick enough, the pursuer is left with the cloak, it was all that he could get his hands on, and the escapee saves her own skin, saves it from capture by way of the cape that got between her and the fingers trailing behind to grasp at her. In the understanding of escape as a finite gesture, one goes from captivity, shrouded through a transitional space, and comes out the other side in the bright light of freedom.

In the US cultural imaginary, escape is often understood as an individual heroic crossing from capture to freedom, from enslavement to self-ownership, from a closed system to one of open improvisational movement. The feeling of reading along with a resilient hero, as Sigmund Freud explains, reveals the invulnerable ego investment in the story's success and continuation. Put differently, narratives are captivating in part because we as readers are ego-invested in the survival of the narrator. "Great escape" stories circulate as mythic cultural texts in the United States, such as the seventeenth-century journals of William Bradford, *Of Plymouth Plantation* (1606–1646), chronicling the Puritan exile from Great Britain and establishment of a new colony in Plymouth, Massachusetts; *The True Story of the Captivity and Restoration of Mrs. Mary Rowlandson* (1682), narrating Rowlandson's harrowing "capture" and release by Native Americans; the *Interesting Narrative of the Life of Oloudah Equiano, or Gustavs Vasso, the African, Written by Himself* (1789), describing the kidnap and sale of a Nigerian man, his work on slave ships, and his subsequent purchase of himself into freedom; and the most widely read of American escape narratives, the abolitionist memoir *A Narrative in the Life of Frederick Douglas, an American Slave* (1845). Such stories explore questions of freedom, constraint, literacy, identity, and humanity. In early American literature, both (anti)slave narratives and captivity narratives depict stories of escape. In (anti)slave narratives, we see the feigned generosity of white abolitionist America as defined by the struggle of the enslaved people whom white abolitionists are purporting to help. Likewise, in seventeenth-century captivity narratives, a white American identity is shored up by the fantastical struggles against the "threatening but enticing wilderness."[12] A burgeoning discourse of the racialization of space, land, and the collective white self emerged in the popular captivity narrative. Recounting life under slavery, (anti)slave narratives develop as a literary genre in which the dangerous act of escape was a key element of the story. Such narratives demanded the end of slavery by way of sentimental and autobiographical accounts of enslaved African men and women, even as they were often heavily edited or written by white abolitionists. (Anti)slave narratives also offer their readers what Ashon T. Crawley calls "an otherwise possibility" by way of their breath-filled "narrative performance" and "enunciative force."[13] Here, Crawley names the otherwise enunciation of the escape narrative, and the breathy intimacy and performance of such speech acts. (Anti)slave narratives demonstrate a readerly white framing and desire—one we see in the Jefferson and Dickinson—even as they introduce Black narrative performances that exceed white understandings and legibility.

As I argue in this book, the dominant understanding of escape is organized around white European Enlightenment notions of freedom and subjectivity. I use the phrase *generic escape* to describe escape narratives which adhere to the conventions of the established genre, a genre that begins in America with captivity and (anti)slave narratives. Such stories sketch freedom as the end point, the aim, and the narrative arrival. Generic escape here is neither a good nor bad object, but it signifies a formal repetition in which redemption and freedom are the universally available telos; this is the philosophical grounding of escape detached from the ethico-juridical-political. And yet, my understanding of escape beyond its generic constraints contains both the passive and the direct, the silent and the spectacular. I advance an idea of escape as in iterative act not defined by the genre constraints of full redemption, but narrative genre that intervenes into normative temporal and spatial logics to articulate an otherwise strategy. It holds within it a mountainous landscape, valleys in shadow, holding and hiding spots. As opposed to branding a new term such as critical escapism, which might make a case for the recuperation of escapism toward the political, I instead wish to retain the term *escape*. I argue that escape holds all these contradictions within its articulation; its meanings run wild and undress themselves, like hedonists and wanderers. In this book escape is a space for thinking through the racialized and sexualized rhetorics of pleasure, freedom, and survival.

Generic escape is employed by white and Black authors alike in the desire for the space and time in which freedom will come. But the generic story of escape imagines the possibility of redemption and freedom as a place of arrival. This is a commonsense white frame which holds the escape story. The generic escape story, however, does not take into account global anti-Blackness, which confines narrative forms and their potential to imagine otherwise. While deviations inevitably do occur within generic escape—where there might also be space for an understanding of escape as iterative, improvisatory, and unpredictable—escape in its genre fidelity tends to imagine movement as finite and as either successful or unsuccessful. In this book I trace the dimensions, aspirations, and limits of escape. I explore the term and the desires that emerge from the neighborhood of the word. I argue that where sanctuary and enclosure are already raced concepts in the United States, settler colonialism and anti-Blackness inaugurate the need for narratives of escape.[14]

Drawing from Black studies as a resource for thinking freedom and liberation, I argue that escape provides a crucial narrative strategy and imaginary for rethinking stories about change from within the enclosures of Enlightenment thought. I ground my understanding in the nineteenth-century (anti) slave narrative and expand outward to consider contemporary performance and other extra-literary invocations of flight by both Black and non-Black artists. I argue for escape as a *genre of change*, as narrative strategy for mapping out visual and literary desires for freedom. *The Only Way Out* argues that escape provides a performative narrative method for imagining social change, critiquing American freedom dreams, and envisioning alternate ways to narrate Black and queer possibility. A narrative genre that does not simply exist in the realm of the literary, escape is also taken up in contemporary performance and visual art to explore questions of embodiment, liberatory praxis, fantasy, desire, and collectivity. This book engages with Black queer and proximally queer artists in concert with white queer artists in an effort to trace the schematics of escape as they get taken up across a range of artistic sites.

I trace the tentacles of escape to plumb questions of narrative, movement, and freedom, not to offer an answer to captivity or anti-Blackness, but to stay with both the trouble and the fantasy of free life worlds. I analyze works of art that show moments of exit, that engage in the language and tropes of escape. Here, I am interested in how artists use the racialized and sexualized historical force of the term itself to reimagine stories of change. I trace narratives of escape as a *genre of change*, playing on the productive tension between the past and the future, between here and there, between what is and what could be. In its generic American understanding, escape has been the province of individualist, progressive, and redemptive narrative structures. Escape is imagined as a clean and universally available move toward freedom. Furthermore, it envisions freedom and humanity as the starting point, and the eventual place to which everyone, irrespective of social class, race, or gender, may return. But minoritarian subjects already come to an alternate version of flight, one not grounded in the fantasy of liberal subjectivity and possessive individualism. Escape imagines *something else*, a utopian potential that exists beyond what José Esteban Muñoz calls the "prison house" of the here and now. Escape draws a path. It is marked by trespass. A fugitive term, it exists in gradations, and it is in these gradations, these plays between negativity and utopianism, where worlds are worked out.

To argue that escape is a *genre of change* that carries forth possibilities for imagining freedom is not simply to say that escape is just one taxonomical category, one way to classify the styles of change that are possible or become coded as imaginable—it is to mark the sensations and styles that gather around such stories. According to Lauren Berlant, "a genre is a loose affectively-invested zone of expectations about the narrative shape a situation will take."[15] Genre is an "affective event" that is understood through the sensual investments that create aesthetic form. Genre convention—such as mystery, sci-fi, and romance—describe the way events become organized and named as such, and the social and sensual feelings that such genres engender. In a piece cowritten with Dana Luciano, Berlant elaborates, "a genre accounts for and makes available collective experience."[16] As a literary genre and genre of change, escape traces the affect that circulates the promise for freedom. Often depicting a break from confinement that constrains mobility or self-determination, escape optimistically signals a liberation to come.[17] The becoming-convention of escape shapes both the generic form of escape and the generic form of freedom; we begin to see the contours of such forms through their narrative repetitions. However, with the introduction of the standard generic we lose a sense of the particular, exceptional, or failed cases that diverge from the conventional expectations of the form. In this sense, genre can have a kind of normative force, and a reenforces majoritarian protocols of legibility and intelligibility.

Philosopher Sylvia Wynter deepens my understanding of genre, linking it to the discursive and conceptual categories through which we come to know ourselves, our species, and our stories. She introduces *"genres of the human"* to describe other modes of being human in excess of the singular universal figure at its white, European-descended conception of humanity. Katherine McKittrick explains Wynter's concerns about "the ways in which the figure of the human is tied to epistemological histories that presently value a genre of the human that reifies Western bourgeois tenets; the human is therefore wrought with physiological and narrative matters that systematically excise the world's most marginalized."[18] For Wynter, this one singular conception of "man-as-human" continues to do violence as it cannot conceive being outside of the static conceptions of the colonial West. Departing from identitarian categories of marginalization, Wynter argues that through our "cosmogonies and origin narratives" we are *"reborn* as fictively instituted inter-altruistic kind-recognizing members of each such *symbolically re-encoded* genre-specific *referent-we*."[19] Genre here is one way of describing the naturalizing force of convention in our cosmogonies and origin narratives. We come to know ourselves as a human "we" through a performative repetition of the origin story of Western bourgeois *Man*. Wynter's "genres of the human" give way to a "being human as praxis," opening up from static naturalist notions of the marginalized and dysselected (an "underclass" McKittrick names as the "colonized-nonwhite-black-poor-incarcerated-jobless peoples") to a sense of humanity as a relational praxis of the living.[20] Wynter's invocation of the term *genre* emphasizes narrative, or what David Marriot refers to as "ethnocultural code," as the ground upon which history is lived, spoken, and known.[21] As such, the genre in which we are living, thinking, and self-narrating is not always immediately clear to us as just one possible cosmogony out of many. Racialization is one code through which we "experience being."[22] In Wynter's work "genre" enables an understanding of enthnocultural code, being, and collectivity; it thus provides a framework for understanding Black studies and minority discourse as a place from which to think alternate cosmogonies for innovating modes of being and being together.

The coding of genre does not provide clear-cut groupings, but is instead relative to the other genres into which "we" may place ourselves. Genre signals a set of affective expectations that orients how the individual and the collective experience being and being *with* one another. It is a charged mode of organizing the feelings that we attach to the different kinds of stories we tell about ourselves and our communities. As McKittrick argues, "Wynter's anticolonial vision is not, then, teleological — moving from colonial oppression outward and upward toward emancipation—but rather consists of *knots of ideas and histories and narratives that can only be legible in relation to one another.*"[23] In imagining humanity as a relational practice, wherein anticolonial vision names the ability to see and imagine outside of the genres that pass simply as commonsense, it becomes clear how genre provides a framework for coding the origin stories we inadvertently reproduce. If escape, as I am arguing, describes a genre of change, then an exploration of the narrative performance of escape might illuminate both the genre-specific codes through which we come to understand the term, as well as the various assumptions that orbit its political and aesthetic form.[24]

The dominant cultural imaginary of escape in the United States is organized around white European Enlightenment notions of freedom and subjectivity. This is a version of freedom that Thomas Hobbes defined in 1651 as "the absence of Opposition" from "external impediments of motion."[25] This negative theory of freedom is one of noninterference; it is a freedom to move without the limitations imposed by external force. In contrast to freedom as noninterference, Jean-Jacques Rousseau articulates a positive theory of freedom, defining it as a project of agency and self-mastery, what we might think of today as a freedom to act or do as one wishes. Such understandings of freedom depict a free agent unencumbered by demand or requirement. Yet, as carla bergman and Nick Montgomery remind us, freedom and friend both share the same root meaning—"love." They explain: "A thousand years ago, the Germanic word for 'friend' was the present participle of the verb freon, 'to love.' This language also had an adjective, *frija-. It meant 'free' as in 'not in slavery,' where the reason to avoid slavery was to be among loved ones."[26] Following from bergman and Montgomery, we might alternatively understand freedom as marking the ability to return to be among one's beloveds. This alternate origin of this word in connection and kin appears to predate a more fearful understanding of freedom as isolated, selfish, and individual. In *Empire of Liberty*, Caribbean political theorist Anthony Bogues likewise explores freedom and liberty as organizing tropes of political action and subjectivity in the United States. He writes that when "liberty" as a strong word "becomes the single organizing truth it provides the ground for one series of political practices."[27] Liberty, Bogues argues, is performative in so far is it has a perlocutionary effect as a "master key in the language of liberal political discourse."[28] Power organizes itself under the guise of freedom within the liberal imperial tradition. And yet Bogues names an alternate understanding of freedom that is born out of a Black practice of poiesis which "requires invention and is predicated upon the radical imagination."[29] While freedom—what we might call a generic freedom born out of a colonial liberal tradition—enables one trajectory of possible political practices, Bogues also names alternate understandings of freedom grounded in Black poiesis and innovation. The task then becomes one of imagining political praxis outside the enclosure of the Enlightenment tradition, where freedom is an open practice of inventiveness and emergent desire.

In generic escape, the liberal Enlightenment philosophy of freedom is the teleological promise, the direction in which escape is headed. Yet, thinking with Bogues, bergman, and Montgomery, new forms of freedom emerge as imaginative practices that are not individualistic, but instead return its practitioners to their people, kin, friends, or loved ones. Enlightenment conceptions of freedom risk obscuring the modes of imagining, dreaming, and desiring that don't move in a direct individual line or path. Imagining that there is a place called freedom flattens the differences between the multiple freedoms that have been and will be imagined. Thinking from a legal perspective, the call for freedom, for free practice of religion or freedom of speech can, and often does, prioritize individualistic, white, Christian, and propertied freedoms over others. As Bogues writes, "We live in a moment in which power organizes itself as freedom and in doing so both obscures and directs our intellectual energies so that it is difficult to think in new ways."[30] The battle would seem to be over imagining, inventing, and dreaming in iterative and interrupting ways.

In 1781, Thomas Jefferson criticized the writing of enslaved British African Ignatius Sancho as escapist and willfully imaginative. Jefferson wrote, "But his imagination is wild and extravagant, *escapes incessantly from every restraint of reason and taste*, and, in the course of its vagaries, leaves a tract of thought as incoherent and eccentric, as is the course of a meteor through the sky."[31] Escape, for Jefferson, stands in for extravagant associative or linguistic connections beyond the realm of "reason and taste" like the fantastic and burning movement of a shooting star. Jefferson's dismissal of, and intrigue in, Sancho's writing links escape to fantastical ruminations outside the realm of proper comportment and reasonable thought. Jefferson's words, in line with many Enlightenment thinkers, further mark Blackness itself as a space of unrestrained and wild rumination. As Sarah Jane Cervenak writes, "Implicit in Jefferson's formulation is an understanding of black men . . . as feminized, unrestrained, and irrational."[32] Escape as an affective practice, a descriptive act, is understood here as an inferior aesthetic position, one removed from masculinity, restraint, and proper commonsense logic. Jefferson's writing reminds us of the tension and link between the aesthetic sense of the escape narrative and the political act of fleeing. The telling of the escape is often considered to be spectacular, flamboyant, and inappropriate.

In the early twentieth century, escape begins to appear as an explicitly aesthetic and affective term. In 1923, *Time* magazine wrote, "For the cities are saturated with the literature of escape."[33] Here, escape is attached to the affective and literary, to narrative aesthetics of "thoughtless transgression" retaining the moralizing Christian connotations of the word that date back to the fifteenth and sixteenth centuries.[34] In this period, escapism arises as a term attached to the moral transgressions of fleeing, specifically in reference to art or fiction. The *Oxford English Dictionary* defines escapism as "the tendency to seek, or the practice of seeking, distraction from what normally has to be endured." The elusion of the law flips here to become an avoidance of a sort of work ethic, where endurance rhymes with Jefferson's Enlightenment reason as defined in opposition to "wild" and "extravagant" thought. Escapism names a desire for aesthetic sensation or pleasure over the persistent practical demands of work, family, and the day-to-day. Over the course of some hundreds of years, escape moves from a criminal and/or emancipatory individual act to a popular affective aesthetic frivolity in the face of a twentieth-century Protestant work ethic and Freudian reality principle. Escape is an expansive and sometimes contradictory genre used to describe both political acts and aesthetic retreats. The word itself does vastly different work in different contexts; it is an agential act, an affective strategy, and an imaginative practice. Today the term is used daily as a metaphor for both the impossible and the transgressive—there is no escape from X or, to escape the bonds of X, or the answer to X escapes me.

In this book, I explore escape as a narrative form of innovation within and in excess of the Western dominance of *Man*, and I trace the stories and futures that escape makes imaginable. Following Wynter, I ask: How might narratives of change emerge "outside the terms of a specific cosmogony"?[35] Put differently, how might a consideration of escape produce futures not predetermined by the commonsense (European Enlightenment) conventions of genre? It is my hope to provide a few points of departure for how escape might tangle together individual and collective narratives of change and contribute to a larger conversation on alternate futures for liberation. That story is how we come to understand ourselves and the place from which we consider political action. Where nonwhite subjects are encouraged to mimetically assimilate into white categories of humanity definitionally unavailable to them, Black artists have variously critiqued such nation-building myths by turning toward narrative models that pressure the demands of legibility, progress, and liberal subjectivity as the only way out. Much cultural analysis is rightfully invested in prescriptive forms of resistance as the primary method for enacting social change. Veering away from more traditional modalities of engagement for racialized and sexualized subjects, I look to artistic scenes of escape that might not initially be read as politically pragmatic. In this book, escape provides an opportunity to explore narratives of exit and risk that intervene into normative spatial, temporal, and progressive logics to articulate other, often unexpected, strategies for Black, Black queer, and white queer collectivity and survival. Escape contains both the passive and the direct, the silent and the spectacular, the affective act and the fugitive practice. Escape exposes the structures of capture which make flight necessary. It is an iterative and episodic modality of survival, relationality, and vision that risks consolidating a white dream of American progress even as its episodic structure allows for improvisation. Escape itself is neither inherently radical nor passive but instead shows us the way stories of change gather around common structures.

(Anti)slave Escape

Fugitive (anti)slave narratives, variously called "freedom narratives," "slave narratives," and "escape narratives," articulate stories of escape through personal narratives that move from chattel slavery to "freedom" and self-possession. This (anti)slave escape genre is typified by the writing of Harriet Jacobs, William Wells Brown, Henry "Box" Brown, and Fredrick Douglass. Such narratives diverge from previous escape stories in that they reframe the US government and landscape as inherently oppressive. While many of these stories tapped into an American notion of freedom as the guiding principle behind the abolition of slavery, they also reflected a more complicated understanding of captivity and freedom, where to escape into freedom often required fugitive slaves to keep moving, as Daphne Brooks writes, in "complex and cyclical patterns of performative resistance."[36]

(Anti)slave narratives were political texts, built around the abolition of slavery, and were hugely popular in the nineteenth century. As Toni Morrison writes in *Playing in the Dark*, such a "publication boom" produced "a master narrative that spoke *for* Africans and their descendants, or *of* them."[37] (Anti)slave narratives were produced at the confluence of autobiography and sentimental fiction, often penned by white editors speaking for, or of, enslaved Africans. While the enslaved man wrote his way to freedom, as was the style of the narratives, Morrison argues that such stories did not change "the master narrative."[38] Instead, (anti)slave narratives—framed and read by abolitionists and anti-abolitionists alike—produced a white encounter with a fantasy of blank Blackness, what Saidiya Hartman refers to as an evacuation of Black sentience, that allowed white readers and editors to know themselves as "not Black," which is to say "free," "desirable," "powerful," and "historical."[39] As Morrison famously observes in relation to the violently desirous fantasies of whiteness: "Black slavery enriched the country's creative possibilities.... The result was a playground for the imagination."[40] White readers of these narratives sought both the truth of the situation and an emotionally stirring narrative of triumph. Yet despite this demand for veracity, the (anti)slave narrative was not a simple relay of historical fact, but a built narrative genre. As Yogita Goyal argues, "The journey to freedom cannot be narrated as the facts alone but requires art," thus creating "the basis for a rich literary tradition that ties freedom to acts of reading and writing."[41] (Anti)slave narratives are both emphatically reflective of true events and simultaneously told through the art of narration, the art of autobiography, and sentimental address. As literary scholar James Olney argues, "The conventions for slave narratives were so early and so firmly established that one can imagine a sort of master outline drawn from the great narratives and guiding the lessor ones." That structure included, among other things, an engraved portrait, testimonials, the first sentence "I was born...," a "record of the barriers raised against slave literacy," and a description of the successful escape.[42] Each narrative is written to depict the reality of slavery, to develop in a chronological, episodic structure, and to serve as a testimonial or evidence.

Following *A Narrative of the Life of Frederick Douglass* by Frederick Douglass, the autobiographical form of the (anti)slave escape narrative proposed first a thinking freedom, then an enactment of freedom, and finally a subsequent writing of that freedom as proof of the author's newly achieved literate humanity. As Samira Kawash explains, "Writing the self was not only constructing a subject of representation but also insisting on the essential (and denied) humanity of that subject."[43] In turning enslaved Africans into subjects of representation, the genre of the (anti)slave narrative marked entry into the realm of subjectivity. "The slave narrative," as Barnor Hesse writes, "was based on a structure of *exposition* as escape.... Slave narratives were 'intensely political documents' writing the agency of escape into the logic of fugitivity that produced the narrating black subject."[44] Escape is defined here as an agential Black narrative form and as the capacity to act inside the logic of Blackness-as-criminality and unauthorized movement. It is not the act of exposition itself that Hess is taking issue with, but rather the narrative demand that the formerly enslaved must self-narrate in a specific style in order to be welcomed, however provisionally, into the category of the "human."

(Anti)slave narratives introduce an example of escape that, on the one hand, seems to fit well with Dickinson's own white fantasy of escape as birthing white creative possibility. Escape is charged with an agential narrative quality. Through this white abolitionist lens, escape is understood to be a movement toward freedom, a step toward incorporation into the category of "the human." And yet escape narratives inaugurate an understanding of escape that exceeds the genre conventions of what we might call a generic escape. Escape narratives speak to multiple audiences; they are what P. Gabrielle Foreman calls "simultextual," playing on the conventions of the genre and improvising within its legible forms. Simultexts are familiar to white abolitionist audiences as sentimental fiction, even as their authors and narrators engage polyvocal techniques "to articulate messages in various social registers."[45] Haryette Mullen further notes that under the legislation of "institutionalized illiteracy," (anti)slave texts transcribed and edited by white abolitionists were often shaped by a complicated play between language, voice, and writing. "In the narrator-amanuensis dyad, the white hand writes for the black voice, turning speech into text and, in many cases, nonstandard dialects into standard English. . . . Or the white editor solicits, corrects, tidies, and introduces black text. The miscegenated text of abolitionist literature constructs the African American subject as a black body with a white sound (an interiority comprehensible to white readers—with the blushing of white skin as the underlying trope of emotional readability)."[46] A white hand shapes a Black voice, makes it legible by way of its own affectively and linguistically white image. Escape narratives emerge as "miscegenated texts," carrying forth both the redemptive progressive desire of white editors and audiences, as well as fugitive Black narrative techniques, messages, and images not available to the white readers or editor. In describing Harriet Jacobs's *Incidents in the Life of a Slave Girl*, Fred Moten writes that while the white editor sought to enframe and regulate Jacobs's voice and style, "the irregular and its other regulations were already operative in Jacobs's work as a special attunement to a certain temporal insurrection in the music of constantly escaping."[47] Emphasizing the sonic and temporal rebellion of Jacobs's text, Moten names the sensorial movement of Jacobs's writing which resists regulation, even as the disciplining editorial white hand tries to reshape a "master narrative."

The Black aesthetic tradition, as poet and critic Nathaniel Mackey intones, is one of "maroonage, divergence, flight, [and] fugitive tilt."[48] Thinking with Mackey, fugitivity describes the improvisatory character that is specific to Black thought, where Blackness is not a property but, to quote Fred Moten, an "illicit alternative capacity to desire," to desire "other than transcendental subjectivity."[49] Fugitivity is an interval between what was and what is not yet, which Stephen Best and Saidiya Hartman understand as the cramped space of the "contemporary predicament of freedom."[50] Where fugitive is alternately a noun and adjective, escape is a verb. Fugitivity is illustrative of a perpetual demand to take flight, where our common understanding of escape is that it moves one in and out of captivity and freedom. Fugitivity is imagined to be an ontological position, whereas escape is imagined to be a finite gesture or movement. While it is helpful to parse out the differences between the two terms, I am interested in not creating a taxonomy, but instead contributing to the rich conversation on fugitive movements and escape acts. I understand escape to sound alongside fugitivity where it neither supplants fugitive thought nor diverges from it, but dances with and inside Black study and emerges as Black thought across a range of contemporary aesthetic life practices and desires. If fugitivity is inaugurated through ontological dislocation, the forced migrations of the Middle Passage, and legal articulations made in the Fugitive Slave Acts of 1793 and 1850, then escape is fugitivity's silent and ostentatious mate that emerges when there is a story to tell. Escape stories, in their breathy excited retelling, put forth "otherwise possibilities" that might exceed the white editorial language of the anti(slave) escape genre to give way to other forms of movement.[51] The escape story then emerges in narrative performance, in the movement between enunciation and the listening ears of the reader. Escape, in its narrative recounting, both retains the vestiges of the white frame, like the skin of a snake, even as it presents the otherwise possibility of Black narrative form.

A Way In

Embedded within Black studies, queer studies, and performance studies, I explore stories of escape as a genre of change, as narratives of movement, and as practices of speculative and imperfect coalition. From the science fiction fanboy epistemologies of Oscar de Leon in Junot Diaz's *The Brief Wondrous Life of Oscar Wao* to the veering escape and capture performed in Sharon Hayes's *Symbionese Liberation Army Screeds*, the sites of escape in this book range from sculpture to literature to photography and theater. I do not wish to flatten the social differences that distinguish the kinds of performance that I take up in this book; instead, it is my hope to touch on variously raced and sexed work to consider what happens when these works uncomfortably, perhaps antagonistically, cohabitate in narratives of escape.

Extending out from the genre of the (anti)slave narrative established by Frederick Douglass, I want to think of escape as a story and critical genre of change. The narrative work of escape attempts the seemingly contradictory task of thinking between the visible and the invisible, the known and the unknown, the autobiographical and the fantastical, the individual and the collective. Escape is animated by the relationships between impossibility and utopianism. While generic escape is taken up by white progressive American narratives and incorporated into the liberal fantasy, escape emerges simultaneously, against its genre transparency, to serve as an improvisatory praxis that frustrates narratives of freedom through nonlinear and iterative movements. It provides a speculative strategy of radical narration for minoritarian subjects. As Alexander Weheliye asks: "What deformations of freedom become possible in the absence of resistance and agency?" Perhaps escape provides one performative mode through which to reconsider the shapes of freedom.[52]

If change is an act of making different, of alteration, then a genre of change does the work of organizing such stories of transition and exchange. There are all sorts of ways to imagine how change occurs. For instance, a primary mode of change in neoliberalism is progressive change. As Eve Tuck explains, this default theory tells us that "if we document the damage, get enough people to pay attention to it, then together our voices will convince so and so (who is in charge) to give up power and resources."[53] Theories of change operate all the time in the political and the literary. These are stories and ideas that do not just document the life of communities and representative individuals, but they are stories that pattern the way the individual or the social becomes different and alters the current script. "Theories of change" in organizational psychology track the causality of change, why it happened, and what can be done to map pathways toward specific outcomes. Discussing escape as a genre change, I am less interested in tracking change as an outcome, and more interested in tracing the way stories of change geared toward freedom and liberation have been told in the United States. What shapes do such stories take and, more so, what do those forms tell us? Is change what is desired? Or is change that which is inevitable as in Octavia Butler's science fiction refrain: "All that you touch you change. All that you change changes you. The only lasting truth is change." The story of escape does not always map out a trajectory toward becoming different. This is particularly the case since it is not predictive as much as it is improvisational. As a genre of change, escape is shaped by map points, a strategy that takes the next right action before reassessing the landscape and going from there. In this book I ask: What capacity for change is embedded in the story of escape as it is taken up as both a racialized and sexual form?

Escape can be used to describe affects, practices, processes, or concepts.[54] Escape is both valorized as an act of heroic bravery and dismissed as response of passive acquiescence. Through a focus on contemporary artistic and cultural texts that employ the paradigm of escape, this book argues that escape enables a critique of the United States' conceptual progressive white investment in freedom and traces alternate modes for imagining free Black and queer life worlds. Emerging as a critical framework for thinking about stories of change, this book is meant as a resource for queer, minoritarian, and Black artists looking to tell the story of movement and liberation. *The Only Way Out* explores escape as a turn from the straight-and-narrow narrative path of political progressivism toward moments of felt belonging, scenes of pleasure, and embraces of care and interiority.

Reading across fugitive (anti)slave narratives, science fiction fandom novels, performances of white captivity, and scenes of queer sexual fantasy, I examine collective forms of entanglement that emerge from escape narratives. Through the lens of performance studies, *The Only Way Out* considers white, Black, and queer scenes of flight and how they push against generic narratives of freedom and change. Performance here is attentive to the social *doing* of an artwork, where sculptural pieces, theater, and performance art are read together to imagine the performative effect of an aesthetic enunciation. Approaching the cultural imaginary of escape through the lens of performance studies enables us, dear reader, to hear stories of defection and exit as performative and citational. Without ignoring the escape act that often happens alone and in silence, centering the story of escape allows a focus on repetition, recitation, and form. *The Only Way Out* focuses on the narrative performance of escape, the social doing of the story. It homes in on how and when the story is told, and the ways race and sex play into each retelling. With a focus on iterability, recitation, and the linguistic force of the term, escape comes into being as both fact and fiction, as an actual event and its aesthetic enunciation and rhythm. Thinking with Jacques Derrida and J. L. Austin, I argue that escape emerges as an act, a social doing, and recitation that does not place primacy on the event but instead provides "different kinds of marks, or chains of iterable marks."[55] Without devaluing the importance of the initial occurrence, citationality shifts from an emphasis on ontology to one of performativity. Considering the iterability of escape, the repeatable enunciation of its story, a performative approach flips the event of the escape on its side to understand the ways in which it ripples out like waves. The initial escape is thus understood as one mark in a chain of utterances and not the central event to which all subsequent retellings must faithfully return. It is my hope that a focus on escape opens other reading and listening practices, other genres of liberatory storytelling and listening. In this regard, it is a critical utopian project, one that believes deeply in the potential for living inside and in excess of the destruction wrought by liberal personhood, and for critical theory as a suggestive resource for imagining and worldmaking. Such a focus on citation also brings our attention to the performativity of whiteness, to the tropes of narrative closure and white stories of liberation, as produced and caught up in the structures of Enlightenment subjectivity and domination.

The generic trajectory of escape tells us that there is first a ruminative dream of flight, then there is the silent and invisible act, and then an infinite recounting of the escape in excited detail. Forward thinking rumination gives over to action, which then results in the theatrical tale. When we speak of the escape act, we typically consider past, present, and future: the anticipatory planning, the current enactment, and the retrospective recounting of the journey. In the planning of the act, the story is moving toward freedom, and in the anti(slave) escape there is a demand for life beyond the criminalizing and pathologizing function of anti-Blackness. In the retrospective recounting, there is pleasure, play, and victory. This is all to say that the temporality of escape is both a recollection and a future trip—it looks forward and back in the telling, even as the authors narrate from inside the event. It is chronological even as the time of the present migrates.

In its infinite recitations, its symbolic repeatability, escape exposes nuanced forms of confinement and previously unimagined moves, or what Michel Foucault calls "practices of freedom." In *Ethics of the Concern for Self*, Foucault writes that "when a colonized people attempts to liberate itself from its colonizers, this is indeed a practice of liberation in the strict sense. But we know very well . . . that this practice of liberation is not in itself sufficient to define the practices of freedom that will still be needed."[56] Instead of reading freedom as a metatheory, Foucault imagines "the practices of freedom" still continuously required; these are small iterative acts. While anti-Blackness and its performative reproduction goes uninterrogated in much aesthetic and linguistic work, escape narratives might be one way in which to bring a white framing into view. To that extent, reading escape in this book is also a way to read white desires for, and fantasies of, Blackness as criminality, as radicality, and as performance and animation.

The story of escape is saturated with pleasure, desire, and longing. The excitement recounted and the futures imagined are not mere descriptions of fact, but affective postures. I turn to queer studies to explore a methodology of desire where, as Eve Kosofsky Sedgwick argues, queer refers to "the open mesh of possibilities, gaps, overlaps, dissonances and resonances, lapses and excesses of meaning when the constituent elements of anyone's gender, of anyone's sexuality aren't made (or can't be made) to signify monolithically."[57] The critical and imaginative work of queer studies is attentive to the ways in which desire and fantasy function as well as the movements that are possible outside of normative logics of genre, linear progression, and causality. Alongside the undertones of the simultextual, queer reading practices and stories are sites that queer subjects invest with love, confusion, and desire. They are narratives in which something is missing, where the logic is misaligned, and where spaces and gaps are open to the relational possibilities between reader and text. These are not scenes of reading *into*. Queer reading is not an interpretive strategy, but a relational move between two bodies, objects, and texts. Sedgwick continues, "Becoming a perverse reader was never a matter of my condescension to texts, rather of the surplus charge of my trust in them to remain powerful, refractory, and exemplary."[58] For Sedgwick, reading the desire into text is not simply a move of projecting onto the narrative, but expecting the narrative to hold much more than any one reader may see at first glance.

Alexander Weheliye's similarly defines queer "not exclusively as a designator for same-sex desires, acts, or identities but instead as a shorthand for the interruption of the violence that attends to the enforcement of gender and sexual norms, especially as it pertains to blackness."[59] Queerness is articulated here in tandem with Blackness, where they are co-constitutive projects of modernity. In "Mama's Baby, Papa's Maybe" Hortense Spillers writes that through the theft of African peoples stolen to the New World and the sea "we lose at least gender difference in the outcome, and the female body and the male body become a territory of cultural and political maneuver, not at all gender-related, gender-specific."[60] Gender, and, what is more, desire and sexuality, cannot be thought apart from histories of enslavement and racialization. Thinking with Spillers, Darieck B. Scott further explains that "examining queer blackness provides opportunities to consider how the history that produced blackness is a sexual history, that is, a history of state sanctioned population-level manipulation of sex's reproductive and pleasure-producing capacities."[61] Queerness is a narrative strategy that is attentive to gaps and excesses as well as to a refusal of the "enforcement of [anti-Black] gender and sexual norms."[62] While generic escape can be read through the lens of redemption, I want to think about the way that it presents a narrative structure that is interested in interruptions that frustrate the telos of generic escape. Queer methods and, more specifically, queer of color methods thus help explore the affective and narrative pathways of escape by constantly questioning the structure upon which such imaginings rest.

Queer narrative structures, like detective stories, go back in time to find the root cause of homosexual desire. Such etiological narratives seek to uncover a truth, but in their backward-looking stance, they give way to a rich conversation on anachronistic movements of queer time and the modes of feeling they generate. Like the nonharmonic escape note in music, queer narratives, as Valerie Rohy argues, do not necessarily fit within the patterning or "linear clarity of a causal narrative."[63] Instead, queer narratives are often characterized by "temporal distortions," where queer desire is out of straight time. Discussing queer time in *Feeling Backward*, Heather Love describes a queer activism in line with the legacy of queer abjection, eschewing a narrative of optimistic historical progress for one of "feeling backward." For Love, this backward turn marks an interest in "imagining a future outside of redemption."[64] Eschewing the redemptive impulse of queer theory, Love makes a case for turning backward to imagine political action in the present. We might ask: How do queer and minoritarian subjects imagine a future outside of redemption? In line with the work of queer feeling, the work of escape is to locate "motives for political action" outside of narratives of progress, revolution, pragmatism, and freedom.[65] I situate my understanding of escape in line with work in queer theory and affect studies to engage alternative models of social activism through an analysis of "minor" or "weak" feelings, to invoke Cathy Park Hong and Sedgwick.[66]

Time and the Structure of the Story

As escape dances between the past and the future, it likewise moves between critical imaginings of the "not yet" and an embrace of radical negativity in the refusal of Enlightenment logics. Put differently, escape resounds with both Black fantasy and Afrofuturism. As Kodwo Eshun writes, Afrofuturism originates as a term in the writing of Mark Sinker and music critic Greg Tate, where Sinkler asked, "What does it mean to be human?" making "the correlation between *Blade Runner* and slavery, between the idea of alien abduction and the real events of slavery."[67] As a story and aesthetic category,

Afrofuturism describes both the creative desires for Black futures and a reframing of the past and present through the lens of science fiction. Eshun argues: "By creating *temporal* complications and anachronistic *episodes* that disturb the linear time of progress, these futurisms adjust the temporal logics that condemned black subjects to prehistory. Chronopolitically speaking, these revisionist historicities may be understood as a series of powerful competing futures that infiltrate the present at different rates."[68] The time of Afrofuturism is marked by both a revision of history and a powerful future that "infiltrate[s] the present." Understood as Black liberation, fantasy, and Black futures, Afrofuturism disturbs linear progress in an attempt to sidestep such a trajectory. Likewise, as free jazz musician Sun Ra suggests in his 1972 film *Space Is The Place*, Afrofuturism is about rethinking the past, present, and future, where he declares: "Black people are myths." As Kara Keeling explains, "Sun Ra points toward the ways that whatever escapes or resists recognition . . . exists as an impossible possibility within our shared reality . . . and therefore threatens to unsettle, if not destroy, the common senses on which that reality relies for its coherence."[69] For Sun Ra, as for Keeling, Blackness escapes the frames of "meaning," "valuation," and "recognition." Such an observation resonates with Thomas Jefferson's quotation in the epigraph that Ignatius Sancho's "imagination is wild and extravagant, escapes incessantly from every restraint of reason and taste."[70] Blackness sidesteps such commonsense logics, exposing them as intrinsically anti-Black. The Afrofuturism of Sun Ra is out of time, and Blackness is an "impossible possibility" with the creative potential to destroy Enlightenment logics of social and political coherence.

Yet even as escape resonates with Afrofuturism's vision of the impossible, it seems simultaneously to be invested in a radical refusal of the terms of relationality and futurity set forth by Enlightenment thought. Afropessimism understands Blackness as an ontological impossibility. For Frank Wilderson, Blackness is an ontological position inaugurated by the continuing violence of slavery, and consequently, it does not possess a before; Blackness therefore represents the antithesis of the "human." Critiquing the filmic form, Wilderson explains that cinema is "almost always anti-black—which is to say it will not dance with death."[71] Reading the 2002 film *Antwon Fisher*, he writes that film "is able to emplot a Black person (invite him into the fold of civic relations) by telling the story of his life episodically and not paradigmatically. It narrates events while mystifying relations between capacity and the absence of capacity. This allows cinema to disavow the quintessential problem of the oxymoron slave narrative. . . . How does a film tell the story of a being that has no story?"[72] Wilderson critiques the episodic as providing fantasy, futurity, and a feel-good understanding of Black life and its capacity for movement. A paradigmatic understanding of Blackness, in contrast, represents the very inability to tell a story from the position of the "Slave" in the Western Hemisphere, where "for Blackness there is no narrative moment prior to slavery."[73] Wilderson continues: "It is impossible for narrative to enunciate from beyond the episteme in which it stands, not knowingly, at least."[74] Afropessimism thus describes the impossibility of speaking or narrating a story from outside of the regime of global anti-Blackness without fundamentally doing away with the categories of Blackness and the human. Escape, a story about liberation in an anti-Black world, thus cannot be told since, in an Afropessimist framework, Blackness is not an identity but a site of fungibility. I read this crucial theoretical project that arrests racial analogy as a conversation between ontological nihilism and critical utopianism. The crux of the question here seems to be about how to tell the story of anti-Blackness, or African diasporic peoples. Or, as Saidiya Hartman succinctly poses in *Venus in Two Acts*: "What do stories afford anyway?" Escape thus arises as a genre of liberation written within the constraints of our current episteme. We might ask: What do stories of change afford and how can they be told?

Returning to Wilderson's critique of the episodic versus paradigmatic, I want to consider the episodic structure of the escape narrative. The (anti)slave narrative is almost always episodic, but this is an aesthetic decision made not by the authors but by the demand of the white abolitionist readership. As James Olney observes: "Any reader of slave narratives is most immediately struck by the almost complete dominance of 'the episodic dimension,' the nearly total lack of any 'configurational dimension,' and the virtual absence of any reference to memory or any sense that memory does anything but make the past facts and events of slavery immediately present to the writer and his reader."[75] The configurational here stands in contrast to the episodic wherein it allows a reader to see a three-dimensional view of the situation as though from a point on high. Drawing our attention to the white framing fantasy of the neutrality and immediacy of the narrative, Olney states that "it is the writer's claim, it must be his claim, that he is not emplotting, he is not fictionalizing, and he is not performing any act of poiesis (shaping, making)."[76] Olney argues that were the formerly enslaved narrator to exceed the "merely episodic" and engage the configurational, or utilize memory or poeisis, then the very validity of the story would be called into question. The (anti)slave escape narrative moves between the genres of autobiography and sentimental fiction and yet is barred from discussing memory lest risking a reception that fails to view the narrative as "a clear, unfailing record of events sharp and distinct."[77] The episodic thus emerges as a framing mechanism which allows for the fantasy of immediacy and truth.

If, as Matthew Garrett argues, an episode is the "relationship between a narrative unit (a scene, an event) and a necessarily larger narrative that comprehends unit," then escape like the (anti)slave narrative appears to be definitively episodic.[78] Escape is an event within a larger structure, paradigm, or configuration. While the episode can consolidate national narratives, such work is dependent on social and historical context in connecting part to whole, nonplot to plot. Garrett explains that "as readers, we can get lost in a single episode—linger over it, reread it, even decide that it can be rewritten as synechdochial representative of the larger narrative in which we stumble upon it. But we can also find our way back to the overall narrative line, however wavering or tenuous it may be."[79] The episodic structure of the escape narrative tends to occlude the paradigmatic previous life under slavery and the life after escape—which often requires continuous fugitive flight. Consequently, the episodic structure of the escape story would seem to consolidate a certain divergent view of Blackness, movement, and freedom that cannot or does not adequately connect back to the larger straight line of the anti-Black plot. Where the episodic narrative structure of escape imagines movement from point A to B, it provides a narrative of redemption instead of one of "paradigmatic impossibility."[80] As Wilderson argues, within a country founded on anti-Blackness, with its structures so deeply woven into the narrative possibilities, the episodic structure reproduces complacency and acceptance of the terms of the narrative. However, I would argue that the episode is not an intrinsically problematic form. Following Garrett's reading of the episode as "a structurational (rather than structural) element of narrative, in the precise sense that it takes shape only through readerly actualization," we may ask in what ways are readers variously activating escape and giving it shape.[81] While escape can be a divergent and pleasurable nonplot, it can also be integral to the larger straight line of the plot. Consequently, escape is used in different moments to different ends, where the episodic structure of the escape is both a scene of national consolidation around white fantasies of progress, and simultaneously told through language and opacity, through narrative that "escapes or resists recognition."

I linger in the conversation on the episodic to consider precisely the importance of the term *escape*—and its relationship to capacity, narrative, framing, audience, and excitement. If Western epistemes—from science to aesthetics—establish how people can move in the world and relate to one another, then (borrowing from McKittrick) we may ask: What stories do the "impoverished and colonized and undesirable and lacking reason" tell to create the human anew?[82] What might each invocation reveal about the ways in which the cultural imaginary of escape is taken up as a holding spot for envisioning the direction and timing of acts toward antinormative and antistatist liberatory desires? How might we imagine different kinds of performative enactments of escape that depart from genre of the Human Man? This work is attentive to what Moten describes as "the air that escapes enframing" in the anti-Black fantasy of enclosure. Escape thus marks the leaking out from captivity and the breathy movements that do not simply rely on capacity or incapacity. Escape moves outside of the precise capture of written text or visual filmic regime to imagine, in Crawley's words, "the excessive possibility of otherwise."[83] Escape emerges as a Black narrative of freedom within the extant white framing genres and marks that movement that cannot always be predicted, legible, or accounted for.

As Moten reminds us in *Taste Dissonance Flavor Escape*, to think freedom is always to think it in tandem with a continued unfreedom. Moten finds the radical potential of the aesthetic in the unresolved dissonance of escape. Discussing what he calls Jacobs's "scrawl space" in *Incidents in the Life of a Slave Girl*—this "loophole of retreat" in which Jacobs hid in the attic for seven years—Moten writes: "Hers is an amazing medley of shifts, a choreography in confinement, internal to a frame it instantiates and shatters. It's the story of a certain cinematic production and spectatorship prompted by transformative overhearing, driven by broken, visionary steps. This lawless freedom of the imagination, in all the radicality of its adherence to art's law of motion, occurs in a space Mackey would characterize as cramped and capacious."[84] The binary between radical and reductive is arrested through Moten's conception of "escape-in-confinement."[85] Thinking with Nate Mackey, Moten understands confinement as both "cramped and capacious," a shifting choreography that is neither fully caught, nor free. This is an escape, he explains, that is "a fundamental audio-visual motif for black expressive culture."[86] Moten continues, "Perhaps constant escape is what we mean when we say freedom; perhaps constant escape is that which is mistreated in the dissembling invocation of freedom and the disappointing underachievement/s of emancipation."[87] Thinking along with Moten as he articulates the sublime in this "aim for freedom"—which is always a "swerv[ing] in and out of confinement," a patience in constraint, and a waiting that is also a radical movement— we begin to see that escape becomes a perpetual dance of hovering bodies moving in and out of visibility and motion.[88] Escape shifts the frame of freedom through an emphasis on ontological enclosure and radical aesthetic worldmaking practices.

Discussing escape routes in this book, I avoid dictating, mapping, or making transparent Black strategies and discourses. Instead, by emphasizing escape, I hope to keep asking questions about how queer and Black artists narrate freedom, collectivity, progress, and coalition. "There is no roadmap to freedom," Kara Keeling writes. "Freedom dreams do not need roads even though it could be said that they make the roads as they move, laying them as common utilities for those that would follow."[89] Escape represents one narrative strategy for laying the bricks on the collective roads to freedom. This is the Black studies engagement with escape taken up as a mode of imagining in concert.

In this book, I pay particular attention to escape as a form of social activism and entanglement. I ask: What is the material specificity of these stories of escape and how are they situated in gendered, sexed, and raced narratives of the United States? Part of my interest in escape has to do with envisioning strategies of flourishing and thinking Black queer studies as a resource for ethical forms of sociality and relationality. How do Black and queer theoretical analyses address larger concerns around social, economic, and political structures of inequality which privilege certain lives and labors over others? *The Only Way Out* examines the sexual and racial performances of escape — iterative narrative movements toward freedom — that teeter between opacity and hypervisibility, individuality and collectivity, hope and political depression. Escape here becomes a critical project of reimagining social and political engagement while remaining attentive to the danger of reproducing the same violences that artists and writers are attempting to escape. The main claim of this book is that a consideration of escape provides a site from which to imagine the shape that change takes. It is not simply that stories of freedom and escape are impossible to tell; it is just that to do so requires a destruction of the current Enlightenment epistemological structures founded in colonialism and anti-Blackness.

The Nearest Exit May Be behind You

Part of what makes escape a complicated site for attaching an unambivalent radicality is its association with theatricality. According to art historian Michael Fried, "theater is the negation of art" as it both demands the viewer acknowledge an embodied relationship with the work of art and, furthermore, creates an experience instead of simply letting the art exist. Fried's grumpy denouncement of theatricality in the name of modernist art is informative as it reminds the viewer that performance is a critical analytic of experience and perception. In other words, theatricality resurfaces all of the messy and excessive bits of the total scene of the artwork as well as the bodies involved in its production and reception. Tracing the narrative performance of escape, I embrace the performative and theatrical in an effort to expand the story to the larger neighborhood or, as Sedgwick calls it, the "periperformative vicinity" of the story.[90] In this way, I look to stories of escape and trace their nonharmonic moments, the lines of narrative that don't appear to necessarily go anywhere at all. Embracing the chaos of escape I also lean into the multitude of meanings for each story, tracing both the detail and the way each story fits into a larger mapping of the term itself. I pay particular attention to the radical and utopian promise of escape to argue for an activist engagement, a manner of imagining, drafting, and mapping a way out, even if the nearest exit may be behind us.

Chapter 1, "The Repetitions of Henry 'Box' Brown," is organized around Wilmer Wilson IV's performance *Henry Box Brown: Forever* (2013), Tony Kushner's play *The Henry Box Brown Play: Political-Historical-Doggerel-Vaudeville* (1992/2010), and Glenn Ligon's art installation *To Disembark* (1993). Each contemporary artwork is based on Henry "Box" Brown's 1849 escape narrative transcribed by a white amanuensis, and his subsequent performances on the abolitionist lecture circuit. Tracing the role of surface, texture, and opacity in the escape narrative, I argue that Brown's story provides a meeting place for flamboyance and anarchy, for theatricality and critique. This chapter imagines escape not as exposition that makes transparent actual events, but as a story that is crafted for different audiences to different ends. The narrative work of escape attempts the seemingly contradictory tasks of thinking between the invisible and the visible, the known and the unknown, the autobiographical and the fantastical. Where each artist envisions a connection between Brown's story and the collective voicing of freedom, Ligon and Wilson provide an opportunity to rest against the demand for constant motion. Dwelling in the story of escape through an attention to embodiment, sense, and touch, this chapter looks to the theories of care that populate the escape narrative.

Chapter 2, "Feeling Out of This World: *That's What I Guess These Stories Are About*," focuses on Junot Díaz's 2007 novel, *The Brief Wondrous Life of Oscar Wao*, and traces the social and political feelings that orbit genre literature. For Díaz "the more speculative genres" contain outlandishly real descriptions and scenarios that approximate the "nigh unbearable historical experiences" of colonialism and its continuities. Díaz writes with and in narratives of the impossible to describe the Afro-Latinx tonalities of daily life. *The Brief Wondrous Life* envisions the feelings of escape endemic to speculative fiction, (de)colonization, and the history of capital in the Americas. I focus on the emotional and affective escapism of science fiction and feeling out of this world, and I introduce the term *genre affect* to outline the turn to genre, the aesthetic, and performance by artists working against white logics of reason and clarity. Reinvigorating the modernist question "What is political about the aesthetic?," I ask: What makes us valorize the act of escape as heroic, while escapism is used as a synonym for the cathartic, the unreal, and the ineffectual?

Chapter 3, "The Optics of Escape: Patty Hearst through the Mouth of Sharon Hayes," examines the performance video work of white queer artist Sharon Hayes in *Symbionese Liberation Army (SLA) Screeds #13, 16, 20 & 29* (2003) to consider Patty Hearst's highly mediated refusal of the national escape narrative. In Hayes's restaging of Patty Hearst's audio ransom notes, she enlivens a scene of political radicalism that does not fit within progressive narratives. In her kidnapping, Hearst was tasked to escape back into the wealthy white culture of her birth, to return to the "us" of the popular media viewership that felt a need to reclaim the stolen property that was Hearst and her allegorical relevance. Cloaked in her position as media heiress, Hearst and her capture were highly visible. Playing on *the optics of escape*, the SLA knew that through her image, their words would be broadcast and repeated; Hearst would become their microphone, a graspable object that would garner public attention. Thinking in line with Black philosophies of freedom that break from white logics of reason and transparency and theories of temporality which move against linear straight time, I contend that Hayes's sonic performance brings the viewer's attention to a confused, but potentially compelling tactic of abandoned whiteness. Hayes's veering strategies of escape are made through nonpragmatic movements of sonic repetition, linguistic infelicity, and constant audiovisual capture. I argue that Hayes's escape does not represent a scene of rescue, but instead provides a critique of the speaking subject at the center of the narrative.

Chapter 4, "This Face Is Not for Us: Grounding Pleasure," looks to the ecstasy and pleasure of the escape narrative. I start by considering the sexual spatial formation of the glory hole as it appears in queer visual narratives. A confluence of scenes of jouissance and sexual self-disclosure (or their refusal), the glory hole is a key site through which to explore the ways in which escape pops up through sex. In many queer white narratives, the homosexual "reveal" marks the center of the sexual narrative instead of representing a side note played among many other sounds of desire and belonging. I read the unexamined whiteness of the liberationist fantasies that have grounded much of queer sexuality studies, to instead think with Amber Musser's conception of the sensual in order to reframe desire outside of the enclosure of the human. The glory hole becomes a site in which to remain curious about theories of public sex while simultaneously critiquing white queer fantasies of negativity, dissolution, annihilation, and becoming undone. In the last section of this chapter, I turn to the work of the artist Tourmaline, specifically her 2020 photographic series *Pleasure Garden*, as a way of thinking pleasure and escape not as a solitary act of self-shattering, but as a move toward building fantasy landscapes among others. Tourmaline's work, I argue, embraces the dance between being a nobody and a somebody, placing pressure on the terms of the desiring subject while still prioritizing sustainability and pleasure in the present.

I conclude the book with a look at Toshi Reagon's 2017 opera *Parable of the Sower*, based on the book by Octavia E. Butler. Reading Reagon's musical manifestation of Butler's 1993 science fiction novel, I argue that escape manifests as both a genre of change and a genre of kinship. Imagining modes of escape and survival as brutal, vulnerable, and collective, Reagon's manifestation in song prioritizes an audience that is open to the coproducing work of storytelling. Considering ways that escape might produce futures not determined by commonsense logics and thinking with Denise Ferreria da Silva's theory of "non-separability," Reagon's opera produces sonic stories that agitate what *is* in order to imagine what *could be*. Tracing Butler's work and influence through song, Reagon uses a future speculative escape to turn the theater audience into a braided community of folk singers. This conclusion reiterates the improvisatory nature of flight and reminds the reader that escape manifests collective scenes of risk, not as movements toward freedom, but as movements that must break, and break again, only to reassess which way to go from here.

THE REPETITIONS
OF HENRY "BOX" BROWN

In his April 2012 performance *Henry Box Brown: Forever*, Wilmer Wilson IV traversed the streets of DC from the Lincoln Theater to the Georgia Avenue post office, from Federal Triangle to the Smithsonian National Postal Museum, attempting to mail himself. Stamps covered his body from head to toe, shiny scales with George Washington's face, the Statue of Liberty, or the American flag. At one post office Wilson asked to be shipped and the postal worker responded, "Baby, I can't mail you. You're a body!" For six hours a day, for three days in a row (a total of eighteen hours), Wilson walked the streets of DC as a body to be shipped, a startling, yet deeply American scene of collapse between person and property. With a ghosted gestural invocation of Henry "Box" Brown's escape from enslavement, Wilson asks what the performance of objects might look like from within. He engages the story of Henry "Box" Brown—not just through the repetition of narrative, but what artist Wu Tsang calls its "full body quotation."[1]

In 1849, enslaved Henry Brown had himself nailed into a wooden crate 3 feet long, 2 feet, 8 inches deep, and 23.5 inches wide and mailed north to freedom.[2] Brown emerged twenty-seven hours later having traveled some 350 miles in the box, most of the journey spent on his head. Brown's postal escape by way of the Adams Express Shipping Company enabled his resurrection from the chattel slavery of Virginia into the free territory of Philadelphia. The

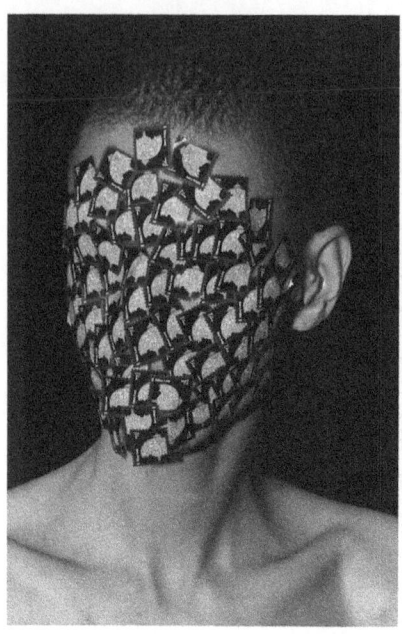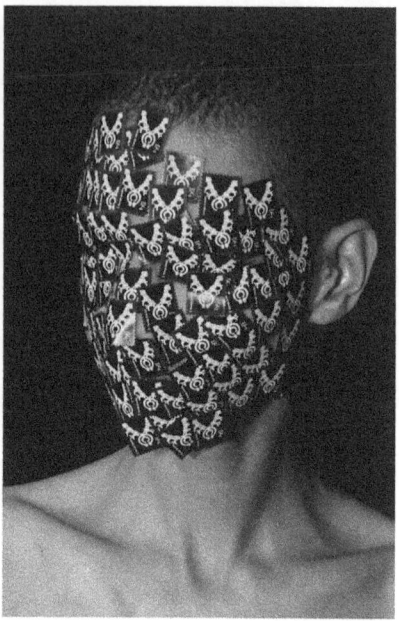

same year as Brown's arrival in the northern free states, *The Narrative of the Life of Henry Box Brown* was published, and Brown put together a touring abolitionist panorama show, *The Mirror of Slavery*. Brown's performance featured an elaborate painted panorama that would move left to right behind him as he reenacted his self-boxing and resurrection into freedom. Yet, Henry "Box" Brown's rebirth into freedom was never quite complete: he escaped slavery of the American south, but after the passing of the Fugitive Slave Act of 1850, he was forced to leave the United States altogether in an attempt to ensure his continued freedom. Upon arrival in England, Brown, with the help of fellow fugitive slave James C. A. Smith, continued to perform his initial escape through repeatedly boxing himself on stages of abolitionist reform and spectacle across England's mill towns. Brown's performance of *Mirror of Slavery* was called both "a brilliant piece of *art*" and "a most interesting series of *lectures* on American slavery."[3]

While much work has been done researching Brown's life story, the circumstance and editing of *Narrative of the Life of Henry Box Brown Written by Himself*, and Brown's subsequent performance work on the abolitionist lecture circuit in England, this chapter focuses on the story of Henry "Box" Brown as it is told today. In Tony Kushner's *The Henry Box Brown Play* (1992/2010), Glenn Ligon's installation pieces *To Disembark* (1993) and *Narratives* (1993),

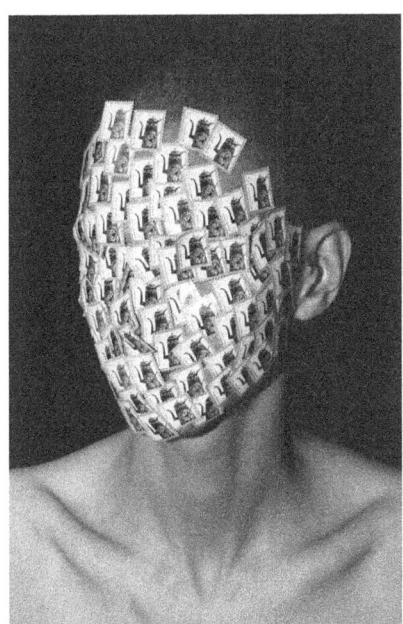

1.1 Wilmer Wilson IV, *Henry Box Brown: Forever*, 2012.

and Wilmer Wilson IV's performance and installation *Henry Box Brown: Forever* (2012), Brown's story of escapology continues to circulate as a mode of imagining. Each of these artworks stages another iteration in a long line of repetitions of Brown's theatrical escape, and his ability to turn fugitivity into a stage trick and sleight of hand. Brown's self-boxing and escape to Philadelphia, to England, and into the twenty-first-century American stages and art galleries illustrate an intertwining of the literal and figurative elements of escape, the fact and the fiction.

Henry "Box" Brown's performance of his initial scene of escape on the abolitionist stage continues to captivate historians, academics, and artists into the twenty-first century. From the illustrated children's books *Freedom Song* (2012), *BOX* (2020), and *Henry's Freedom Box* (2007) to the HBO Family animated story narrated by Alfre Woodard, Brown's story continues, its endurance owing in part, according to Henry Louis Gates Jr., to the story's allegorical symbolism. What continues to animate Brown's story of escape? What might we hear in such performative repetitions of the story? Brown's story of vision, mobility, and self-mastery stands out among escape narratives because it operates as both entertainment and fantasy. Brown turned fugitivity into a stage trick, an escape act. Predicting the modes of self-making and theater that would be enacted at the turn of the century by Harry Houdini, Brown

The Repetitions of Henry "Box" Brown 33

worked as an escapologist, performing what Daphne Brooks calls "black abolitionist escape art."[4] While many sentimental abolitionist narratives were geared toward eliciting white sympathy to bring about the end of slavery, Brown's narrative had, and continues to have, a different sort of resonance. As Daphne Brooks argues, Brown's self-boxing act, his own repetition of the initial scene of escape, "used the black body as a tool of defiance, as a site of illusion, theatrical mastery, and reinvention."[5] Brown effectively disappeared his body in the ever-vigilant "panoptic culture of slavery" that saw Brown as a thing, as property to be safeguarded for speculative earning potential.[6] Brown's repossession of the Black body through tools of self-discipline and "theatrical mastery," according to Brooks, demonstrates a repossession of that which had been previously stolen from him. In his magician's feat of disappearance, transformation, and reemergence, Brown rewrote the story of the Middle Passage as one of "resurrection."[7] He became the author of his own story and, as Cynthia Griffin Wolff put it, transformed the Middle Passage narrative "into its opposite by converting the very stringencies of an African slave ship into a blueprint for freedom."[8] According to this logic, Brown's self-boxing is productive of an escape route—establishing his access to freedom and subjectivity by way of his ability to reassert narrative authority over his own life, story, and image.

In this chapter on contemporary invocations of "Box" Brown's performance and escape, I look to the works of Tony Kushner, Glenn Ligon, and Wilmer Wilson IV. Brown's story is primarily taken up for its pedagogical import and its engagement with individual humanist narratives of self-possession, but in my reading, these artists move the individual story toward the collective, asking questions that tie change to concerns of care, rest, and reprieve. Brown's story exceeds the narrative of individual success found through mobility and instead opens onto the opacity of collective textures and care-filled surfaces. Each artist engages Brown's story through a performance of embodiment, skin, sense, and touch. This is a reengagement with Brown not just on the visual level, but also through the sonic and haptic. And while each artist still reproduces the individual hero at the center of the escape story, they also gesture toward the possibility of liberation for the more-than-one of the collective. Care emerges in the work of these artists displacing the emphasis on Brown's autonomous movement, and instead envisions escape as a space for imagining collective reprieve. Where change, as I argue in the introduction, imagines an alteration, care emerges as an overlooked arm of the escape story privileging not the spectacular retelling but the ways in which escape also signals a turn inward and away.

Henry "Box" Brown's Theatrical Flare

Henry "Box" Brown's story of escape from slavery was criticized at the time of its publication as popular entertainment, as a form of abolitionist minstrelsy belittling the severity or radicality of fugitive practices and lives. As Frederick Douglass writes in his 1855 autobiography, *My Bondage, My Freedom*, exposing the details of escape as "Box" Brown did actively prevented others from attempting similar escape routes by directly addressing the enslavers and not the enslaved.

> It is, perhaps, proper that I should frankly state, in advance, my intention *to withhold* a part of the [story] connected with my escape from slavery.... The practice of publishing every new invention by which a slave is known to have escaped from slavery, has neither wisdom nor necessity to sustain it. Had not Henry Box Brown and his friends attracted slaveholding attention to the manner of his escape, we might have had a *thousand Box Browns per annum*.... I honor those good men and women for their noble daring, ... nevertheless, the good resulting from such avowals, is of a very questionable character. It may kindle an enthusiasm, *very pleasant to inhale*; but that is of no practical benefit to themselves, nor to the slaves escaping. Nothing is more evident, than that *such disclosures are a positive evil to the slaves remaining*, and seeking to escape. In publishing such accounts, the anti-slavery man addresses the slaveholder, not the slave.[9]

Brown is accused of prioritizing the titillation and pleasure of the story over its practical use and re-use for other enslaved men and women. Douglass charges Brown—along with the equally theatrical Ellen Craft, who escaped slavery by passing as her white male master—with bringing unwanted attention to a serious matter, for which revealing strategy is always, he argues, to directly address a white audience and system of surveillance. While Douglass refuses to represent his escape in detail, his imagining seems no less fantastical than Brown's, as he speculates "we might have had a thousand Box Browns per annum." The dialectic that is set up between representing escape versus refusing to relay method marks Douglass's story as one of abolitionist practicality, where Brown's story tilts the genre into pleasure, explication, and gratification at the expense of the escapes that could have been. Indeed, there is something about Brown's story that is often both "very pleasant to inhale" and grossly spectacular for a contemporary audience precisely because of the form or genre which Brown employs. Unlike Douglass's sober narrative of quiet patience, Brown's story lends itself to theatrical reproduction, to a white fantasy of an entertaining redemption. It is a feel-good story, a Hallmark movie; it is an escape that feels to its audience like it ends in an episodic triumphant freedom without challenging any of the structural problems which support slavery and its afterlives.

I begin with the story of Henry "Box" Brown because it outlines the question of freedom posed in fugitivity narratives, not the birth of the subject through the trails of escape and the trace of the pen. In Tony Kushner's 1993 *The Henry Box Brown Play*, he explores the connection between Henry "Box" Brown and British-born American anarchist Samuel Fielden—a workers' rights advocate arrested during Chicago's Haymarket riots in 1886. In his autobiography, Fielden credited Brown as having inspired him to resist exploitation, which in turn propels Tony Kushner to explore the relationship between anarchy and abolition in a small English mill town. Glenn Ligon's own invocation of "Box" Brown comes in his series *To Disembark*, which takes its name from a Gwendolyn Brooks poem. In Ligon's piece, he stages boxes (the same size as Brown's) around a gallery space; each one is filled with the sounds of Billie Holiday, KRS-One, or Ligon's own voice. Wanted posters with queer accounts of Ligon written by his friends frame the boxes. While Kushner's approach to the story of "Box" Brown is one of Brechtian contemplation, Ligon's work brings his audience's attention to the sonic, sculptural, and narrative framing mechanisms which capture the Black body (and Black queer body) in a space just out of sight. Wilmer Wilson IV's work takes the idea of the shipment to the post offices of Washington, DC. Walking through various capital neighborhoods as a postal object, Wilson's meditation on skin-as-box provides a gesture for rethinking Brown's story and its consideration of surface and interiority, subjectivity and its refusal.

Each story of escape is descriptive of an act, but each of these artists reminds us that the act is simultaneously conveyed through narrative form. As H. Porter Abbott writes, narrative "is the representation of events, consisting of story and ... discourse."[10] Story describes the event itself and discourse shapes the narration of the event. To be conveyed, the event requires someone to tell the story, and, shaped by discourse, the story can take different forms. The political is always caught up in the aesthetic and poetic shapes it makes, even when that form is, to use Douglass's term, a "withholding." Each of the artists in this chapter uses different practices—which I read through the lens of performance—to contribute to the discourse around Brown's iconic escape. Here I pay particular attention to the ways in which the performative genre of escape uncovers theories of care.

Tony Kushner: Storying Escape

The Henry Box Brown Play: Political-Historical-Doggerel-Vaudeville, written by Tony Kushner, envisions Henry "Box" Brown's abolitionist panorama performance and lecture, *The Mirror of Slavery*, as it happened one fall day in 1851 in the town of Todmorden in South Lancashire, England. Initially written in 1992 as part of a residency at the Julliard School of Drama, *The Henry Box Brown Play* was not staged until the fall of 2010 when it premiered at NYU's Tisch School of the Arts, directed by Mark Wing-Davey and with lyrics and music by Matt Citron and Wing-Davey. In a 2010 interview, Kushner explained, "I had put the play away and my memory of it was that it was an honorable attempt at something that I wasn't pleased with, and that I thought I wouldn't have any time to work on."[11] The play was originally meant to premiere at the National Theater in London as a coproduction of the New York Shakespeare Festival. George C. Wolfe—director of the Broadway premiere of Kushner's *Angels in America* (1993) and *Caroline, or Change* (2003)—was slated to direct *The Henry Box Brown Play*, but that production never transpired. As of the writing of this book, *The Henry Box Brown Play: Political-Historical-Doggerel-Vaudeville* has yet to be produced beyond its weeklong run at NYU in 2010.[12]

In Kushner's research on the history of anarchy in the United States, he came across a British immigrant named Samuel Fielden (b. 1847), who was one of the speakers at Chicago's Haymarket demonstration on May 4, 1886.[13] Fielden was a self-proclaimed anarchist and workers' rights advocate who was arrested during the Haymarket riots to support striking workers and was wrongly accused of inciting the crowd to violence. In Fielden's 1887 autobiography, written from behind bars, he remembers seeing Henry "Box" Brown speak in his hometown of Todmorden as a child. Fielden writes, "This gentleman brought with him a panorama, by means of which he described places and incidents in his slave life, and also the means of his escape. He used to march through the streets in front of a brass band, clad in a highly-colored and fantastic garb, with an immense drawn sword in his hand."[14] An 1864 article from the *West London Observer* reports that Brown was often dressed as an "African Prince" to promote his performances, while another source describes Brown as an "African King, richly dressed, and accompanied by a footman."[15] Brown's tour was not one of "proper" or modest reform that many British abolitionists demanded. The parade and procession of Brown, his box carried by coach to the venue (as is reported to have happened leading up to

Brown's performance in Leeds in May of 1851), upset many abolitionists and reformers who were focused on temperance.

Kushner's title *The Henry Box Brown Play: Political-Historical-Doggerel-Vaudeville* names doggerel and vaudeville as artistic genres alongside the play's call to the historical and political. With the comic and political emphasis, this naming gesture points to Kushner's own Brechtian leanings. The scripted jokes keep the audience laughing as Kushner relays the realities of labor and alienation in the ongoing horrors of racial capital. The alternation of humor and seriousness is meant to spur the audience into action in the present. Doggerel describes a clumsy poetic verse that turns the serious trivial through an often-bawdy humor associated with American burlesque. Where burlesque, as Jayna Brown argues, was "organized around the principles of excess, luxuriance, and pleasure, [giving] license for release into the real of the senses,"[16] doggerel is likewise characterized by a sense of excess in its irregular and "low" rhyme. And while doggerel is not necessarily a physical form, the bodily and sensual are emphasized in its verse. The burlesque form was invested in "fantasies of the working woman's body," and consequently, its staging was always racialized, owing to the fact that American burlesque was modeled on early nineteenth-century minstrel shows.[17] Jayna Brown's description of burlesque helps fill out an understanding of doggerel as related to the lewd and excessive raced and sexed bodily histories of such performance genres.

Only slightly distinct from doggerel, the category of vaudeville describes a genre of musical farce invested in levity and itself a direct descendant of minstrel performance with "songs, clogs, comedy skits, and one act abbreviations of musical farces."[18] According to Douglas Gilbert, the first vaudeville house is rumored to have been opened in New York in the late 1840s or 1850s, but by the 1890s, distinct performance circuits had developed to distinguish the sensual burlesque from the family-friendly version of vaudeville that was on the rise. As Jayna Brown details, "Ethnic impersonation typified the U.S. vaudeville stage. Developed by Irish, Jewish and Italian players, such acts reflected the tensions and contradictions around class and cultural belonging for the new immigrants.... These vaudevillians attempted to reconcile themselves with an ethnic loyalty, while at the same time divorcing themselves from their 'repulsive pasts,' which barred them from access to the status of whiteness that accompanied the process of 'Americanization.' But the vaudeville stage excluded most black performers from its circuits."[19] Both American vaudeville and burlesque were inheritors of the complicated histories of what Eric Lott calls "the racial counterfeit" of minstrelsy. And as vaudeville began to appeal to "respectable" white middle-class women, it also began excluding Black acts and audiences from its "cleaner" performance circuits.

In the 1890s of Samuel Fielden's retelling both doggerel and vaudeville were familiar genres, yet Kushner's titling seems like a missed opportunity to more clearly and fully connect the histories of American and British theater to the white supremacist logics that continue to structure the artistic discipline of theater. Brown's stage was already heavily populated with phantasms of Blackness with which he was forced to politically, visually, and economically contend. Many British cotton-manufacturing towns were filled with fantasies based on white actors in blackface playing the part of Shakespeare's *Othello* or based on minstrel songs that had traveled across the Atlantic. For instance, a quarter of a century before Samuel Fielden's arrest at the Haymarket riots in 1886 two plays about slavery were both hugely popular on Broadway: Dion Boucicault's *The Octoroon* (1859) and George Aiken's stage adaptation of *Uncle Tom's Cabin* (1852). It is likely that Fielden himself would have been familiar with both of these plays.

As *The Henry Box Brown Play* opens, clunky amateur theater lights snake up the wall in plain sight. A banner appears high above the Todmorden Oddfellows Hall with the image of a factory "belching dark smoke" and reading: "In Industry We Prosper."[20] The play opens on a dark stage with Sam Fielden, "a local boy and bobbin doffer," who works in the textile factory clearing the machines of empty spools. A tall and thin Sam is played by the grown-up version of himself reflecting back on his memory of seeing Brown lecture as a "wee tot." Sam sits upstage in a recreated version of the contemporary Todmorden Oddfellows Hall, while the "Todmorden Audience" begins to wander slowly onto the main stage to watch the fugitive slave tell his tale. As the wheezing tune of the organ begins to wane, the tall and serious Sam rises and turns to address what is noted in the script as the "Real Audience." Walking slowly toward the edge of the stage, our narrator locates the events that are about to unfold before us as originating in his memory of "one September night, [when] half the population gathered in the grand theater of the Oddfellows Hall, to hear the wondrous story of Henry Brown, and his miraculous escape from slavery—in a box!"[21] Sam explains, "This here of which I speak happened long ago." He has "forgot the half of it, and made up that bit, and most likely the rest I have misremembered, but that's not the point."[22] This is not the truth, and, furthermore, aiming for a truthful telling of this tale misses the mark. "The rest" stands in for that which is perhaps lost to Fielden's own memory. His statement recalls Brown's reboxing at the hands of amanuensis Charles Stearns—including Stearns's turgid interpretation of

Brown's story—as well as the myriad of other "official" historical accounts that Brown had little power in shaping.[23] This "forgetting the half of it" sounds the echoes of Henry "Box" Brown's story and its current circulation and life in the virtual world of ideas in the present, in what Kathryn Bond-Stockton calls its "viral memory."[24] The opportunity that arises in "getting it wrong" has little to do with validating the historical record, but instead allows for an acknowledgment of the work such a story does in the present and tells us about contemporary political needs and wishes.[25] This is a memory play, an illusion that takes its cue from historical facts but does not remain faithful to them. Like Abbot's understanding of discourse, Kushner's play illustrates the conversation that circulates the viral memory of Brown's story.

Pulling a little black flag from the inside pocket of his coat, the character of Sam Fielden continues his monologue tracing the origins of his anarchist politics and activism to an evening in Todmorden when he witnessed Brown's panorama performance. Standing tall at center stage, he explains: "Now I am an Anarchist, one of those who wave the Black Flag proudly, under which banner of absolute freedom the downtrodden masses will someday rise up to overthrow the whole patchy bloody bleeding bloodsucking belly-full and fat-bottomed pig-pack of the rich who clip coupons with clean hands washed white by the Wealth us what got the dirty hands produces. Property is theft! Authority is the mask of violence! Anarchy! Liberty!"[26] With manifesto-like passion, Sam critiques the greed of the rich using the promise of anarchy as the avenue into "absolute freedom" and the ideology that shall unite the diverse "downtrodden masses." Like any opening monologue, it provides a framing, a meta theory through which to understand Sam's memory play. Kushner's character recalls early white American abolitionists such as Henry David Thoreau, William Lloyd Garrison, Josiah Warren, Theodore Dwight Weld, and Henry C. Wright who were frustrated by the failure of the US government to respond to the call for immediate abolition of slavery and, following anarchistic ideals, advocated for a withdrawal from the violence and coercion of government. Such protoanarchist contemporaries of Brown advocated for a range of responses to government from Christian nonresistance to immediate and uncompensated abolition. They did not desire the moderate and pragmatic abolition of slavery.

Sam's answer to private wealth is the anarchist cry for "absolute freedom." His monologue is a call to arms as he aligns his project—through props, his all-black outfit, and a familiar adamant political rhetoric—to the cause of anarchists throughout history. Quoting nineteenth-century French anarchist Pierre-Joseph Proudhon, Sam proclaims: "Property is theft! Authority is the mask of violence! Anarchy! Liberty!" As envisioned by Proudhon, anarchy called for an "unbounded emancipation" to contrast the current situation where "government, of course, enslaved man [and] economic injustice merely prolonged ancient systems of class ownership of other classes."[27] Indeed, anarchy emerged as not simply a call for no government, but a declaration that, in the words of Thoreau, "government is best that governs not at all."[28] For Proudhon, anarchy was the antithesis of slavery as it imagined liberty from the restraints of a government that no longer served its people and a critical suspicion of domination. In retrospect, it becomes clear that radical and immediate forms of lasting abolition were already anarchic, as such moves toward emancipation refused to abide by governing laws. Framing Brown's initial escape as a form of anarchy, Kushner ties abolition and anarchy together in a systemic critique of a world that could conceive of private property, let alone private property in the form of a person. Brown's performance is affirmed here as having a pedagogical importance, where the tale of Brown's individual escape suggests a larger critique of private property, capital, and the state. To call the abolition of slavery a protoanarchist move refuses Christian secularist traditions that, after the Emancipation Proclamation, sought to recuperate abolition as part of the natural political progression. In Kushner's reading, Brown's work was more than individual self-making, but represented a performative critique of a noisy American sense of freedom and the economics of white supremacy.

As Proudhon explains in his 1840 treatise *What Is Property?*, if slavery is murder, then it should be equally apparent that property is theft. Slavery was the logical extreme of the intervention of man-made laws where "enslavement was only the most complete invasion, or theft, of the life of another."[29] For Proudhon slavery was every time a man was robbed of "his thought, his will, his personality;" he referred more generally to the concept of slavery as though it was a relic of the past which had been universally eradicated. Instead of an attention to the actual institution of US chattel slavery and those suffering under its violent structures, Proudhon was more interested in articulating the harmful and dehumanizing logic of ownership and demanding the need for a large-scale restructuring of society. Following in the long tradition of political philosophy, slavery was an evil discussed metaphorically and abstractly. Consequently, the abolition of racial slavery was still a minority position distinct from the philosophical concerns of "wage slavery."

Standing upon the wooden panorama stage-within-a-stage, the Shakespearean orator character of Henry "Box" Brown begins his story with the help from his fictional assistants, Althea Edwards, "fellow thespian and also real-life former slave," and Fiacra MacFhiacra of Belfast, "associate thespian and crank-turner."[30] Both Fiacra and Althea appear to be drawn in vaudevillian shades, assisting and teasing Brown at the same time. Just before Brown begins to speak, the Todmorden audience breaks into song. Compelled by the ghosts that precede Brown, they sing "Camptown Races" in full chorus only to be interrupted by millworker Noah Greenwood's emergence on the stage in blackface reciting a soliloquy from *Othello*. Sam Fielden explains, "the effects of the novelty were such that the Todmordenites was all transported and aroused."[31] The Todmordenites—all adorned in a faint and ashy whiteface paint that makes them look ghostly—project their desire and fantasy onto Brown. The women from the temperance and suffrage league dance in ecstasy and clutch their skirts as they push up against the stage and sing, "He is the handsomest handsomest man that I have ever seen." Kushner reflects the white fantasy projected onto and manipulated by Brown in his performances. His retelling is a negotiation of this white fantasy and its lockdown in the register of the visual where the overdetermined Black body is rendered hypervisible and immobile. Foregrounding the erotic charge embedded in white discussions of Blackness and escape, Kushner is aware of Black theatrical traditions from Shakespeare's *Othello* to the minstrel performances of Lincoln Theodore Monroe Andrew Perry (aka Stepin Fechit); but while he acknowledges these tendencies of theatrical storytelling genres, he is unable to step outside of vaudeville and doggerel styles of their reproduction.

After Henry tells the tale of his wife and children being sold from him, he has nothing left to lose and makes his move to escape. He has a dream full of luminous beings and glowing cotton balls and knows he shall be free, entombed in a box. Henry hatches the idea of passing as the product of the labor upon which British and American industry depends. Dressing up as cargo, unmoving as a blowing "pearlescent" cotton bale, Henry inters himself for this twenty-seven-hour journey to the free states. The play shifts from Brechtian illumination and wonder back to clunky vaudeville lines as Henry disappears through the cotton cargo box center stage. After Henry has made his way thorough, millworkers Cyril and Lumb pick up the box and walk in place miming the distance and duration Brown traveled. As they mime movement at the center of the stage, the panorama painting backdrop turns into a train track, they argue about where they are coming from, where their journey north begins, unsure if it is Georgia or Virginia, depending on whether Henry wants to implicate the cotton or tobacco industry. As the two characters argue on stage, Cyril asking, "Ain't you got no imagination Lumb? This is a play," Henry makes his way through a trapdoor in the bottom of the stage and reemerges above the panorama. Cyril and Lumb joke and remind us that it is a vaudevillian artifice. Finally, Henry reappears upside down, head crooked to the side at the bottom and feet floating above him trapped in the traveling box. The set design places the actor's head inside a box of fake cloth limbs twisted like a pretzel. The image is puppet-like, depicting a body that is twisted and cartoonish. It looks strangely similar to an earlier work, "32 Hours In a Box... And Still Counting" (1987) by artist Pat Ward Williams, that featured a window-paned photograph of a Black man twisted in the size of a shipping crate, the short pedestal under which read, "Henry Box Brown who escaped slavery enclosed in a box 3 feet wide and 2 long." That Williams's work proceeds Kushner's by some five years speaks to both the art moment of the late '80s and early '90s, but also to the ways in which the figure of Brown himself was being imagined in that moment.

On Kushner's stage, from inside this even smaller box above the stage, Henry speaks:

> And up into the North, as in a dream, I saw leveled forests, desecrated earth, and terrible cities in a terrible time where the great-great-grandchildren of former slaves live not slave but free in cities which are fertile breeding ground for rats, where one of every four women is raped and the chief cause of death among young men is gunshot wound and black women die from breast cancer ten times more than white women and black infants die in rates that exceed those of most third world countries and twenty million live without homes and a hundred thousand die unmourned of plague and education and health care are luxuries for the rich and we are not saved, all this time and we are not slave any longer free, and—[32]

Henry's story of escape provides connective tissue to continued white supremacy and systemic inequality in the United States today. Kushner attempts to approach the topic of anti-Blackness in the early '90s as interconnected with environmental degradation, poverty, sexual violence, houselessness, and the AIDS crisis. While entombed inside the wooden crate, Brown has a vision of destruction. He sees the detritus of the past heaped onto the cities of today. These are places that do not breed equality, but are instead filled with diminished life chances. Henry's vision of horrors, his "threshold of revelation," echoes the themes of painful progress from Kushner's *Angels in America*.[33] Freedom is foreclosed while fugitivity is an impossible dwelling place. Like Walter Benjamin's angel of history, Henry sees the rubble heap of history growing sky high. Henry's escape is not a direct line to freedom, and the legacy of freedom continues to be an ambivalent one.[34] For those gifted with the rights of "humanity" postemancipation, to quote Hartman, "it also served to obscure the coercion of 'free-labor,' the transmutation of bonded labor, the invasive forms of discipline that fashioned individuality, and the regulatory production of blackness."[35] In short, emancipation did not follow through with its implied promise of freedom and self-possession, but instead inaugurated new forms of theft and ownership in bonded-labor and indebtedness. Instead of introducing a clean break from slavery into freedom, the Thirteenth Amendment ushered Black people into different forms of labored compulsion, as well as social and economic bondage.

Kushner's play in 1992 is seemingly meant to challenge capitalism's relation to white supremacy in a Brechtian style. He adopts anarchy and illusion as methods for retelling Henry "Box" Brown's story. Kushner wants to retain the promise of freedom through anarchy as means to connect the works of Black abolitionists and the working-class white proletariat then and now. I am reminded of his line in *Angels in America*: "An angel is a belief, with wings, and arms that can carry you. It's naught to be afraid of. If it lets you down, reject it. Seek for something new."[36] Kushner believes in belief, whether it takes the form of Mormonism, homosexuality, Judaism, or socialism. Freedom and anarchy emerge here as belief systems of coalitional uprising born from Brown's mobility and a critique of capital, or what Moten calls "the resistance of the object."[37] In a 2012 interview in the *Paris Review*, Kushner explained, "I simultaneously discovered Marx, Brecht and Shakespeare and I realized they're all playing with the same thing—the way things both are and are not what they seem. All three ask us to see the surface, but also what's beneath the surface. They ask us to think about intended effects and about what's being concealed within the effect."[38] Inspired by language and illusion, by the theatrical sleight of hand, Kushner identifies the stage as a place to reveal the connections between finance capital, systemic racism, and worker's rights. Invoking Marx, Brecht, and Shakespeare, he is interested in the magic of alienation, the display and dissonance of the purportedly "natural" law which gives such supernatural power to the commodity or the stage.

Bertolt Brecht, famous for his theorization of epic theater and the "alienation effect," understood the theater as a space for instruction and inspiration. The "magic" of the theater involved its ability to make that to which the audience had become accustomed, that which had begun to appear natural, appear strange again. Influenced by Marx's analysis of the commodity as possessing a special power untethered to use-value, Brecht believed that the proletariat should be made aware of their own class consciousness and exploitation under the illusions of capitalism. He writes, "The actress must not make the sentence her own affair, she must hand it over for criticism, she must help us to understand its causes and protests."[39] With use of Brecht's practice of alienation in acting, the actress should "show the horror of a bloody epoch" like a "messenger returning from the lowest of all hells."[40] It is with this alienation that the audience then becomes removed from the givenness of the scene and can then consider the "possibility of remodeling society."[41] Alienation puts the onus to act on the audience and viewer. As Walter Benjamin wrote, Brecht's estrangement effect was "less concerned with filling the public with feelings, even seditious ones, than in alienating it in an enduring manner, through thinking, from the conditions in which it lives."[42] Such estrangement distances the audience from the actors, providing a critical understanding of the world previously obscured by language and sentiment. Elaborating on the work of Brechtian feminist Elin Diamond, Daphne Brooks describes what she terms "afro-alienation" as "calling attention to the hypervisibility and cultural constructions of blackness in transatlantic culture" in an effort to "'disturb' cultural perceptions of identity formation."[43] Brooks argues that Henry "Box" Brown used performance to "defamilialrize" his own body, effectively "yield[ing] alternative racial and gender epistemologies."[44] Afro-alienation thus diverges from techniques of realism to do the work of defamiliarizing the spectacle of white supremacy and its immobile production of Blackness. Brown was a protoanarchist, but he was also an early spiritualist performer of ghostly disappearance and escape. Late in his life, he worked as a conjurer and magician on the London stages. Brown mobilized the theatricality of escape, where to escape just once is never enough. As Daphne Brooks observes, the magic of the illusionist is that he figures out how to move without appearing to move at all.

However, the magic that Kushner sees in Brown's story and performance career emphasizes the image of Brown's body inside the box. This is an attempt to access Brown's interior motives and explain to a contemporary audience the ongoing effects of white supremacy in the present so they themselves might be inspired to action. Akin to the trespassive eye of the white abolitionist speaker or editor, Kushner renders Brown visible in a frame within a frame within a frame that is his vaudevillian rendering of Henry's box. Movement and transparency are key to Kushner's mobilization of Brown's story, and they are done for a white anarchist end. Instead of using alienation to challenge the assumptions of "racial and gender epistemologies," Kushner's alienation is caught on the surface level of the stage, pronouncing the absurdity of property and ownership instead of the white logics that render Blackness as always already alien and stuck in place.

Does Kushner need to pass through Brown's own story in order to arrive at, and validate, Fielden's anarchy and its potential? Put differently, what does the Black escape narrative do for white creative desires? While there is a clear and crucial connection between abolition and anarchy, Kushner is unable to think alongside Black radical movement and wandering without putting it at the service of a central white anarchist voice. As Saidiya Hartman asks in *Scenes of Subjection*: "Can the white witness of the spectacle of suffering affirm the materiality of black sentience only by feeling for himself? Does this not only exacerbate the idea that black sentience is inconceivable and unimaginable but, in the very ease of possessing the abased and enslaved body, ultimately elide an understanding and acknowledgement of the slave's pain?"[45] This is what Hartman calls the "precariousness of empathy." It is not that Kushner attempts to write a Black character, but more so that he cannot conceive of a Black story without a white frame, without his experience as the entry point, without reboxing Brown all together. Perhaps this is a failing of the theatrical form in which Kushner is so deeply invested, where theater carries with it a particular history when it comes to white fantasies of Blackness. While attempting critique, Kushner's play also emanates from these precise histories of minstrelsy, melodrama, and white spectatorial pleasure. As Hartman argues, by way of her reading of the letters of the white abolitionist John Rankin, "the elasticity of blackness enables its deployment as a vehicle for exploring the human condition although, ironically, these musings are utterly indifferent to the violated condition of the vessel of song."[46] The elasticity of Blackness for white "amusement" or as a "sentimental resource," writes Hartman, evacuates Black being, replacing Black interior thought, experience, and feeling with the violence of white fantasy projections.

Written inside a New York City both ravaged by AIDS and the "war on drugs." Kushner uses Henry "Box" Brown's story to imagine a socialist reprieve. But in the process, he effectively turns Brown's story into a vessel for contemporary white anticapitalist politics. Approaching the "paradox of freedom" through the lens of anarchy, Kushner brings questions concerning anarchist and abolitionist aesthetics to the forefront of his work. Reflecting on nineteenth-century white desires, which called for both the spectacle of the reformed Black subject and the artifice of the Black minstrel show, Kushner presents a didactic drama; however, he does not himself know what to do with the legacy of escape and anti-Blackness nor with the ongoing white traditions of capture. Following Brown's pedagogical performance to teach a white audience, Kushner gets stuck in the frame of the white stage. He harnesses the enunciative force of the escape story to connect struggles for "freedom from domination." Such an attempt at telling Brown's story as the basis of a coalitional anticapitalist politics is myopic insofar as it recenters whiteness, even as it illuminates escape as a genre for coming together in liberation. *The Henry Box Brown Play* then poses the question: Is escape as an ideology open to the collective and, if so, how? Furthermore, how might the narrative of escape through its connection to anarchist beliefs become a space of care that pushes against the strictures of the individual to embrace collective liberation, or friendship, in the present?

Withholding the Countenance of Brown:
Glenn Ligon's *To Disembark*

Where Kushner chooses to reappear, Glenn Ligon, in his 1993 work on the visual language of escape and narrative, makes sure that Brown stays hidden. Ligon creates conceptual work across painting, sculpture, lithography, and text. From neon signs that read "America" and "negro sunshine" to 1970s coloring book drawings of Malcolm X to the retextualization of the Million Man March slogan—"I *Am* a Man"—printed across an otherwise blank canvas, Ligon connects Black history to the present. He visually animates difficult questions concerning race, sexuality, vision, and language. As Huey Copeland notes, "Ligon was influenced by conceptualism's linguistic turn, minimalism's phenomenological address, and feminist critiques of media imagery."[47] Ligon's work pulls the gallery audience into the space of a given historical moment by making the viewers recognizable, responsible, and complicit in the way history continues to be shaped in the present.

Glenn Ligon's installation *To Disembark*, which was inspired by Henry "Box" Brown, was originally mounted at DC's Hirshorn Museum and Sculpture Garden in 1993. In 2011, the installation was included as part of Ligon's midcareer retrospective at the Whitney Museum of American Art in New York and at the Los Angeles County Museum of Art (LACMA), where the work was presented alongside the series *Runaways* and *Narratives*. Across the space of the gallery floor, Ligon stages four crates the size of Brown's own box. Such boxes look almost indistinguishable from the boxes one might find on the loading dock of a museum. Shipping crates are common at art institutions, with artists' names written on them, cradling valuable pieces expertly packed by art handlers. Visitors are meant to move through the space of these minimalist boxes and listen to their surplus speech and sound. In each crate there is a noise, sometimes quiet and barely audible that makes you bend down closer, a breath's distance, to listen to who or what might be inside. Ligon uses the disappearance of Brown's body as the starting point for his repetition of Henry "Box" Brown's story of escape. Unlike Kushner, he does not try to recreate the visual imagery, to present an unmediated glimpse into the past, or to hyperanimate Brown in voice and body. Instead, Ligon's work begins with the absence of Brown's body, reminding us that any access to this historical figure and his art will also be partial and speculative.

The wooden crates are nailed shut and blank on the outside except for a few simple shipping and handling icons painted in black. Some boxes read "FRAGILE," or "handle with care," and show breakable wine glasses stenciled on the long side of the crate; others are marked by short thick arrows indicating which end is meant to face up or by umbrellas indicating that the boxes be kept dry. The crates do not open, so the contents remain just out of reach of the gallery visitors. Instead, they are filled with sounds that emanate out through their wood barriers, each quiet enough that the audience must lean in and slow their breath to hear and recognize the words or melody. Like Brown's own fabled emergence from the box in Philadelphia while singing the tune of "Uncle Ned," these boxes are animate and vocal. Depending on which box the gallery visitors approach, they might hear Ligon himself reading *The Narrative of Henry Box Brown* (1851), the "whoop, whoop" of KRS-One's rally against racism and police brutality in *Sound of da Police* (1991), the melo-

1.2   Glenn Ligon, *To Disembark*, 2011.

dies of Billie Holiday's lynching protest song, "Strange Fruit" (1939), or Bob Marley crooning "emancipate yourself from mental slavery" in "Redemption Song" (1980). Each "song of freedom"—to borrow from Bob Marley—echoes the impulse of Brown's own 1851 narrative while simultaneously chronicling the ongoing effects of anti-Blackness.

The title—*To Disembark*—describes an exit. It is a verb that signals the moment when a ship meets land and its people go on shore. Disembarking recalls the ships that stole Africans to the Americas, a history of violence and theft, as well as Brown's own movement through the postal system, which landed him in northern "freedom." Disembarking does not mean that one has reached their destination, but that they are terminating one segment of a potentially ongoing journey. Ligon's title is itself a recitation of Gwendolyn Brooks's 1981 book of prose in which she speaks to the experience of institutionalized racism in the United States and the resistance of collective action. Ligon's *To Disembark* is a poetic invocation that focuses on our ability to understand language as it is obscured through both form and context. Along with the lithographic series *Runaways* and *Narratives*, the piece is both a historical memory of Brown's "abolitionist activist work" and a reflection of the mode of memory and its function in the present. Through his work, Ligon asks: "What are the conditions under which works by black artists enter the museum? Do we enter only when our "visible difference' is evident? . . . Who is my work for and what do different audiences demand of it?"[48]

To Disembark orients the viewer's attention to the sonic dimensions of Brown's boxing, of his voice, and its spectral echo at the end of the twenty-first century. Demonstrating the spatial and temporal reverberations of Brown's journey, the work recalls the Middle Passage, slave galleys, and coffins. The KRS-One song in particular brings Brown's narrative to the present as it reminds the attendee of anti-Black police violence, the prison industrial complex, and unequal incarceration rates which reflect six times as many Black men in jails as white men. Standing alone in the space of a gallery, folding your body in half to reach down to hear the slow acoustics of Marley, or the bouncing refrain of KRS-One, creates a mode of engagement distinct from a spectator in a dark theater. Gallery attendees are asked to come in close, even if they aren't required to stay for the whole show.

Both *The Henry Box Brown Play* and *To Disembark* focus on the box. For Kushner, Brown's box is an opportunity to consider the illusion of capital and to unmake its fetishistic hold on a contemporary audience. The box shows the breakdown between person and property, but in an effort to explain this collapse, Kushner allows the audience to look inside. While Ligon likewise invokes this history of racial capitalism, he presses the audience to consider not the true story of "Box" Brown, but the circulation of the box itself. He tells the gallery visitors all they need to know: Brown escaped from slavery to freedom by mailing himself north in a box much like the ones at your feet. Ligon does not excavate Brown as a historical character; he does not explain to the audience that Brown himself restaged his escape on the abolitionist lecture circuit, that his narrative was written by a white editor, or that Brown continued to perform as a magician and spiritualist after he finished touring his panorama show. The audience is denied the pleasure of looking at Brown, and instead positioned to look at the framing mechanisms that shape and constrain him. Sounding Brown's iconic escape in the repeated figure of the box and Brown's 1851 narrative—as read by Ligon himself—the installation puts visually absented bodies together, present only through their referents and descriptions. Here, Brown's box is not arrested in singularity, but it repeats in time and space.

On one wall of the *To Disembark* installation is a series of prints titled *Runaways* (1993). These ten 16×12-inch lithographs are in the style of runaway "wanted" posters or handbills that became common in the north after the Fugitive Slave Act of 1850 was passed. Such posters used racializing terms to describe the enslaved by height, body type, and social demeanor. Ligon's *Runaways* consists of a series of narrative descriptions of the artist himself as given by friends who were instructed to describe him as though they were giving a missing person's report to the police. Ligon uses these words to recreate his own "wanted" posters. He then places these accounts into the visual language of these handbills along with historically sourced lithographic icons of lone Black travelers or enslaved persons.[49] One image playfully reads,

> RAN AWAY, a man named Glenn. He has almost no hair. He has cat-eye glasses, medium-dark skin, cute eyebrows. He's wearing black shorts, black shoes and a short sleeve plaid shirt. He has a really cool Timex silver watch with a silver band. He's sort of short, a little hunky, though you might not notice it with his shirt untucked. He talks sort of out of the side of his mouth and looks at you sideways. Sometimes he has a loud laugh, and lately I've noticed he refers to himself as "mother."

Ligon's friends seem to have completed the assignment with a sense of humor, describing him with affection, "cute eyebrows," "cat-eye glasses," or teasing him, "a little hunky, though you might not notice it with his shirt untucked." The descriptions are queer and playful, and yet, in other *Runaways* posters the seemingly straightforward descriptive statements carry a historical weight. Such observations as "short haircut," "nice teeth," or "does not look at you straight in the eye when talking to you," are presumably meant as affectionate quips, but recall the historical force of anti-Blackness and its recitation in the present. As Huey Copeland explains, enslavers created a coded vocabulary to describe the fugitive. "Adjectives like proud, artful, plausible, cunning, amiable, polite, wily, and deceitful reappeared with astonishing frequency in the descriptions given by masters, registering the individuality of the slave but also constituting a shifting portrait of the fugitive."[50] Where language appears at first glance as somewhat benign in *Runaways*, it nevertheless carries forth an aesthetic lexicon of objectification and anti-Blackness. In Copeland's list of historical descriptors, we see the sharp performative edges of language that uphold the same minstrel portraits that Kushner was attempting to critique.

Even though Ligon's friends describe him in sweet, clever, queer, and funny ways, such narratives of hypervisibility resound with contemporary surveillance structures like the racial profiling of New York City's "Stop and Frisk" program that mark Black and Black queer life as something that must be contained and physically monitored. As the echoes of KRS-One quietly resound across the floor of the installation, the "whoop, whoop" sounds of the police emphasize the anti-Black logics that undergird American notions of safety and "free" movement. Ligon produces a tension between the comic aesthetic present and the deep-seated history of anti-Blackness in the United States, outlining not their opposition but their continuity in what Copeland calls Ligon's "antiportrait impulse."[51] Placing pressure on the portrait of the "black subject," Copeland explains that antiportraiture "is meant to refuse the gaze, to deny any presumed access to the sitter's personality, and to refute both the classificatory drives and emotional projections."[52] Denying presumed access to the subject behind the work, Ligon emphasizes his own image only to challenge the viewers' sense of what it is they want or expect in reading his work. Employing opacity and refusal as portraiture techniques, Ligon gives the viewer a sense of a ghosted subject and withholds access to the figure at its center. In each series he presents the viewer with the absence of the Black body. In this way, what the story of Henry "Box" Brown makes available to Ligon is also the sleight of hand trick, the ability to be present without being made understandable to white eyes.

Elsewhere, Ligon engages Zora Neale Hurston's essay "How It Felt to Be Colored Me" in an oil stencil painting in which he repeats Hurston's line: "I feel most colored when I am thrown against a sharp white background." Hurston's words repeat until they are undone in the repetition of the charcoal bleed against the white "blankness" of the canvas. Ligon draws the viewer's attention to the production of visual contrast, to the production of Blackness in opposition to its sharp white backdrop. In the introduction to her 1935 book of folklore, *Mules and Men*, Hurston writes about southern Black resistance to question from outsiders and anthropologists, explaining, "The theory behind our tactics: 'The white man is always trying to know into somebody else's business. All right, I'll set something outside the door of my mind for him to play with and handle. He can read my writing but he sho' can't read my mind. I'll put this play toy in his hand, and he will seize it and go away. Then I'll say my say and sing my song.'"[53] Here, Hurston demonstrates the work of opacity, refusal, and engagement. She emphasizes the ability of Black and Indigenous people in the American south to evade the trespassive white eye by either outright refusal or presenting the white outsider with something to look at to distract them from further attempts to "know into" Black thought. Simone Browne uses the term *dark sousveillance* to describe a strategy for remaining out of sight of racial surveillance as well as a place from which to develop strategies of "antisurveillance" and "countersurveillance."[54] Dark sousveillance, Browne argues, "speaks to black epistemologies of contending with antiblack surveillance, where the tools of social control in plantation surveillance or lantern laws in city spaces and beyond were appropriated, co-opted, repurposed, and challenged in order to facilitate survival and escape."[55] Dark sousveillance strategies remake the logics that undergird surveillance in order to enable practices of freedom. Browne argues that lantern laws established in New York City were meant to regulate Black movement and knowability, literally requiring that Blackness be lit and visible at all times or face physical violence at the hands of the law. Discussing both historical and contemporary antisurveillance techniques from biometric technology to airport security, Browne's theory of dark sousveillance draws out Ligon's own critique of a racializing surveillance as it extends from the lantern laws of the early 1700s into the art museum of the 1990s. By placing a "play toy" in the hands of the museum, Ligon is able to do the simultextual work of emphasizing Black freedom practices, survival, and play without having to remain visually decipherable and available to the structures of the NEW YORK CITY art world.

On the opposite wall of the installation is Ligon's *Narratives* series. These frontispieces to slave narratives are historical documents promising autobiography and authenticity for a white audience. Again referencing the lithographic style and conventions of the mid-nineteenth century, Ligon places himself in the frame of these popular slave narratives nominally penned by the formerly enslaved, and usually heavily rewritten by white editors. Legacies of nineteenth-century Black autobiographies—often ghostwritten and prefaced by white authors and editors—are made to share time and space with contemporary Black art and writing. One piece from *Narratives* reads, "THE LIFE AND ADVENTURES OF GLENN LIGON A NEGRO; who was sent to be educated amongst white people in the year 1966 when only about six years of age and has continued to fraternize with them to the present time." Succinctly framing one version of Ligon's "life story," the piece evokes all of the ways in which biographical narratives are framed today depending on the audience that might read, and more importantly purchase, a given type of life story. As Hartman writes, "The paradox of Brown's narrative and that of the majority of slave narratives is that the literary machinery harnessed to resurrect the dead subject (if we understand the condition of slavery as social death) most often results in killing the protagonist a second time."[56] Not only are the authors of slave narratives themselves prevented the possibility of life under slavery, but the narrative framing through the "literary machinery" of the white editor and amanuensis kills the author a second time by removing their voice from the very story purporting to provide their entry into subjectivity. Ligon plays on the double bind of these narratives as cherished historical documents that provide an archive of antebellum Black voices and their symbolic erasure of the subject imagined to be at the center.

Other pieces from *Narratives* contain similar titles such as "Black Rage; or, How I Got Over," "The Narrative of the Life and Uncommon Sufferings of Glenn Ligon, a Colored Man, Who at a Tender Age Discovered His Affection for the Bodies of Other Men, and Has Endured Scorn and Tribulations Ever Since," and "Incidents in the Life of a Snow Queen" with legitimating quotes by Hilton Als and bell hooks mimicking the editorial voices of Lydia Mary Childs or William Lloyd Garrison. Placing his own life and likeness inside the archive of escape narratives and their confines of genre he almost pokes fun at his own engagement with the white art institutions with which "he has continued to fraternize." Instead of using white abolitionist voices as framing devices, Ligon uses the editorial presence of a Black feminist writer and a queer Black cultural critic. He changes the narrative frame to preface the story of his life with queer and feminist Black thinkers aligned with his political project. Even while the legitimating voices are not white, there remains a certain type of voice—the rational writing of published authors and respected public intellectuals—that is given framing importance to explain his work. To be made knowable, then, looks like being translatable and culturally verified in proper linguistic comportment.

1.3
Glenn Ligon, *Narratives*, 1993.

Still another print reads, "To Disembark, or the Price of a Ticket, Comprising an Account of the Author's Birth, Parentage, Early Years, and the Many Hardships and Sufferings He Endures on His Journey toward Freedom." A third of the way down the page, in the style of nineteenth-century slave narratives, is a brief subsection signed with the initials G.L. The two-sentence paragraph echoes the humble plea for literary acceptance and authorial authenticity often found on the title page of (anti)slave escape narratives that required framing devices so that they might be considered legitimate and truthful. Ligon's personal inscription explains that this imaginary novel is meant to allow the reader insight into the soul so as to "view my colored heart at close range." He continues, "If this effort may avail to stir myself and others to a more active pursuit of freedom and self-love, then the object in sending it forth will be accomplished." His inscription, both serious and playful, alerts us once again to the framing devices at play in hearing Black voices and reading Black texts. It also invests his minimalist sculptural pieces with a political imperative—the "*active* pursuit of freedom." Such a statement adheres to the genre convention of the nineteenth-century narratives for freedom and, in my reading, speaks to the genre expectations of the gallery as well. As Ligon asks, "Why do so many shows with works by colored people (and rarely whites) have titles that include 'race' and 'identity'?" Indeed, such a statement brings our attention back to the genre demands of the art institution when showing work by Black artists. In this way, unlike Kushner, Ligon's invocation of Brown is not geared toward teaching a contemporary white audience, but reads more as a response to the demands of the art world itself and its own abilities to see or not see Black work. Thinking back to Wilderson's articulation of the episodic as a narrative structure that supports redemption over a paradigmatic critique of anti-Blackness, Ligon appears to suggest that the art world, the temporality of the work and the gallery attendees passing by the boxes or lithographs, lends itself to the episodic form as it produces consumable narrative cross-sections that leave the viewer feeling good. And yet, I would argue that Ligon leans into the episodic snapshot in order to explore the knowability of the figure that appears at the center of each box, handbill, or frontispiece. *To Disembark*, *Narratives*, and *Runaways* animate not just Brown's panoramic performance and emergence, but also his disappearance inside various social and literary boxing mechanisms of the time. In other words, the archive is animated even as it keeps Brown's and Ligon's likeness out of sight. The episode emerges as necessarily not the whole story.

Post-Enlightenment subjectivity, as Andre Lepecki explains, is defined by an ability to move autonomously through the world. He writes that the fantasy of modernity creates "autonomous, self-motivated, endless spectacular movement."[57] What gets taken up as generic escape features the redemptive progress narrative of subject-making through autonomous movement, self-narration, and spectacular self-making. As Sarah Jane Cervenak writes, "while self-direction and self-mobilization were key to anti-slavery consolidations of humanness, other modalities of movement across the plot were just as important."[58] The anti-slave plot is both narrative and geographic as the word "plot" describes not only a sequence of events but also a small piece of marked-out land. For Cervenak, the plot provides the ground for an "aesthetics of diversion" characterized by a "informational withholding and aleatory prose" that protects Black interiority from white trespass and possession. This terrain of freedom is one of withholding and opacity, articulating a wandering that Fred Moten might characterize as a "subplot, a plot against the plot, contrapuntal, fantastic, underground."⁵⁹ This contrapuntal underground subplot is a strategy of protection from the white abolitionist reader and the enslaver alike. The "other modalities of movement across the plot" prevent attempts to fix, know, and render legible Black thought and life within the capture of white reason. As Fred Moten, Harryette Mullen, and Gabrielle Foreman name in the introduction, such simultextual wandering eludes the trespassive eye of the white amanuensis, editor, or reader.

Throughout his oeuvre, Ligon plays on the question of light and dark in visual representation, exploring the manner in which the color and clarity of images, the tradition of black text on white canvas, reproduces social inequalities or aesthetic assumptions regarding form and color. *To Disembark* pushes the audience to ask: How do we see inside a closed box where no light is permitted? Ligon calls out the hypervisibility of his body in a white-walled art institution bringing attention to racial scrutiny with which institutions present Black artists. Showing the box and no body, he recalls a Black history of bodies that are immediately and readily available to a white audience for violent amusement and consumption.⁶⁰ Ligon's work enables Brown's own sort of movement in excess of the white captive frames that Kushner, his contemporary, cannot seem to see outside of. Ligon engages with the story of "Box" Brown, placing his own image alongside Brown's own "un-visible" body, speaking to the limits on Black mobility within artistic spaces, and an experience of alienation from artistic establishments.⁶¹ The otherwise movement across the narrative plot here emphasizes the ongoing narrative work of escape within institutions and logics of white containment as they move into the contemporary art gallery and museum.

Baby You're a Body: Wilmer Wilson IV

Some twenty years after Kushner and Ligon, Wilmer Wilson IV's *Henry Box Brown: Forever* returns us back to the figurative, but further displaces the mythical fantasy of the subject by focusing instead on sticky paper skin. Wilson centers the excess of Brown's story, almost like he is gathering the tiny scraps of Post-its or stamps to see what is left of Brown's stage trick. The spectacle, to think back to Frederick Douglass's comment on Henry "Box" Brown, is upsetting. This is a different audience than those who attended the abolitionist lecture circuit. While Brown's performance, for Douglass, was a direct address to a white (potentially slave-owning) audience, Wilson's performative enunciation on the streets of DC has a different circulation. As opposed to convincing a public of the cruelty of anti-Blackness, the impetus for Wilson's performance was to "visualize the interiority of [Brown's] gesture."[62] Privileging interior kinesis over readability, Wilson's performance employs the stamps as both a visual and a sensory frame.

In his work, Wilson creates performances and installations that obscure his body or face variously with black Post-its, "I voted" stickers, brown paper bags blown-up like balloons, "flesh tone" Band-Aids, and clear hydrogen peroxide strips. He calls these pieces "skin works," pieces in which Wilson plays with the film of the body and its symbolic resonance. In a 2015 interview discussing these works Wilson explained, "Thin things are things that have marginal and fleeting presence. These can be materials and objects, like . . . lottery scratchcards in urban space; they can also be images and bodies. The way thin things escape this state is by accumulating together with other thin things, which transforms them into a film."[63] Thin things are like thin skin, like thin film, porous or perforated. Wilson tells us here that thin things don't last long, don't last as long as the thicker things like moss, or gelatin, or mirror disco balls with hard surfaces. Those surfaces are thick like protective membranes. He explains that "thin things escape the state by accumulating

1.4   Wilmer Wilson IV, *Henry Box Brown: Forever*, 2012.

together with other thing things."⁶⁴ This kind of provisional collectivity of small gestures, small acts, small things creates a space of escape, an evasion of the regulation of the state, and a reprieve.

I am reminded of the performance studies method of thick description, of laying bare the stakes of a performance to an often subaltern or minoritarian audience looking for belonging. For Wilson, a lithe figure, thinness seems to rhyme with performance's ephemeral nature. Wilson asks: "What does it look like to employ these facets of historical specificity that don't lend themselves to a fetishization or voyeurism of the interiority, however indexical or not, of the figures depicted?"⁶⁵ Wilson imagines ways history can be evoked, ways for the complicated story of Brown to be indexed, without necessarily making itself available to an immediate fetishization, voyeurism, or evacuation.

As Wilson tells it, having been born in Richmond, Virginia, the story of Henry "Box" Brown was well-known to him. Curious to understand the effect of his second skin performances outside of the white-box gallery, Wilson's *Henry Box Brown: Forever* performed, in his words, "skin-as-box." Creating a faceless postal object, Wilson wanders through the old ornate America-proud buildings of DC. Stamps cover the curves of his body from his torso to the round sides of his shaved head. He wears only underwear with the stamps sticking tight to his skin. He walks between the hypergroomed national gardens, and the working-class Black neighborhoods. Wilson's second "forever" skin possesses a monetary value; the nondenominated postage stamps mark him as an object for shipping. These pieces of paper—tacky on one side and nationalistic on the other—are indexical. Captured in glossy photographs by Wilson's gallery and curator, his 2015 performance was archived for a future audience while he circulated in the present of the performance.

In one image, Wilson stands at the post office waiting his turn as onlookers snap photos of him on their cellphones. All that you see are Wilson's eyes, framed by a sea of flag stamps collaged across his body. In another image, Wilson walks in front of the Old Post Office pavilion, directly facing the camera. In this shot, he engages the facelessness of most escapes—both Douglass and Brown are shrouded by night, by the cramped space of the box or by a refusal to disclose the scene. In still another picture, Wilson walks by a shoe repair business, Black working-class patrons watch him in what appears to be amusement and distrust as he passes. Looking at these images, I am reminded of both the vulnerability and the precariousness of performance. Durational performance is exhausting, with artists often pushing themselves to the limits and placing themselves in situations that are risky—the work of artists like Pope L., Marina Abromovic, and Adrian Piper come to mind. Wilson's white curator, Laura Roulet, tells the story of an encounter with an older Black woman during Wilson's performance who was growing increasingly upset by the spectacle of Wilson as a faceless postal object to be shipped. Roulet explains, "First commenting that Wilson appeared anorexic, [this woman] tried to interpret the situation and the racially mixed entourage, . . . insisting, 'Don't let them do this to you . . . George Washington had slaves!'" Roulet explains that Wilson then broke character and pulled the stamps from his lips to reassure the onlooker that he wanted to be doing this performance. According to the curator, the women then pulled out her belt as though she were prepared to protect him and started calling Wilson her son. Both the reaction and the narration of the onlooker's response raise the question of the intended audience for this week. I do not know what the woman on the street saw when she saw Wilson, nor do I necessarily trust the curators framing of the incident, but the story speaks to the vulnerability felt around the work from both Wilson and the witness of his performance.

In a subsequent series, Wilson created large-scale works from staples and community fliers, the same staples one might find attached to a phone pole long after the paper flier has disintegrated. Looking at these images I see thorns, or a texture like the ones readers are invited to touch in a children's book. I see the tactile shiny pillows sold at the 99-cent store, gold sequins on one side and black sequins on the other. I see the shapes the wind makes in the snow as it blows the flakes into drifts against a building. But these silver grains aren't soft like snow, or gently abrasive and exfoliating like sand. These are industrial staples, long square brackets, each one discharged, ka-thunk, into a large photographic pigment print, pressed onto a body-sized piece of wood. An echo of red or pink peeks through the waves from underneath. And when I zoom out I can see the body-sized gesture. Shoes peek out from the sea of staples. These are colorful sneakers with neon laces. A red color under the staples begins to resemble a shirt and the body-sized wooden frame exposes the representation of a body, or perhaps a portrait. The shoes at the bottom of the image are shy in the way they tuck into each other, almost as if they know they alone can be seen.

This piece is part of a series of works that feature enlarged versions of promotional materials that Wilson collected in West Philadelphia. Like much of Wilson's work, these pieces are time-based. They were made over twenty-five to thirty hours each in which the images are slowly covered over with staples. In another piece, the staples shine like the sun, emanating in rays from a corner exposing, again, a pair of shoes. This time, they are heels with Black feet and dressed-up, manicured toes. Underneath the staples is more color,

1.5 Wilmer Wilson IV, staple series, installation view at the New Museum triennial, 2018.

what looks like letters in yellow, and red, or orange, maybe, in unidentifiable shapes. The wall text of the exhibition reads: "A woman's shoes are left uncovered by staples, suggesting the possibility for *escape*. As Wilson repeats the act of stapling en masse, his physical obliteration of paper and obscuring of the image takes on a dimension of care. The figures underneath are protected from visibility, a reprieve for bodies otherwise hypersurveilled and hypercommodified in Western visual culture." The shoes suggest the *possibility* of escape, as though because the shoes are uncovered, they can move. The usage of escape would seem to imply that the staples are the force that confine, and the shoes represent some sort of fantasy for the potential to move, one foot in front of the next. Following along with Wilson's own emphasis on thin things, and an indexical view of history that does not fetishize its Black subjects, it seems that it is not the exposed shoes, but the staples themselves that offer an "escape." This invocation of escape recalls Simone Browne's articulation of dark sousveillance as undersight, as a refusal of anti-Black policing and surveillance, and as a strategy for evading the fetishization, hypervisualization, and consumption of Black artists and their likenesses. Similar to Ligon's own antiportraiture, part of Wilson's project engages the problem of how an artist might appear their body without that appearance signaling, also, its capture. As he explains, "I don't want to abandon the body. I want the surface to remain a viewing device, like a lens and not like a wall." For Wilson, the film of the surface—stamps or staples—covers the face without letting the viewer forget the human-like silhouette. He continues: "That push and pull between sub-human or superhuman was really important to me. I think of my work as trying to reach outside of the discourse of the human."[66] This stepping outside of the confines of the Western Enlightenment notion of the human-as-man allows Wilson to play with the shapes of representation, the ways portraiture or the body become legible and visible. Wilson's work is open-ended, resisting the enclosure of narrative redemption and resolution. Narrative here functions as a space for ongoing interior experience made only available in the archive of images left behind, in the archive of stamps as a shedding second skin after the performance.

    The staples that cover over the figures in Wilson's staple series enact a bracketing off, a reprieve, proposing a sense of place that is seen from the inside out but cannot be seen from the outside in. Instead of the woman's shoes suggesting the possibility of escape, Wilson proposes that escape lives inside the duration of the staples, the thin staples repeated together like sand, accumulating on the community fliers. The staples create an index of local

1.6 Wilmer Wilson IV, *Henry Box Brown: Forever*, 2012.

pamphlets, small things that are not archived except for in people's homes. The staples are a different kind of skin or armor, and they gesture toward escape outside its normative understanding. Perhaps the wall text misplaced the word *escape*. What if the placement of "escape" were moved to read: "A woman's shoes are left uncovered by staples. As Wilson repeats the act of stapling en masse, his physical obliteration of paper and obscuring of the image takes on a dimension of care suggesting the possibility for escape." Instead of the shoes offering up the possibility of escape, it might be the staples that offer care instead of obliteration. This is perhaps another way of saying: "thin things escape." The staples are troubling toward freedom; they upset skin, figuration, performance, and light. A path of escape is not only found through the movement that the shoes make possible, but I argue that Wilson demonstrates an alternate form of escape in the reprieve of the rest of the body inside and underneath the staples. The opaque body is afforded rest. Here reprieve and opacity work together. Wilson picks up not just on the mobility of Brown, but also his engagement with the dark sousveillance of the undercover cloak.

Wilson's work illuminates the structures of escape, its directionality and relation to narrative form. What Copeland calls the "masquerade" of Brown is so alluring to artists and audiences today because his mode of escape gives over to a range of responses that are attuned to anarchy, illusion, sound, and skin. From the pedagogy of the children's book to the refusal of contemporary artists to mobilize Brown's work for transparent and redemptive ends, Brown's story and subsequent performative enactment have served as a place to puzzle through the complexities of freedom. As Sarah Jane Cervenak writes, "The opacity in the spectacular is the undetectable place of an errant movement, an interior kinesis that resists forces attempting to trace, follow, and read."[67] Wilson imagines the interiority of escape as a gesture in its repetition. He imagines the fleshy and unreadable movements and how they resonate both for himself and for others. He explains, "Part of my project against portraiture is to try to identify the line at which visual information is taken away from an image and our imagination or subconscious rushes in to fill the gaps."[68] Where the imagination fills in the gaps there is diagnosis and conclusion, a demand for taxonomy and understanding.

Asking for the story to remain one of visual information, Wilson returns the narrative of escape to its formal structures in excess of their juridical pull and demand to be understood. This is not to say that real freedom from confinement, enclosure, and systemic injustices that make Black bodies targets of white fantasy is insignificant, but more so to bring our attention to the limitations of the definitions of freedom itself. Wilson demonstrates how practices of freedom exist outside the sayable and surveillable. And furthermore, it is outside these realms of Enlightenment understanding and rationality where spaces of care, curiosity, poiesis, and abstraction can be manifest. Returning to his work with staples, Wilson explains, "It feels like an archive to see this accumulation of staples on a pole. An archive of a circulating public discourse happening. It's exciting to me to think about ways of employing that labor to certain protective ends, or certain care-filled ends."[69] This archive of care and circulation illustrates the accumulation of discourse around freedom; in this way, we might argue that the escape narrative represents an archive of freedom, its practices, its white codification and legibility, and all of the ways the return to escape also signals a return to ongoing conversations about Black improvisation and interior movement.

The Frame of Escape

The National Great Blacks in Wax Museum in Baltimore features over 150 life-sized historical figures rendered in wax—from abolitionist Sojourner Truth to gospel singer Mahalia Jackson. Of all of these representations, the only moving figure displayed in the museum is Henry "Box" Brown. Wearing a wide straw hat, hands poised as if to peek over the edge, he retreats inside and then reemerges from his shipping box on repeat. I mention this appearance of Brown to emphasize the mobile self-mastery that makes Brown's story stand out. As others have written, Brown invented strategies for moving through captivity and developed new modes of engaging the public in his touring panorama show. He created narrative trajectories and forms that were previously unavailable to him. This seems to be the primary reason that the story of Brown is invoked as a celebratory and pedagogical tale of self-discipline and invention. Performing his emergence outside of the box, Brown's story is one of imaginative survival. Yet he is compelled to constant movement, never allowed an opportunity for rest even in the archive.

While Kushner attempts to freeze Henry "Box" Brown in an effort to horrify a contemporary audience into action, Ligon and Wilson embrace opacity and invention through refusal and, to quote Simone Browne, an "un-visible" bodily presencing that makes the viewer question the legibility of the body itself. Throughout his performance career, Brown was constantly reinventing himself. Danielle A. D. Howard compares Brown's performance work to the Afrofuturism of Sun Ra, explaining that "both Brown and Sun Ra's embodiment of inventive or even outrageous identities served as acts of wizardry, disempowering the genealogical grip of slavery on the African American psyche."[70] Brown's acts of wizardry seem to embrace a form of interiority and care, disentangling his vision of self from the psychic capture of the slavery. Where Kushner reminds us of the connections between the ideological practices of abolition and anarchy, he is unable to bring the practices together beyond their mere juxtaposition. Yet all three of these artists seem to return to Brown in order to say something about care and coalition. In the retelling of Brown's escape—the performative repetitions on the stage, in the gallery and on the street—each artist focuses on movement that is aesthetic, by which I mean having to do with aesthesis, with touch and sense. The archive of work inspired by Henry "Box" Brown utilizes the frame of escape while constantly displacing the white fantasies that latch onto Black performances of freedom. Replacing such framing with questions of care and interiority, Brown's story becomes one not only of reinvention, but of imagining the ongoing work of care against surveillance and captivity.

If escape is a genre of change where genre "makes available collective experience," then the repetitions of Brown's abolitionist spectacular wizardry tap into a story of the unexpected sensory work of freedom. Brown came to know himself through the genres of performance in which he worked, as a master of the box, and as an African prince. Where Kushner wants to tell a story of coalitional anarchy, Ligon creates space for Black play and refusal within spaces of white artistic confinement. Moving away from the art spaces of the theater or white cube, Wilson focuses on the protection of the figure of Brown. The throughline among these strategies is a desire to shift away from escape as in individual story to one that names the collective experiences of wanting change. And both Ligon and Wilson pay particular attention to the consideration of the materials that enable an experience of the self as both protected and under scrutiny. If we think generatively of Kushner's anarchist lens, we can see that anarchy itself is focused on a responsibility to each other. But instead of upholding anarchism as a universal salve to cure the ills of the present, perhaps we might read each artistic invocation of Brown as lifting up various forms of engagement, care, and cooperation within the genre of escape. It is in this way that escape becomes a (not uncomplicated) space for thinking freedom alongside the experience of others.

Care, as I introduce the term here, in the artistic structures, propositions, and gestures put forth by Wilson and Ligon, is meant to demonstrate not "care for," like wardens or doctors or superintendents, but instead the introduction of a space where care is prioritized and imagined as an encounter and conversation. Care suggests a sense of interdependence as a structure or, thinking with Leah Lakshmi Piepzna-Samarashina, as "a collective responsibility that's maybe even deeply joyful?"[71] Care is tied to having a body that cannot exist independently in a white supremacist and ableist society that imagines discrete hyperproductivity and bodily infallibility. Care names that bodies are interconnected and dependent upon one another. Instead of conceiving of this interconnection under the sway of Euro-Enlightenment thought as a problem or inadequacy, it might be considered through these works as an embrace of the joy of care, as a practice of freedom, of the pleasure of connection and being "among loved ones." The act of gathering, or assembly, allows people to make collective decisions. As Wilson reminds us, "thin things escape the state ... by accumulating together." In this vision, escape becomes a collective action of accumulating together, of small gestures, or repetitions, and of freedom seeking outside of the regulative eye of European thought and understanding. The care and rest of escape might not be a blueprint for how to bring collective bodies together to escape the watchful eye of the state, but it does give Brown's image and narrative a reprieve from constant movement and, in so doing, suggests a refusal of the incessant demand for Blackness to perform.

Hers was the generation that would launch the Revolution, but which for the moment was turning blue for want of air. The generation reaching consciousness in a society that lacked any. The generation that despite the consensus that declared change impossible *hankered* for change all the same. At the end of her life, when she was being eaten alive by cancer, Beli would talk about how trapped they all felt. It was like being at the bottom of an ocean, she said. There was no light and a whole ocean crushing down on you. But most people had gotten so used to it they thought it normal, they forgot even that there was a world above.

—JUNOT DÍAZ

As soon as genre announces itself, one must respect a norm, one must not cross a line of demarcation, one must not risk impurity, anomaly, or monstrosity.

—JACQUES DERRIDA

FEELING OUT OF THIS WORLD

That's What I Guess These Stories Are About

To argue that speculative fiction is a robust form of world-making is not a particularly contentious claim. With its focus on both the macro and the local, speculative fiction shows the individual capable of change as well as the worlds around them that do not (and perhaps never did) work. However, speculative fiction is also one of the most expansive genres, as it has very few hard and fast rules. What is unique to the genre is its focus on the world-building aspects of narrative, wherein the world itself is often the primary narrative character. In this chapter I turn to speculative fiction—the genre that includes all the stories that ask "what if?"—as one of the main sites where stories of escape congregate. Speculative fiction provides a counter to established stories of escape that are invested in real-life containment and release, opting instead to track the social and emotional tonalities of escape. If part of the argument of this book is that escape is a genre of change, then this chapter looks to escape as an affective category for imagining change in the here-and-now of literary life-worlds.

Afrofuturism, as I argue in the introduction, disrupts temporal progress through an attention to the episodic as a strategy for making the impossible feel if not possible, at least imaginable. Where white supremacy and colonialism function to imagine blackness as a thing of the past, Afrofuturism envisions a futurity unbound by the dictates of white capture. Narratives of escape as they are present in Afrofuturism, magical realism, and other speculative genres outline other worlds that exceed the here-and-now. The types of escape that emerge in these various artistic and literary genres necessarily differ and call on different audiences. Where the golden age of science fiction carries with it a history of white men conquering new planets, what Walidah Imarisha and adrienne maree brown in their book, *Octavia's Brood*, call visionary fiction focuses on the fantastical as a space to build "freer worlds." As Imarisha explains, "We believe this space is vital for any process of decolonialization, because the decolonization of the imagination is the most dangerous and subversive form there is: for it is where all other forms of decolonization are born. Once the imagination is unshackled, liberation is limitless."[1] The felt world of the imagination, like the material laws of the nation-state and the linguistic, has been shaped by white colonial logics. Consequently, as Imarisha writes, to imagine in spite and in excess of these restrictive structures requires strange and unexpected visionary work. And yet, the challenge of detethering the frameworks of colonial violence from the psychic structures of self is not a simple task. In this chapter, I turn to a text that engages escape as both strategy and theme. I do so not to ignore the controversy surrounding its author, but to return to the complicated spaces of escape, where escape fails to be either a good or bad object, either the answer or the problem.

The Brief Wondrous Life of Oscar Wao, written in 2007 by Junot Díaz, traces the social and political feelings that orbit speculative fiction. The book received a Pulitzer Prize in 2008, and in 2012, Díaz was awarded the MacArthur Fellowship for his writing. Six years later, in 2018, Díaz was accused of sexual violence, bullying, and harassment by several women of color. These testimonies followed on the heels of an essay Díaz wrote for the *New Yorker* in which he described his own sexual assault and rape at the age of eight. While I do not wish to solely focus on Díaz's personal life within this chapter, the topic of sexual trauma as it relates to the feelings of escape, colonialism, gender, and genre are relevant. In mentioning these accusations I neither want to vilify nor redeem Díaz, but instead to consider accountability, repetition, and healing as they get written into the felt sense of escape. Reading Díaz against himself, looking for the visionary grains Díaz provides for his reader, as well as the way he disappoints, this chapter considers the affective tonalities of speculative fiction. The controversies surrounding the author amplify themes of complicity already embedded in the characters and afterlife of the novel. Díaz's work has itself been taken up and uncritically celebrated by white middlebrow audiences, and his characters reproduce the colonial and masculinist language of domination. And yet, there is something deeply queer and feeling about the book. Through *The Brief Wondrous Life of Oscar Wao*, I argue that speculative fiction emerges as an episodic genre of change that speaks to the feelings of the escape story. Furthermore, such affective textures are inextricable from the violences of enclosure, the individual, and the normative.

The Brief Wondrous Life of Oscar Wao imagines "a world above" the unbearable weight of a "whole ocean crushing down on you."[2] Belicia Cabral—the mother of our main character—recounts the experience of living under the confinement of dictatorship as the sensation that one's lungs are collapsing under the weight of the ocean. Beli, "suffering from the same suffocation that was asphyxiating a whole generation," reminds the reader of the hankering for an impossible change that persists even when you don't know how or what that change could look like.[3] For Díaz "the more speculative genres" contain outlandishly real descriptions and scenarios that approximate the "nigh unbearable historical experiences" of colonialism and its continuities.[4] Díaz writes with and in narratives of the impossible both to describe the Black and Latinx tonalities of daily life and to imagine the potential to feel otherwise. *The Brief Wondrous Life* envisions the feelings of escape endemic to speculative fiction, colonization, and the history of capital in the Americas. A discussion of the *feeling of escape*, what I also call *genre affect*, highlights the potential for genre, the aesthetic, and performance (analogs often read as escapist and antipolitical) to work against scenes of white supremacy, reason, and clarity. Indeed, it is precisely this escapist derision that interests me. Reinvigorating the modernist question "What is political about the aesthetic?," I want to ask, what might be political about escape? Or, put another way, why is the act of escape valorized as heroic, while escapism is often dismissed as cathartic and ineffectual?

In *The Brief Wondrous Life*, the aesthetic and "the real" are written together in an overlapping history that describes both the Trujillo dictatorship in the Dominican Republic and the science fiction feelings of New Jersey, unbelonging, and diaspora. As in the previous chapter, we are reminded that real escapes are recounted as stories about escape. Giving the reader a historical novel that is told through personal narrative and marginalia, through the lens of narrators and main characters who are writers themselves, Díaz places the act of historical narration in the hands of Dominican American sci-fi nerds. Highlighting the feelings of escape instead of the liberatory movement from confinement to freedom that generic escape implies, Díaz takes his reader backward across the lives of Oscar de León's "cursed" family on an emotional journey of wanting an escape. We follow the life story of Oscar as it is peppered through with interruption and supplementation by the stories of his mother, Hypatía Belicia Cabral (Beli), growing up at the height of Trujillo's bloody reign, and of his older sister, Lola, an *oya soul*, always running and yearning for elsewhere. The novel traces the affective and social potential of escapism—by way of genre literature and romantic love—at the same time that it narrates a "real" physical escape from political peril and violence. As readers we are reminded that the movement of escape is inextricable from the feeling and fantasy that such a movement invokes and encourages. Díaz's cleverly crafted novel weaves together themes of escapist fantasy with stories of familial escape moving across the ragged borders of colonialism and empire.

In this chapter, I explore the scene of wanting change, what Oscar's mother Belicia describes as "hanker[ing] for change" despite the feeling of "being at the bottom of an ocean" with "no light and a whole ocean crushing down on you."[5] This is the "freedom drive" that coincides with the "disappointing under achievement/s of emancipation" to quote Fred Moten.[6] Focusing in on the novel as a meta scene of escape—the reading of the novel is an escape from the "real world" dramas of everyday life, and the subject of the novel, Oscar, is infatuated with the more escapist literary genres—this chapter examines the affective texture of escape for both the characters and the novel's readers. Moving from the sounds and containers of escape charted in chapter 1, this chapter explores escapism in literature and the role the more speculative genres, what Díaz shorthands simply as "genre," play in this felt psychic space of escape. Speculative fiction, I argue, illuminates the genre affect of escape, connecting adolescent longing to anti-colonial visioning.

The Politics of Genre

Readers choose their genre based on the world they want to experience, the feelings they want to have—emotions such as fright, romance, adventure, or angst. But why are some artistic works categorized as difficult, time-consuming, thoughtful, and productive, where others are easy and amusing and encourage only superficial engagement? Furthermore, what is the qualitative difference between the two? From the mid-eighteenth century onward, literature has had an intimate relationship to escapism. With the rise of printing, the novel became available to a newly middle-class audience reflecting life as it is lived within a social and economic context. Initially, the novel created misgiving because, unlike verse drama or philosophy, it was "easy reading." The prevalent attitude toward genre literature in the twentieth century seems to have continued this belief that new commercial and popular literature encourage escapist activities and should not be taken seriously as an artistic or critical cultural contribution. In *Reading the Romance*, Janice Radway argues that the escapism of romance literature has a compensatory function. "It supplies [readers] with an important emotional release that is proscribed in daily life because the social role with which they identify themselves leaves little room for guiltless, self-interested pursuit or individual pleasure."[7] In genre literature, readers can establish and access affective life-worlds in which they take pleasure in both themselves and their surroundings. Radway specifically notes the affective and political intervention genre reading makes in the day-to-day lives of female romance readers. She argues that reading romance "is also a figurative journey to a utopian state of total receptiveness where the reader, as a result of her identification with the heroine, feels herself the object of someone else's attention and solicitude. Ultimately, the romance permits its reader the experience of feeling cared for and the sense of having been reconstituted affectively, even if both are lived only vicariously."[8] The good feelings that such genre engenders sustain readers; romantic fiction makes up for a reader's less-than-satisfactory present, and at the same time, it serves a utopian function demonstrating how readers would like to be socially recognized or emotionally "cared for." The compensatory function of art can be critical and sustaining, or it can simply reaffirm a false sense of satisfaction that, as Theodor Adorno argues, merely maintains the status quo of dissatisfaction and alienation which is already present in the culture industry.[9]

Questions concerning the function of the aesthetic echo throughout the late-nineteenth and twentieth centuries. Frankfurt School thinkers such as Adorno, Walter Benjamin, Herbert Marcuse, and Ernst Bloch were concerned with the power of the aesthetic to inform and change the larger social world. Marcuse describes art in bourgeois culture as generative of liberatory ideals not grounded in material politics. The commodity-based sense of happiness and freedom created by affirmative culture glosses over material practices that might effect change and alter current conditions. In response to the illusions created by affirmative culture, Marcuse calls for a practice of negativity that would reveal what is lacking in current social and economic constellations. His critique of affirmative culture is also a rejection of the capital-oriented performance principle—what he refers to in *Eros and Civilization* as "The Great Refusal"—in favor of a potentially powerful pleasure principle or aesthetic dimension.[10] Instead of living for work, he proposes a living for pleasure. For Marcuse the aesthetic has the power to both critique the failings of this world and illuminate a potential "new social order."[11] Elsewhere Marcuse writes, "The incompatibility of the artistic form with the real form of life may be used as a lever for throwing upon reality the light that the latter cannot absorb, the light which may eventually dissolve this reality (although such dissolution is no longer the function of art). The untruth of art may become the precondition for the artistic contradiction and negation. Art may promote alienation, the total estrangement of man from his world. And this alienation may provide the artificial basis for the remembrance of freedom in the totality of oppression."[12] Marcuse suggests that art enables "the remembrance of freedom" in the distance it creates from the reality of the day-to-day. For him, it is just such a memory of freedom—a sensation of a world beyond capital and oppression—that stirs in the viewer or reader a desire to critique her contemporary situation. Distinct from Brecht's distancing effect which causes his audience to think *this should not be so*, Marcuse's remembrance of freedom shows the audience the way things could be. For Marcuse, the alienating function of the aesthetic enables a critique of the false happiness found in affirmative culture.

Similar to the aesthetic, the work of escapism can set the reader off on a pleasurable and carefree adventure in literary fiction, or it can provide a critical engagement with another world that recalls the political imperatives of our own. *The Brief Wondrous Life of Oscar Wao* is not properly a genre novel, but it works with genre through its science fiction sensibilities and cross-generational map of escapist desires. Escape emerges here in its felt sense as it is performed on an affective register. Thinking escape as a genre of change with the power to alter the logic of freedom and confinement, escapism marks a political escape strategy that is often overlooked. *Brief Wondrous Life* demonstrates an affective promise of escape, one that is grounded both in felt life experiences and in strategies of psychic survival.

THAT'S WHAT THESE STORIES ARE ABOUT

The novel's very title tells us that Oscar is not long meant for this world. His is the story of a first-generation Dominican boy growing up in Patterson, New Jersey, finding both solace and opportunity in the affective landscapes built through speculative fiction novels, films, and comics. Personal, national, and familial history is told through the fragments of memory and imaginative supplementation. Díaz pulls from a vast cross section of popular references, often speaking in shorthand, and always invoking a level of insider cool, even when the topic is the nerdiest of all: science fiction. And while the novel itself is considered realist fiction because it does not fit within science fiction genre conventions, it invokes the feelings of genre; it reads as epic, mythic, wild, and insatiable. Díaz describes the feeling of social exclusion and what it means to be a Dominican American immigrant with the heavy history of family and colonialism tugging at your heels. Yet, the manner in which Díaz details Oscar de Léon and his gigantic feelings resonates with the otherworldly.

The novel begins with our narrator, Yunior, telling the tale of Oscar de Léon, nicknamed Oscar Wao, as he collects Oscar's manuscripts, memories, and letters to fill in the *"página en blanco"* of history.[13] Oscar's story, which becomes Yunior's story and the story of the Americas more broadly, begins with the moment of colonial contact as Admiral Cristóbal Colón touches down on the New World. The European colonization of the Americas, the enslavement of Africans, and genocide of Indigenous people set the stage for Oscar's story; his "brief wondrous life," begins at this moment of extraction and exploitation as it carries through the years to Ronald Reagan and Rafael Leonidas Trujillo.

The novel opens with Oscar and his growth into a person who does not fit easily in the world that surrounds him. Oscar feels like an outsider, and in this way there is something slightly queer about him from the beginning. He is "too fat," his racial affect and self-presentation do not coincide with Dominican or American norms, and his extracurricular interests are anomalous and "uncool." Oscar is a chubby nerd who "talks like a star trek computer" and dreams of being the Dominican J. R. R. Tolkien.[14] The only thing that Oscar loves more than what he calls "the more speculative genres" is love itself. But women find him incomprehensible and want nothing to do with him. Consequently, Oscar spends most of his time ensconced in his genre worlds, studying them and bringing them to life in his own volumes of speculative writing. And despite his deep emotional attachment to, and investment in, his imagined worlds, Oscar feels himself to be a failure and is constantly struggling with "the darkness" of New Jersey, social isolation, and the diasporic discontent that plagues him.[15] He fails to achieve the stereotype of "normal" Dominican man: "He wasn't no home-run hitter or a fly bachatero, not a playboy with a million hots on his jock."[16] He is socially ridiculed for being fat, submissive, and introverted. He speaks in the verbose and nerdy jargon of one of his genre novels. Because he does not feel Dominican enough and for all of the other reasons that diaspora forces a reevaluation of where one fits in the world, Oscar turns to speculative fiction; he never heeds the call to "grow up" and leave his childish attachment to genre behind. His genre books, movies, and comics allow Oscar a form of affective and psychic escape, a stubborn resistance to the more coercive and traditional narratives of being and belonging. Oscar is an affective escapologist, but his creative imaginings are never quite enough. He repeatedly escapes from the feeling of loneliness into his literary and filmic worlds of fantasy, if only momentarily. The escapes that Oscar wants to make—permanent escapes from affective states such as depression or social exclusion—are frustrated and foreclosed. Escapism, what we might call the daily desire for escape, is Oscar's strategy when he cannot physically escape a place in which he finds himself sticking out like a sore thumb. Just as Henry "Box" Brown in chapter 1, Oscar can never truly escape, so he turns to escapist literature. As the "tendency to seek, or practice of seeking distraction," escapism operates on an affective and intrapsychic register; it emotionally safeguards one from an inability to endure the world.[17] In its arsenal of practices, escapism includes a psychic withdrawal into fantasy and seclusion. As a genre practice, escapism is not entirely distinct from the literary and performance practices that emerge in the first chapter. Indeed, escapism appears in the world of Oscar Wao as a necessary element of the escape narrative, one that emphasizes the affective tonalities of both genre as well as the flat, heteronormative, whiteness of modernist literary conventions.

Recounting Oscar's early years, Yunior explains: "Being a reader/fanboy (for lack of a better term) helped him get through the rough days of his youth, but it also made him stick out in the mean streets of Paterson even more than he already did.... You really want to know what being an X-Man feels like? Just be a smart bookish boy of color in a contemporary U.S. ghetto. Mamma mia! Like having bat wings or a pair of tentacles growing out of your chest."[18] The humor and emotion with which Díaz writes helps us come to know the felt sense of Oscar's daily life. Deeply attached to his literary worlds, Díaz parallels Oscar's experience of being a "smart bookish boy of color in a contemporary U.S. ghetto" with that of being an X-Man.[19] The X-Men allusion refers to the human mutant superhero who possesses a power that makes them unique but also makes them stand out and, maybe more crucially, makes them feel like they stand out. While being a "reader/fanboy" helps Oscar get by, it also prevents him from fitting in. Connecting the experience of a diasporic Dominican nerd to that of a comic book mutant gives the reader entry into the emotions and social experience of Oscar. Díaz uses speculative fiction to get at an experience and feeling that is difficult to explain in a language that takes the white American middle-class experience as its unspoken norm. Using speculative fiction examples such as "having bat wings or a pair of tentacles growing out of your chest" to explain the feeling of standing out also puts a visually rich and affectively open image on an experience that might otherwise feel like a dead end.[20] Like the Afrofuturist imagery of Sun Ra bringing Black aesthetics of liberation into the future, or the magical realism of Gabriel García Márquez imagining worlds despite the "lack of conventional means to render [Latin American] lives believable," the X-Men invocation imagines a way out of what can feel like a closed circuit.[21]

The feeling that escapism engenders allows the reader to take felt experience seriously as a basis for social and political strategy to combat racialization, coercive gender and sexual norms, and the abjection of diasporic belonging. This is the felt work of escape and the allure of freedom that it promises. As I discuss in the introduction, escape enables a critique of freedom by exposing its unacknowledged boundaries and glossed-over promises. In the story of Oscar de León, the generational persistence of this desire to escape—as well as the speculative fiction realities that the de Leóns experience time and again—demonstrates the resonance of such a feeling.[22] Furthermore, the attention to escapism illuminates the potential inadequacy of discrete realist literary genres to explicate and relay the feeling of lived experience in the Americas. Escapism resounds through Yunior's science fiction lens and beyond to describe the fantasy work of "getting out."

I want to pause on this idea of escapism as a perpetually derided activity, as the opposite of engagement or activism, to think through both the ways in which escapism is in fact a form of engagement worth considering. Whereas escape, particularly in relation to national borders or hostile and dangerous situations, is often considered to be an imperative, a heroic method of survival, "escapism"—the habitual version of the otherwise heroic and solitary grand escape—is derided as a diversion from "what has to normally be endured," that is, "reality."[23] As the "tendency to seek, or practice of seeking distraction," escapism operates on an affective and intrapsychic register; it emotionally safeguards you from an inability to endure reality—whether through a fault of your own, or due to external circumstances beyond your control.[24] The practice of escapism is tied to "the more speculative genres," but as Díaz demonstrates, it is not unique to them. Like failure and passivity, the felt and psychic work of escapism suggests an alternative to the choice between either "cynical resignation" or "naïve optimism."[25] Passivity and failure often point to the structures that frame action, engagement, and success as binary and uncomplicated. Escapism opens up the potentially critical and generative work of passivity, fantasy modes of belonging, and the imagination of elsewheres. As psychoanalyst Adam Phillips observes, "To escape—or, of course, to be unable to escape—is often linked to a certain sense of failure."[26] The opposite of engagement, escape marks a defection, a withdrawal, and passivity. I would argue that the failure of escapism is tied to daydreaming and fantasy, to the alteration of the terms of engagement for another, perhaps illegible, tactic. For Oscar de Léon, escapism is the desire for another land, a homeland traced through the throes of diaspora, the alluring promise of belonging and self-acceptance, and the sci-fi worlds of unending adolescence. Oscar reminds us that there is something to be learned by attending to the feelings of escapism and the scenes in which such feelings congregate.

Throughout the novel, Díaz switches from Spanish to English, from the New Jersey and New York Dominican language of Yunior to the verbose science fiction vernacular of Oscar. To understand the specifics of Dominican history or get the backstory of a particular plot point, the reader must jump back and forth between the narrative and the footnotes at the bottom of almost every page. As literary critic T. S. Miller observes, Yunior recounts "a history told from the margins and in the margins."[27] In the polyvocal language of Dominican diaspora and sci-fi fandom meaning is made in excess of European American conceptions of speech, history, and subjectivity. While it is easy to understand the larger sweeps of the story through Díaz's playful conversational tone, every reader will inevitably miss a word here or there and need to read through it. The language used illustrates the multiplicity of experiences, readings, and audiences of the book. With the narrative often interrupted by a side note, a remembrance of the story from multiple perspectives, or important contextual facts that have been added in the extended footnotes at the bottom of the page, the story is told in fits and spurts, recounting history through the fragment. Díaz reminds us that history itself is a genre not altogether distinct from the "more speculative" ones. The reader is reminded time and again that we cannot fully possess or know the life of Oscar de León. What we can begin to hear, however, are the feelings that attach to this tale of personal, national, and diasporic history.

While Díaz never talks exclusively in the Dungeons and Dragons speak of the geeky 1980s, or complete sci-fi slang, he writes in a manner that regards speculative fiction scenarios as real. In a 2012 interview Díaz explained that as a kid, "there was an enormous amount of pressure from all sides for me to pick one discourse (reflecting my high test scores, identity as Dominican immigrant, and experience growing-up in a poor black and Latino neighborhood). That was the smithy in which this language was formed. All these motherfuckers wanted me to pick one simplification so that they could feel better, and I know that that would've been the death of me."[28] This code switching between the language of the ivory tower and that of the predominately Black and Latinx streets of Paterson, New Jersey, illustrates Díaz's effort to keep the seemingly contradictory experiences and identities together despite the social pressure to bracket them for the ease of others. He names the pressure to compartmentalize as a "deadly" psychic excision. Díaz speaks through the narrator Yunior in the words and vernaculars of home that are most comfortable to him.

Oscar's story begins with Yunior. He is the narrator and the closest thing that Oscar has to a friend. Yunior fancies himself a model Dominican man: tough and sexually irresistible, but also secretly sensitive and intellectually savvy. He is the jerk who cheats on Oscar's sister, Lola, and fails to protect Oscar from social ridicule, yet he is also the guy who continues to show up for Oscar. While Yunior excels at performing normative Dominican masculinity, he also geeks out with Oscar on comic book worlds. The main difference is that Yunior can pass as stereotypically Dominican and masculine while Oscar cannot. Yunior begins the tale of Oscar's life by explaining fukú, a curse born in the moment of Dominican colonization at the beginning of "the new world" and on the backs of the enslaved. Fukú is the promise of doom brought on through Admiral Cristóbal Colón and the brutal "homegrown" Dominican dictatorship of Rafael Leonidas Trujillo Molina.[29] Yunior explains the Dominican Republic dictator, saying, "Homeboy dominated Santo Domingo like it was his very own private Mordor."[30] Genre fiction is transposed over lived peril; Trujillo becomes Tolkien's evil-eyed Sauron ruling over the realm of Mordor.[31] Dictator of the island nicknamed "El Jefe" from 1930 until his death in 1961, Trujillo is best known for his national policy of Antihaitianismo, resulting in the Paisley Massacre and the death of an estimated twenty- to thirty-thousand Haitians. Trujillo created a climate of fear and violence during his bloody reign and insistence on Dominican control of the island.

Fukú is at once the ghost story of colonization and the everyday belief in resistance. It is a "curse or a doom of some kind," something that "your everyday person could believe in."[32] Both Trujillo and fukú set the stage for Beli's escape, a very "real" escape from a regime "of silence and blood, machete and perejil, darkness and denial, [which] inflicted a true border on the countries, a border that exists beyond maps, that is carved directly into the histories and imaginaries of a people."[33] According to Yunior, the fukú of Trujillo, the doom brought on by colonial contact and the dictator, is so powerful that to utter his name, to even think it for that matter would send sudden death your way for generations to come. He explains, "Traditionally in Santo Domingo . . . anytime a fukú reared its many heads there was only . . . one surefire counterspell that would keep you and your family safe. Not surprisingly, it was a word. A simple word (followed usually by a vigorous crossing of index fingers). Zafa."[34] The story of Oscar de León, or more precisely the telling of it, becomes "a zafa of sorts," a "counterspell." The zafa that Yunior's narrative performs is meant to keep the family safe from the insistency of the curse, to stop it before it begins to cohere into fully formed doom.[35] This zafa also becomes Yunior's excuse to talk about his feelings, something he was never very good at. As he explains, "A heart like mine, which never got any affection growing up, is terrible above all things."[36] Yunior's literary zafa is his belief and escape; it is his excuse to sort through personal and historical loss.

The words "fukú" and "zafa" are what J. L. Austin calls performative utterances. In saying these words, one is also *doing* something, that is, bringing a curse upon your family or protecting it from tragedy. For Yunior, the story of Oscar de León is itself a performative act, a doing beyond the pleasure and entertainment of the tale, a narrative zafa made to protect future generations from the bad luck brought down by Trujillo and the reverberations of colonialism. Sidestepping the language of liberation and confinement and acknowledging the sways of power and money that dictate the relative definitions of these terms, zafa and fukú acknowledge the interconnected social network of feeling, politics, and religion. Fukú is Yunior's interpretation of Oscar's journey, his cursed Dominican American "brief wonderous life." But he is careful to explain that this is only his interpretation, as Oscar would not have liked this designation. "He was a hardcore sci-fi and fantasy man, believed that that was the kind of story that we were all living in. He'd ask: What more sci-fi than Santo Domingo? What more fantasy than the Antilles?"[37] The comparison, made in the book's introduction, between fukú and sci-fi establishes that genre is itself a belief in line with other cultural beliefs or superstitions. Genre is a style or aesthetic transaction that also possesses what Raymond Williams calls "affective elements" to describe the unspoken but felt atmosphere.[38] Yunior understands Oscar's life, its emotional valleys and shadows, to be in line with "fukú americanus" and this doom brought on by Trujillo and colonial contact, while Oscar always knew himself to be part of a fantasy novel—ridiculous, tragic, dramatic, and magical—a novel which he fought his hardest to pen.[39] Fukú and science fiction are two means through which to explain intimate access to the same set of emotions and spectacularly real experiences. In his footnotes, Yunior calls Trujillo "a personaje so outlandish, so perverse, so dreadful that not even a sci-fi writer could have made his ass up."⁴⁰ Superstition and genre fiction are the modalities, the lenses employed to explain "the outlandish," "perverse," and "dreadful."

Yet these two descriptive categories are more than just avenues in which to articulate feeling and event. Both fukú and zafa are performatives. If the performative is a linguistic utterance that is simultaneously an enactment, a *doing*, then we might extend the performative to include utterances that have a social and cultural effect beyond the initial scene of utterance. The performative is not bound by the strict linguistic utterance, but can and does operate in excess of content, time, and location. In *Performance and Performativity*, Andrew Parker and Eve Kosofsky Sedgwick discuss the scene of performative utterance, commenting that not only is the marriage an event that requires a ritual history for validation—one must socially recite the specific tradition in order for the wedding to be recognized as such—but the wedding event also requires a witness in both convention and law.⁴¹ Through the act of witness, this "interlocutory space" of the performative does not just exist in the mouths and deeds of those on the marriage proscenium. This space of the performative, what Sedgwick elsewhere calls the "periperformative," is dependent on a variety of heterogeneous elements in which social *doing* exceeds the moment, vicinity, and initiation of its utterance. Fukú and zafa are themselves performative utterances that invoke invisible audiences of environment, culture, and history. For Yunior, these words call forth and simultaneously safeguard a history of the Dominican Republic, family, and the de Leóns. They are a way to trace diaspora and to call a community and geography into being.

Both stories of fukú and sci-fi tell of a world where things are more than what they seem, in which communication exceeds mere linguistic content. This genre scene of performativity, wherein the invocation of science fiction does something for Oscar beyond conveying a categorization of literary preference or communicating linguistic content, works for Oscar as a protection, a "metaphorical Hail Mary" that guards him from the painful circumstances in which he finds himself. These performative genres (fukú and sci-fi) are the means through which a powerful imagery is conjured into existence and given a name. These are experiences of doom, frustration, and the inconsistencies in lived reality between Santo Domingo and New Jersey. Fukú and sci-fi are the powerful desires of magic and failure invoked to protect and ward off the bad vibes. How else does one describe the lived and felt realities ranging from teen depression to survival under a brutal dictatorship? Words such as trauma, tragedy, or immigration, heavy with broad strokes of juridical and psychoanalytic connotations, cannot fully describe such experiences. Instead, the more speculative genres are characterized by their very excess—they are anomalous and unrealistic—which is why they become an ideal medium through which to articulate that which does not fit into current epistemological understandings. Genre is a way for Oscar to make sense of his surroundings and feel a sense of belonging, just as it is a way for Díaz to explain the experience and feeling of colonialism and alienation.

In the beginning, there was Oscar's mother, Belicia Cabral. And Beli wanted out, not just from "the Dictatingest Dictator who ever Dictated," nor from his national culture that was suffocating her generation, but she simply wanted to escape. "Beli had the inchoate longings of nearly every adolescent escapist . . . but this was a country, a society, that had been designed to be virtually escape-proof. Alcatraz of the Antilles. There weren't any Houdini holes in the Plátano Curtain."[42] Not only does Beli want to geographically escape from the Trujillo dictatorship, but in line with other frustrated adolescent escapologists, she longs for a psychic and affective escape even as she cannot name precisely what she is escaping from. But Beli, "the Child of the Apocalypse," never had the chance to escape the sweet and controlling grasp of her parents because they were taken from her, disappeared like so much of Dominican history under Trujillo before she was given a chance to know or love them.[43] Sold as a child servant, a "criada, a restavek," to a family in Outer Azua, Beli was lost to her birth family and community until her second cousin La Inca discovered her eight years later.[44] Beli went to live with La Inca, her "mother-aunt," who tended her until they became family, "sanctuary."[45] It wasn't until Beli became a teenager and discovered she could use her sexual power to get what she wanted from the men who found her irresistible that she was hit by an intense longing, an impulse for escape. "But where she wanted to escape *to* she could not tell you."[46] All Beli knew was that she "wanted out."[47]

Díaz marks Beli's longing as familiar to "nearly every adolescent escapist," even as this feeling of escape is grounded in Trujillo's dictatorial curse. And what is key to Díaz's theorization of escape is this overwhelming sense or knowledge that, in truth, there is *no way out*. Calling on the performative escapologists of the start of the century such as Harry Houdini and the infamous Alcatraz Prison—"the island"—Díaz places Beli's feelings of escape from "the Alcatraz of the Antilles" in line with heroic narratives of escape and their attendant grand theatrical gestures. Díaz invokes both the hope and hopelessness within this very desire to escape.

For Díaz, this desire for escape also reflects the relationship between the United States and diaspora. As Jill Casid writes, diaspora and exile mark not only the historical situation of the "Middle Passage, slavery, and forced transplantation from Africa to the Americas," but also "the action of a long journey and a feeling of desire never extinguished by a destination object that takes the place of a homeland."[48] Casid argues that diaspora is not only nostalgic, but a "contemporary critical process of border crossing" and "future making."[49] As a futurist project, diaspora is forever tinged with the initial violent tragedy of a stolen homeland. Yunior reflects on Beli's rushed departure from the Dominican Republic, asking, "What did you know about states or diasporas? What did you know about . . . children whose self-hate short-circuited their minds?"[50] Critiquing her easy and rushed desire to escape, a desire to escape which manifested New Jersey as its arrival, Díaz gestures toward this complicated relationship of migration, loss, and the psychological effects of social exclusion and disenfranchisement.

For Beli, a way out of her situation, a way out of this dictatorship, was an escape act calling forth the ingenuity and fearlessness of Houdini. But as Díaz asks: How do you escape from the accumulative detritus of colonization and anti-Blackness, of internalized sexism and racism, of the greed that power calls forth? The answer he gives is that one cannot escape. After suffering a serious beating at the hands of Trujillo's goons, miscarrying her first child, and narrowly avoiding a cursed death in the cane fields, Beli is put on a plane to Nueva York by La Inca. This is where Beli's story turns into the stories of Oscar and Lola, where her desires for escape continue to flow into those of her children.

On the streets of Paterson, New Jersey, Oscar's sister, Lola, similarly craves escape. At fourteen, "desperate for [her] own patch of the world," she begins to plot.[51] Trying to get out from under her overbearing "Old World Dominican mother," Lola would "lay in [her] room with stupid Bear-Bear . . . imagining where she would run away to when [she] grew up."[52] Reading book after book about runaways, as soon as Lola hit puberty she could no longer keep the "wildness" inside her at bay. Constantly fighting with her mother, who was sick with breast cancer and trying to keep Lola in line and taking care of the family, Lola rebels. "All my life I'd been swearing that one day I would just disappear. And one day I did."[53] Lola runs away to the Jersey shore, only to be pulled back home again by her mother and sent as punishment and salvation to Santo Domingo.

Lola's desire for escape seems quite typically a teenage one. This is a time in life we might associate with the desire to run, to flee, to get out—as in sneaking out of your parent's house—but it is also a time in which one begins to realize the systemic inequalities that dictate the ways in which we fit in the world. Instead of experiencing the social order as full of insurmountable rules, teenagers and young adults are released into the chaos and fury as newly minted social actors. The adolescent years of yearning to escape also represent the moment in which the nerds among us might sink into the unserious genres often relegated to young adult fiction. Oscar calls this feeling "a particularly Jersey malaise—the inextinguishable longing for elsewheres."[54] But how might we understand this intergenerational teen discontent that dovetails so neatly with the racial and colonial melancholia that runs through Beli to her daughter Lola and then to Oscar?

When Belicia calls Lola back from Santo Domingo to New Jersey, Lola's response is to run and never look back. "That was the dream I had. But if these years have taught me anything it is this: you can never run away. Not ever. The only way out is in. And that's what I guess these stories are all about."[55] Escape is usually described as an evacuation, an exit, a getting "out" of a bad situation. Returning to the etymology of escape, to get out of one's cape, we see escape as a theatrical transformation of appearance and situation. But to claim that "the only way out is in" is to argue that in order to escape a situation, one should make the potentially absurd choice of turning around to delve even further into the jaws of capture. These words coming out of Lola's mouth perhaps represent her perpetual haunting by all of the problems of family expectations and the feelings of being caught between New Jersey and the Dominican Republic. I read this phrase not as a demand to stand up and face your problems, as an echo of pragmatism or atonement, but as a vertiginous moment of escape and an interrogation of the direction it might take. It is also possible to read her words, "I guess that's what these stories are all about," as referring to the psychic escape into the novel and into "stories" themselves.[56] This escape becomes not one of physical movement but an escape into the life of the mind as encouraged through the act of reading fiction. "The only way out is in" might at first sound like a doubling down, like a chiding that you can't escape your problems. But I want to suggest that Beli's is an escape strategy that champions the counterintuitive and the absurd; it is one which suggests escapist forms of escape, ones that do not immediately appear viable or legitimate. When you can't find a way out, maybe you can find a way in. And once you are in, maybe you can alter the underlying structure that dictates the terms of engagement. Author Lev Grossman asks:

What kinds of escape do you find in George R. R. Martin's Westeros? Or in the grim, rain-soaked Britain of Kate Atkinson? Or in Suzanne Collins' brutal, subjugated Panem? . . . They make you forget your own problems, sure, but they replace them with a whole new set of problems even more dire (hopefully) than the ones you left behind. . . . When you read genre fiction, you leave behind the problems of reality—but only to re-encounter these problems in transfigured form, in an unfamiliar guise, one that helps you understand them more completely, and feel them more deeply.[57]

Genre, the contemporary poster child of escapism, gives us an example of Lola's adage, "the only way out is in," because while genre involves an escape, as Grossman explains, that escape is not always one that simply makes you forget your problems. Such an escape into fiction enables us to "re-encounter" our problems in a way that provides affective access to them.

Genre Affect and Racialization

Early science fiction, as John Reider argues, is significantly influenced by colonial "encounters between European travelers and non-Europeans—such as Thomas More's *Utopia* (1516), Cyrano's *Comical History*, and Jonathan Swift's *Gulliver's Travels* (1726)."[58] The "Golden Age" of science fiction in the 1940s was characterized by heroic stories of science and wonder in the writing of authors such as Isaac Asimov and Ray Bradbury. By the '60s and '70s "new wave science fiction" authors had turned away from the technology and exploration of "hard sf" toward the literary, toward experimentation and interior landscapes. Ursula K. Le Guin, Samuel R. Delany, and Joanna Russ, among others, wrote about the relationship between oppression, socialist utopian longings, and posthuman desires. While race, sex, immigration, and colonialism had always been present in science fiction and fantasy, with new wave authors, such themes seemed to be brought into the center. Contemporary science fiction authors such as N. K. Jemisin, Nalo Hopkinson, China Miéville, and Octavia Butler continue an investment in speculation that considers structural problems of capitalism, anti-Blackness, climate collapse, and immigration.

In an interview in *Bomb* magazine, Díaz explains the science fiction undertones attached to racialized experience in the United States: "If you're looking for language that will help you approach our nigh unbearable historical experiences you can reach for narratives of the impossible; sci-fi, horror, fantasy, which might not really want to talk about people of color at all but that takes what we've experienced (without knowing it) very seriously indeed."[59] Díaz points to the parallel between narratives that discuss the felt experience of racism and immigration and the extraordinary voyages of sci-fi. This is an attention to the impossible happening in the present, the "nigh unbearable" experiences of people for whom meager safety nets do not exist. These "more speculative genres" become a way to describe the feelings of social abandonment and dislocation. Díaz continues, "Time-travel made sense to me because how else do I explain how I got from Villa Juana, from latrines and no lights, to Parlin, NJ, to MTC and a car in every parking space? Not just describe it but explain the missing emotional cognitive disjunction?"[60] These are the jarring affective tonalities of late capitalism. Such a jump in daily experience points to a global disparity in wealth and access. There is little language and sparse metaphorical comparison for such an "emotional cognitive disjunction." However, this felt dissonance parallels genre conventions that are more accustomed to making radical switches in time and space. As readers we expect genre to leap through time and space. But in daily experience it is startling and unmooring to travel to extremes within a matter of hours. Such affective and geographic moves feel unbelievable in the same way that genre often does; in both experiential worlds we are required to suspend our disbelief in order to suture these experiences together. The de León family responds to this felt dissonance of experience through the thematic of escape.

While Beli's escapist desires focus on the romantic and Lola's orbit around the act of running, Oscar's escape focuses on the "more speculative genres" and the internal worlds of magic and fulfillment that are caught in the pages of his graphic novels and books. Oscar experiences the world in and outside of genre as galactic and overwhelming. Díaz writes, "His affection—that gravitational mass of love, fear, longing, desire, and lust that he directed at any and every girl in the vicinity without regard to looks, age, or availability—broke his heart each and every day."[61] His feelings are the size of planets, and he forms deep affections for almost every girl that comes within his orbit. We might understand Oscar's highly affective story to be one of inappropriate, excessive, and anomalous affect often attached to Latinos and people of color, thanks in part to a nationally "impoverished" white affect that masquerades as the norm.[62] For José Esteban Muñoz, "affect is descriptive of the receptors we use to hear each other and the frequencies on which certain subaltern speak and are heard or, more importantly, felt."[63] Affect describes the way minoritarian subjects hear and relay feelings on a subfrequency, underneath the dominant thrum of the normative. Oscar feels too much, too strongly; his feelings take up too much space. If his affect is racially marked because it does not conform to the monotony of a white US national affect, what are the ways in which this "feeling brown," as Muñoz calls it, dovetails with a "sci-fi fanboy" affect marking a failure to grow up, be a man, and stop playing games? Affective expectations and feelings are part of a reader's relationship with any given genre from science fiction to historical fiction. The feelings that we expect to have in reading a novel are coded in genre categories such as romance, mystery, fantasy, and so on. Part of what Díaz invokes in his novel is the feeling of science fiction, the feeling of other worlds, fantastical languages, epic quests, and the negotiations of (un)belonging. I want to call this feeling of escapism specific to Oscar genre affect. This is a feeling that is attuned to, if not focused on, (speculative) genre work as a vehicle for escape. This is a feeling that marks an intense emotional attachment to genre worlds. It is indicative of an outsider status and the sense of not being part of the rest of the world. A subset of the feelings of escapism present throughout Oscar's family all the way back to his grandfather, genre affect is for Oscar a way to both engage in the world and perform one's understanding of self. Genre affect describes the feelings of escapism as they are attached to the experience of reading and investing in literary genres. It describes both the wide-reaching longings for escape present throughout *The Brief Wondrous Life of Oscar Wao* and the feelings that get put onto the themes and tropes present in Oscar's love of speculative fiction and comic books. Genre affect becomes for Oscar an identity—a cluster of themes and desires built into an understanding of self—as well as a marker for social experiences of (un)belonging that bring various people together under its umbrella, if only momentarily.

Genre affect as it plays out in the story of Oscar de León has everything to do with the social ordering of the world by way of the lived experiences of the unreal, the unbelievable, and the inexplicable. Oscar comes to know himself through books, through genre and its accessories. In psychoanalytic terms, Oscar uses the object that is genre (a grouping of books, comics, and films) by projecting his psyche onto it—which D. W. Winnicott marks as a natural occurrence in "object-relations." And through "object-use," Oscar incorporates the "other-than-me" substance of the object back into himself.[64] This is to say that Oscar is formed through his relationship to genre. Just as Oscar comes to find his sense of self through diaspora, New Jersey, his failed Dominican masculinity, and the Cabral curse, so too is he shaped by his love of the speculative. This is an object that is defined by its degradation and relegation to young adults and nerds, to its perpetual vulnerability to social and psychic destruction as not properly rigorous or real. By association with such a precarious love object—a genre that is all too often relegated to lowbrow and juvenile readership—Oscar embraces this vulnerability of self. His psychic structure is built around his keen awareness that, like speculative fiction worlds and objects, he is perpetually vulnerable to destruction.

Genre affect, the mood of Oscar's "more speculative genres," is the way that he comes to know himself, his way of feeling and being in the world. This is the psychic life of Oscar Wao, in which mood informs the way one comes to see, experience, and be in the world. Genre for Oscar is both an affect and an identity. Whereas we could argue, as Brian Massumi and others have, that affect, as opposed to emotion, is characterized by the fact that it exceeds subjectivity, exceeds being and stagnation through its emotional intensity, it is also habitual and thus marks Oscar as, more often than not, in a genre mood. His speculative fiction desires and negotiations become integrated into his thought process and his speech patterns. Oscar "could write in Elvish, could speak Chakobsa, could differentiate between a Slan, a Dorsai, and a Lensman in acute detail, knew more about the Marvel Universe than Stan Lee, and was a role-playing game fanatic. Dude wore his nerdiness like a Jedi wore his light saber or a Lensman wore her lens."[65] He shows commitment to walking through the world as an out and proud nerd. In fact, he cultivates this look through excelling at the genre-specific knowledge by learning the invented languages of *Lord of the Rings* and *Dune*. If he feels shame about this, it is something he carries with him as part of the package of what it means to take speculative fiction as your sense of self, to feel and wear genre in this often-hostile world that values normativity. His escapism, his genre affect, provides a sense of self and home, when "real world" scenes of belonging violently exclude him.

After painfully making his way through the brutality of adolescence, Oscar follows his sister to Rutgers University in New Brunswick, New Jersey. At first, Oscar feels like he is free at last; he is on his own with an initial "optimism that here among thousands of young people he would find someone like him."[66] But his hope for a renewed sense of community and life beyond the confines of Paterson and the social exclusion of Don Bosco Tech High School quickly wears off as he realizes Rutgers is more of the same. The white kids treat him "with inhuman cheeriness," and the students of color dismiss his authenticity after seeing him and hearing him speak—"You're not Dominican."[67] Again, he is left outside of community and friendship. Part of the pain of reading Oscar's story has to do with the relatable feeling of reaching, of always stretching for something impossibly beyond grasp. During his junior year, Oscar ends up living with Yunior, who by this point has become Lola's on-again-off-again boyfriend, in "Demarest Homo Hall"—"Home of all the weirdos and losers and freaks and fem-bots."[68] Yunior puts up with Oscar because he is in love with his sister, Lola, but also because he sees part of himself in Oscar. Yunior is a writer with a love of genre fiction, but one that knows how to keep such embarrassing affections secret. He knows how to temper his genre affections and let them out only when they are socially appropriate. Although Yunior is by all accounts a "normal" Dominican man—"who ha[s] pussy coming out of his ears"—he identifies with Oscar.[69]

Telling the story of Oscar's nickname in a series of anecdotes, Yunior recounts:

> Halloween he made the mistake of dressing up as Doctor Who, was real proud of his outfit too. When I saw him on Easton, with two other writing-section clowns, I couldn't believe how much he looked like that fat homo Oscar Wilde, and I told him so. You look just like him, which was bad news for Oscar, because Melvin said, Oscar Wao, quién es Oscar Wao, and that was it, all of us started calling him that: Hey, Wao, what are you doing? Wao, you want to get your feet off my chair? And the tragedy? After a couple of weeks dude started answering to it.[70]

Oscar dresses as his hero, coming out by wearing and performing his object of attachment. In this moment, not only is Oscar called a nerd because of his Dr. Who outfit, but he is also called Oscar Wilde, the markedly effeminate literary novelist famously jailed for gross indecency and the love that dare not speak its name. Like "abject" homosexual Jean Genet, Wilde sought to escape his jail cell through writing. This appellation and literary kinship is intended to inflict shame on Oscar, embarrassing him for his failed masculinity and intimate relationship to the pen. But "the tragedy" as Yunior notes, is that Oscar doesn't reject the accusations. Instead, he seems to embrace the Dominican Wao, not seeing the offense that such a connection is meant to inflict, or perhaps, preferring to be queerly noticed instead of having his presence ignored. In an Austinian sense, Oscar's uptake of the injurious speech changes something of the agreed-upon power structures implicit in the name calling. Both Wilde and Wao represent the generative fantasy of reading and writing the way out of. Even when there is no literal escape, they seem to say that the very act of dreaming changes makes an exit possible.

And while Díaz has been duly critiqued for his reproduction of "*machista* values," particularly, as Israel Reyes notes, "the obsessive gaming involved in the seduction and sexual conquest of women," there is also a queer sensibility in his writing.[71] For Michael Warner, queer scenes are those in which "people are brought into great intimacy by their common experience of being despised and rejected."[72] Queer here names a shared feeling of social abjection. Although Díaz at no point specifically marks Oscar's character as sexually queer, it is hard to deny a queer reading of him, particularly since his primary love object, genre, demonstrates the interruption of normative sexual or social development. What we might call genre scenes bring together the outcasts by way of a common set of obsessive and nerdy desires. However, genre diverges from queer in that queer, most often, professes a desire for other bodies, other people who are similarly located or identified in these subcultural communities. However, instead of gathering around other like-minded social outcasts, genre, at least in the case of Oscar, is focused on objects of fantasy: books, comics, and movies that imagine other worlds. Genre does not pull Oscar into greater intimacy with others, but leaves him feeling perpetually alienated, even from within his would-be community of misfits.[73] In this way genre affect is not simply a celebration of the psychic structures and possibilities opened up through an attachment to genre; it also carries with it the uglier side of speculative fiction: depression, isolation, and the experiences of failure and capture. The utopian longings of genre worlds involve what Muñoz has called "the hangover that follows hope."[74] This is the disappointment that comes after a wishful version of what the future could look like. Genre affect is descriptive of a manner, mood, or feeling through which we engage, understand, and come to be in the world. It is not a fixed feeling, as the term "emotion" might suggest, but is instead in constant flux. As such genre affect is sometimes melancholic and disappointing. Jonathan Flatley explains that affect is both "relational and transformative."[75] Furthermore, according to Kathleen Stewart, the significance of affect is found in what certain feelings might tell us, not the meanings they will uncover, but more precisely their "potential modes of knowing, relating, and attending to things."[76] Genre affect, then, illuminates the forms of knowing and relating that can be found through an attachment to genre worlds and conventions.

Raymond Williams elaborates on the political potential of affect by expanding "feeling" out from the personal psyche to cultural climate.[77] For Williams, feelings happen in the present and consequently are "lacking semantic availability."[78] Such feelings cannot be brought into precise language because of their widespread present resonance, but are nonetheless constitutive of a shared affective atmosphere. Affect is thus both a personal mood, as well as the mood of a larger group, neither of which can be explained from within the affective atmosphere that one finds themself currently inhabiting. Thus, genre affect is not only found in the affective and psychic worlds created by

Oscar Wao, but it is also a mood that might be said to pervade a certain political moment or social space. And, following Flatley, affect differs from mood or emotion in that affects come into being in relationship to objects.[79] Beli's escape was always found in love objects, but for Oscar, the object that he attaches to is genre—including the syntax and landscapes manifested therein. Oscar's relationship to speculative fiction is lived; for him it is an ethics and an aesthetics—it is both an action and a way of being in the world. As Flatley further explains, the "dwelling place" of affect exists in its object, in the imperfections and idiosyncrasies of the loved one's face, in the material world "unmediated by concepts."[80] It is through affect that we come to know each other and the world. Speculative fiction, as the "dwelling place" for this set of complicated sensations, becomes the site for Oscar's material attachment to the world and experience within it. Far from being an uncomplicated disengagement from "reality," genre is the object through which pathways of sensation are brought into being outside of their precise semantic availability.[81]

Oscar's feelings of escape, as concretized in his imaginative worlds of genre, provide him with a survival tactic. And while Jean-Paul Sartre—perhaps wrongly—argues that affect does not change the politics of the larger world, Sartre does believe that affect influences the way we come to experience the world in our body. However, I would argue that a change in individual bodily experience is, in fact, a political change. Feelings often do change the social situation in which they are experienced and to which they respond. For Sartre, emotions surface when we lose ourselves in relation to the world and become adrift in a response unmediated by language. Following Enlightenment logics, pragmatism and level-headedness are valued characteristics, while emotional response is associated with an almost dangerous wild abandon. Yet, as Muñoz explains, "because stigmatized people are presented with significantly more obstacles and blockages than privileged citizen-subjects, minoritarian subjects often have difficulty maintaining distance from the very material and felt obstacles that suddenly surface in their own affective mapping of the world."[82] To assume that emotions impede one's engagement in the rational world is to deny all of the ways in which an emotionally "flat and impoverished" white national affect is reinforced as the standard. Oscar's escapist feelings demonstrate how affect is more than just an intrapsychic experience of being in the world. Instead, genre affect introduces a critical language for speaking about subaltern and antinormative feelings as strategies for change.

In speculative fiction, the themes of difference and unbelonging are prevalent as the basis for creating communitarian feelings and exposing underlying

Feeling Out of This World   89

systems of inequality. Oscar finds solace in these worlds even as he continues to feel utterly alone and lost in the day-to-day. Oscar's worlds signal an intense desire and longing that is simultaneously coupled with a melancholy of all things lost. Eventually, even Oscar's Dungeons and Dragons buddies, Al and Miggs, abandon him once they reach high school so that they can grow up and socialize beyond the confines of their nerdery. The loss that Oscar feels is not only a loss of social skills due to his genre pastime; it is a loss rooted in a history of dictatorship, colonialism, and forced migration. Where diasporic subjects are often accused of "just not fitting in," here the reader is reminded of the assimilationist demand to flatten one's feelings and affectively conform.[83]

After Oscar graduates from college, he returns to Paterson to live with his mother and teach at the high school that he was so desperate to leave as a teenager. Recounting his experience, Díaz writes,

> Every day he watched the "cool" kids torture the crap out of the fat, the ugly, the smart, the poor, the dark, the unpopular, the African, the Indian, the Arab, the immigrant, the strange, the feminine, the gay—and in every one of these clashes he saw himself. . . . In a burst of enthusiasm he attempted to start a science-fiction and fantasy club, posted signs up in the halls, and for two Thursdays in a row he sat in his classroom after school, his favorite books laid out in an attractive pattern, listened to the roar of receding footsteps in the halls, the occasional shout of Beam me up! And Nanoo Nanoo! Outside his door; then, after thirty minutes of nothing he collected his books, locked the room, and walked down those same halls, alone, his footsteps sounding strangely dainty.[84]

Oscar's love of science fiction and fantasy often elicits in him a bursting enthusiasm, a desire to reach out and connect with others, as well as a quiet retreat back into the safety of his genre worlds. He sees himself reflected in every school kid who is ridiculed. When he tries to reach out to his students through the genre fiction, laying his eager attachments out on the table "in an attractive pattern," he is laughed at and ignored. Oscar's enthusiasm often retracts into his disappearance and diminishment. Elsewhere, Díaz recalls Ray Bradbury's *All Summer in a Day*, a story of a girl named Margot who is locked in a closet by the other little children on Venus for the only day that the sun will shine in seven years.[85] Bradbury's short story marks the sadness of such fantasies, the threat that they can be so easily taken away by cruel schoolchildren and their disdain for difference (in this case, it was the difference of the little girl who had seen the sun before and loved it with all her heart).

To love genre in the way that Oscar does is at first an exciting point of connection, but eventually turns into a lonely and disappointing solo endeavor.

There are moments when Oscar is driven to suicide as an escape. In college, he tries to kill himself by jumping off the New Brunswick Train Bridge, but "instead of finding himself in nerd heaven—where every nerd gets fifty-eight virgins to role-play with," he lands on the garden divider and wakes up in the hospital.[86] After college, Oscar half-heartedly attempts to commit suicide again. He drove all night to escape his life. During these moonlit adventures he often found himself nodding off at the wheel only to wake up in the nick of time to save himself. "Nothing more exhilarating [he wrote] than saving yourself by the simple act of waking."[87] Oscar's persistent threat of suicide underscores that escape is not always an easy desire. To exit from the scene of the "real world" sometimes means that you cannot return to it. Such suicidal ideation might be read as self-directed violence, as a continuation of the colonial and anti-Black forms of masculinity which figure Oscar as a queer impossibility and an embodiment of science fiction himself.

When Oscar finally dies, it is not by his own hand. In fact, he tries his hardest to stop it because he has found love with "a semiretired puta" named Ybón Pimentel. "Oscar considered her the start of his real life."[88] He pursues Ybón despite her state trooper boyfriend who threatens to kill him. Masculine colonial violence reemerges in Oscar's need to prove that "real life" begins with heterosexual love. Oscar goes up against the state trooper, "the capitán," a literal representative of state power. But eventually Oscar is caught and taken to the cane fields. After he recovers from this "colossal beat down" Oscar is sent home to New Jersey. Then, a few months later, he sneaks back to Santo Domingo. At first, Ybón refuses to answer his notes, but finally, she tells him to save himself and go home. Oscar responds, "This is my home. You're my real home, mi amor. A person can't have two?"[89] The inevitable happens and the faceless goons—the mythic ones who terrorized his grandfather and his mother—chase him down and kill him. He must put away childish things, refuse a queer ending, and die in a last-ditch attempt to fit the gendered genre of man. In the end, there is no escape for Oscar Wao, for his mother or his sister, and, if we flash-forward to Díaz's third book, *This Is How You Lose Her*, perhaps there is no escape for Yunior either.

At "the end of the story," Yunior recounts the aftermath of Oscar's death—the return of Beli's cancer and Yunior's breakup with Lola. "And then, almost eight months after he died, a package arrived at the house in Paterson." In a letter to Lola, Oscar wrote to "watch out for a second package. This contains everything I've written on this journey. Everything I think you will need. You'll understand when you read my conclusions. (It's the cure to what ails us, he scribbled in the margins. The Cosmo DNA.)"⁹⁰ But this second manuscript never appears; the pages are forever lost in the mail, holes left in the archive of lived experience. A reference to the American anime television show *Star Blazers*, the "Cosmo DNA" was a device that would remove all the radiation from the atmosphere, thus enabling Earth's inhabitants to return from subterranean exile back to the "aboveground" world of life. Oscar's lost insights, the "Cosmo DNA" cure that could map an escape into the stars, are never found and Yunior is left to fill in the gaps with his own narrative.

The creative writer, as Sigmund Freud explains, enables us to enjoy the world of fantasy—both our own secret fantasies as readers as well as those of the author. In a 1908 essay Freud wrote that "the adult . . . is ashamed of his fantasies and hides them from other people. He cherishes his fantasies as his most intimate possessions, and as a rule he would rather confess his misdeeds than tell anyone his fantasies."⁹¹ The fantasy manifest in creative writing allows the adult access to childhood play and wishful thinking, a world in which humans are not "repel[ed]" by each other's fantasy wish fulfillments, but one in which the fantasy can be experienced vicariously and pleasurably. The writer "bribes us by the purely formal—that is, aesthetic—yield of pleasure which he offers us in the presentation of his fantasies."⁹² The escape artistry of genre, of creative writing, is often synonymous with fantasy and the unreal. In their paper on game design, Harald Warmelink, Casper Harteveld, and Igor Mayer delineate two different types of escapism: "cause based" and "effect based."⁹³ Cause-based escapism describes a negative escape from something painful or unpleasant, whereas effect-based escapism provides positive reinforcement in its move toward pleasure and enjoyment. Genre is both a cause- and effect-based form of escapism; the more speculative genres get Oscar out of the pain and violence of the normative real world, while simultaneously providing a pleasurable space of ideation. An attention to the feeling of escape illustrates the creative fantasy woven into the structure of escape, and the unexpected dreams upon which innovative escape attempts rest.

In 2018, Díaz wrote in the *New Yorker*, "No one can hide forever. Eventually what used to hold back the truth doesn't work anymore. You run out of escapes, you run out of exits, you run out of gambits, you run out of luck. Eventually the past finds you."⁹⁴ Discussing his experience of sexual violence and the way it has wreaked havoc on his interpersonal relationships, Díaz returns to the language of escape. He tells us that escapes and exits are made to avoid the grief and pain of personal injury. Between his own admission of having been sexually assaulted as a child and the women who have accused Díaz of misconduct, it is clear that the past must be accounted for. Experiences of trauma do not stay in the past, but they continue to shape the lives of people who survive them. Díaz continues, "And since us Afro-Latinx brothers are viewed by society as always already sexual perils, very few people ever noticed what was written between the lines in my fiction—that Afro-Latinx brothers are often sexually *imperilled*."[95] Escape, he argues, can help one wiggle out of their pain for brief moments, but not forever. And what is more, escapes in this context might enable interpersonal repetitions of violence.

In the wake of publishing his essay, Díaz was criticized for anticipating the accusations that would follow and trying to get ahead of them by naming his abuse. Stories of intergenerational sexual abuse are not uncommon, and while it does give context to the accusations against Díaz, it does not excuse abusive acts on either end. Masculinist violence begets more masculinist violence. Or, as Aya de Leon explains, we live in a society that would allow rape, misogyny, and harassment. She writes, "People either want to excuse Junot or vilify him. We need to hold both: he's a brother with a history of abusing and being abused. I believe that a man like Junot can be redeemed. But let's be clear, he hasn't redeemed himself yet."[96] Leon expresses a refusal to cancel Díaz, but neither does she want to let him off the hook. It is possible to hold him accountable and simultaneously understand the larger ways in which his own record of harm is built in and through anti-Black and patriarchal structures.

This seems particularly important given that libidinal economies are built into the history of colonialism. As Israel Reyes writes of Díaz's work, "Even as the narrator portrays the deadly consequences of these games of masculine domination, he is also engaged in a playful and not entirely innocent game with the reader, who is seduced into taking pleasure in the textual performance of violence, conquest, and colonization."[97] The complicity of the reader in such forms of violence echoes the desirous white reader of the (anti) slave escape story. The middlebrow readers of Díaz follow along in his recitation of a sexualized colonial power, relishing their ability to feel good about reinhabiting that power through the lens of minoritarian literature. Instead of Díaz's accomplishments being lauded on a formal level, focusing on the way language itself is (perhaps ambivalently) remade against proper colonial comportment, the bourgeois reader instead sees the novel as a way into understanding something about true Dominican identity.

What can be learned from Díaz, from the harm he caused and the harm he suffered, and from the way these forms of harm are connected? What is the felt sense of this tangle of patriarchal and masculinist violence, its depiction on the page, or the way it plays out in graduate seminars and lecture halls?

What do we make of the desire to escape this dense weave of both structural and interpersonal harm and abuse? How as readers is it possible to engage with his work and also hold him accountable? In her work on the author Ursula K. Le Guin, artist Tuesday Smillie critiques the failures of Le Guin's writing around race and gender, explaining that "the moments of imaginative and political failure are painfully problematic, re-inscribing the very hierarchal social structures Le Guin set out to unmake, as well as structures adjacent to them. Through these constrictions however, something else is made visible."[98] The something else that Smillie is referring to is radical imagination. And part of this radical imagination that characterizes Le Guin's imperfect science fiction novels is also her willingness toward autocritique. Smillie continues, "Le Guin offers a model where fucking up and being called out by our peers does not mark the end of a project, but provides the opportunity for a crucial turning point in the imagining of what that project could accomplish."[99] While fucking up representationally and causing physical and emotional harm through sexual predation, abuse, and bullying are distinct, Le Guin's move toward autocritique in a series of revised essays in which she engages critical feedback might serve as one model for thinking through how to engage both Díaz and his characters — both Yunior and Oscar.

In *The Brief Wondrous Life*, Oscar is killed—that was always promised. And in the real world of the author, we as readers and writers are reminded of the impossibility of escape from trauma and its repetitions, and from the anti-Blackness and sexual violence of colonialism. In this sense, for Oscar the paradigmatic reigns, whereas for Yunior, the episodic enables an avoidance of having to be held accountable. I wonder if there is a way for us to read Díaz against himself, to see Yunior and Oscar as different sides of the same coin, and to consider the ways in which escape and its feelings orbit these impossible/incomposible feelings of trauma. I am reminded again of both the beauty of feeling out of this world, as well as "the hangover that follows hope."[100]

On one hand, the feelings that cohere around genre fiction are predictable; they are coded by the visual marketing of paperbacks, television shows, and comic books. When you pick up a romance or a mystery, you have a sense of some of the emotions you might feel. It is this affective transaction that gets coded as escapist because reading these genres, feeling these genres, can be straightforward. But Oscar's story imagines the ethical potential of passivity, escapism, and withdrawal. Genre affect names the emotional resonances of escape, and escapism as a felt experience. *The Brief Wondrous Life of Oscar Wao* imagines the eccentric life-worlds of escape that turn away from dominant structures of language and feeling that organize the social lives of minoritized subjects. And as Lev Grossman reminds us, "fiction is never real, but feelings always are."[101] In *The Brief Wondrous Life*, genre affect, as it is articulated in and across real scenes of escape, becomes a placeholder for the affective tonalities of getting out and moving toward pleasure. The novel insists on the importance of the felt experience of escape. It illustrates why change cannot be enacted alone. Escape can be lonely and cut off from others, but maybe it doesn't have to be. What becomes possible in the uptake of the more speculative genres, in their reception not as prescriptive, but as an ongoing conversation?

THE OPTICS OF ESCAPE
Patty Hearst through the Mouth of Sharon Hayes

3.1 Sharon Hayes, *Symbionese Liberation Army Screeds #13, 16, 20 & 29*, 2003. Installation view at the Whitney Museum of American Art, New York, 2012.

Whiteness is always shocked by its own scenes of captivity. Exceptional at its core, whiteness imagines itself to be definitionally free from confinement, while white logics imagine Blackness and Indigeneity to be caught in a perpetual state of self-inflicted and organic confinement. American captivity narratives, as I mention in the introduction, provide a shocking momentary break from the unlimited movement of whiteness. Captivity narratives shore up whiteness by showing what it is not, and how the precarity of its sanctity and purity are threatened. In the United States, the captivity narrative was born out of cultural contact, imagined through Native capture of the white settler. As Laura Mielke writes, "The drama of the traditional Indian captivity narrative, like that of the horror film, resides in the white protagonist's traumatic dislocation and injury, witnessing of spectacular brutality, and miraculous survival."[1] This narrative genre, born out of early settler stories of fear and encounter, became a founding American story of self, white identity, and progress. Mary Rowlandson's narrative *The Sovereignty and Goodness of God: Being a Narrative of the Captivity and Restoration of Mrs. Mary Rowlandson*, which depicted in great detail her capture by Native Americans, set up the genre conventions for subsequent captivity narratives and justified the colonial project as a way to purify and save the nation.[2] Richard Slotkin calls the captivity narrative "the most basic story form of the Frontier Myth" where "the structures of Protestant Christian mythology which the settlers had brought from Europe were applied to the secular experiences of colonization."[3] The purification of the captive woman's body and soul becomes a stand-in for the cleansing required for the racialized nation. Slotkin continues, "Her captivity is figuratively a descent into Hell and a spiritual darkness which is akin to 'madness.' By resisting the physical threats and spiritual temptations of the Indians, the captive vindicates both her own moral character and the power of the values she symbolizes."[4] The founding myth of the captivity narrative produces a gendered and raced story of encounter between light and dark, between sanity and madness. The captivity narrative illustrates the demand to escape as a mode of white salvation.

In considering the white radical uptake of escape, I turn to the resonances of the captivity narrative in the work of artist Sharon Hayes. Her quotation of Patty Hearst is a scene of both reverence and genre disobedience as she points to the coercive force of the law of genre. *Symbionese Liberation Army (SLA) Screeds #13, 16, 20 & 29* (2003) by Sharon Hayes begins with the title card, "Patricia Hearst's First Tape." An androgynous white woman with short hair that eagerly curls out around the ears begins speaking in a near monotone. She gives very little away. On screen, Sharon Hayes takes the place of Patty Hearst, reciting the audio-screed ransom notes that were initially broadcast on Berkeley's KPFA radio station in 1974. The frame fits neatly around her face as she stares out to the deferred audience beyond the lens. Emotionless, she speaks directly into the camera, "Mom, Dad, I'm okay. I had a few scrapes... and stuff... but they washed them up and they're getting okay?" On "okay," her intonation trails up at the end, so that it sounds more like a question than a statement. Around fifteen seconds into *Screed #13*, the first of the four Patty Hearst ransom tapes that Hayes respeaks, she misses her line and it becomes clear that Hayes is not alone on screen. There is something like a live studio audience for her recorded performance, a room full of people whom we cannot see, but who are present for the performance recording. An audience member positioned behind the camera, somewhere in Hayes's line of sight, corrects her, feeding her the line that she should be performing instead of the one that she has incorrectly uttered. Hayes nods ever so subtly and easily picks up the line, "I am not being starved, or beaten, or unnecessarily frightened." Performing for the recording, Hayes maintains steady eye contact with the camera as she stumbles through the words. Gradually it becomes apparent that the live audience is in possession of Hearst's audio transcript. They have been instructed to correct Hayes when she deflects from the script and to prompt her with Hearst's exact lines, however inarticulate or awkward they may be. Hayes concentrates to remember the proper words, fluttering her eyes and momentarily closing them, or scrunching her nose and squinting as though she is straining to see something in the distance as she reaches inside to find the words in their correct order.

This version of the story begins in 1974 when self-proclaimed "soldiers" of the Symbionese Liberation Army (SLA) kidnapped nineteen-year-old white Californian media heiress Patty Hearst. Having grown up with the 1950s era promise of innocence, insularity, and safety, America's white college youth were confronted by the inadequacy of their middle-class ideals and felt disappointed by the level of change brought about by the civil rights movement and the publicly televised, and often personal, trauma of the Vietnam War. The majority-white radicals of the SLA seemed to realize that the world was dramatically unfree, and the only way they saw to respond to the violence of imperialism, poverty, incarceration, and racism was through terms that would garner public attention, fear, and—they hoped—respect. Adopting the rhetoric, mannerisms, and vocal inflections of radicals such as the Black Panthers and the Soledad Brothers, the SLA sought to align themselves with Black and Latin American radicals, and were thus seen—in the dominant public eye—as racialized voices of radicalism.[5] Held hostage and kept in a closet for two months, Patty Hearst eventually came to identify with her captors, going so far as to change her name to Tania in solidarity with the SLA.

At the time of the kidnapping, the FBI and Hearst's parents vigorously pursued rescue efforts, and the American public rallied behind the Hearst family, identifying with the pain and frustration they must have felt at losing their daughter to a racialized militant "terrorist" organization. Yet public opinion quickly changed as Hearst began to record "audio communiqués"— publicly broadcast on the radio—allying herself with the political aims of the SLA. Hearst's radio missives ranged from radical ideas confusedly spoken as through the mouth of a ventriloquist's dummy to the rehearsed words of a revolutionary committed to the cause. The content of the audiotapes followed the rhetoric and style of previous SLA documents, as Hearst demanded free food for California's poor and proclaimed, "Death to the fascist insect that preys upon the life of the people."[6] Advertising this confused alignment of rhetoric and the racial makeup of the organization was one of the ways that the media sought to discredit the SLA and undermine radical politics more generally. No longer a "victim" captured against her will, Hearst became a criminal coconspirator, an "urban guerilla."[7]

Hearst's story altered the genre script that captivity narratives—starting with Mary Rowlandson's 1682 narrative—move teleologically from free to hostage to free, ending in a glorious, if slightly wounded, return home. In Hearst's publicly perceived failure to escape from the SLA—an escape that should be performed but is instead refused—she allied herself with the kidnappers who had emotionally and physically abused her under the guise of revolution and "free sex."[8] Perhaps her alleged refusal to escape was a psychological defense mechanism, intelligently worked out as the most viable option, or perhaps Hearst realized the ways of the tyrannical "bourgeois pigs" of America and decided she would rather stay and fight in the "people's army" than return to her home culture.[9] Notably, Hearst was tasked to escape back into the wealthy white culture of her birth, to return to the "us" of the popular media viewership that felt a need to reclaim the stolen property that was Hearst and her allegorical relevance. In the end, she was legally faulted and found guilty for choosing wrongly, for failing to reject the potentially radical and violent ideologies of the SLA, and was sentenced to serve seven years in jail for her participation in the Hibernia Bank robbery, her image forever captured on security camera footage.[10]

But, why did Hearst participate in the activities of the SLA? This question of Hearst's motivation seems to continue to haunt her. And while I am not primarily interested in Patty Hearst as a radical subject, I do perversely care about her tongue and her linguistic fidelity, or infidelity, to certain narratives. Hearst's audio communiqués are messy and confusing documents, scenes in which self and voice diverge. As I will argue, Sharon Hayes's tactics of repetition and reverberation demonstrate a virtuosic stuttering break—what Fred Moten might call "an irruption of phonic substance"—in the asymmetry between voice and body, between Hearst and her proliferating media representation.[11] In Hayes's restaging of Hearst, I trace the expanded audiovisual field of the escape story. Where seeing escape is always simultaneously sonic and sensational, Hearst's narrative is a story that plays across genre conventions and into the periperformative vicinity of the escape narrative. Cloaked in her position as media heiress, Hearst and her capture were highly visible. The SLA knew that through her image, their words would be broadcast and repeated; Hearst would become their guerilla spectacle, a microphone and graspable object that would garner public attention. Through visual and linguistic capture, Hayes brings Hearst's odd narrative survival into the present. This is not simply the radical story of Patty Hearst that neatly ends with Hearst married to her bodyguard, nor is it the camp resurgence of Hearst in five of John Waters's films.[12] Looking backward at Hearst's kidnap through the lens of Hayes's *SLA Screeds*, I configure an optic of escape that agitates the stagnant narrative that fixes Hearst in just one pose. In Hearst's failure to escape, she performs an infidelity to the captivity narrative genre, and is instead haphazardly understood through a lens of criminality and proximal Blackness. As I have argued in previous chapters, escape is an American myth that places pressure on commonsense conventions of genre, opening up spaces of possibility. Instead of escape birthing white creative possibility, as in the work of Emily Dickinson, in Sharon Hayes's performance of Patty Hearst's failed escape and sonic capture we see the slippages and infidelities of the genre.

In this chapter, escape turns from the straight-and-narrow path of narrative to veer into the complicated radicality of sonic textures. Where Hearst's kidnap and story had everything to do with the sound of her voice, in Hayes's respeaking, the optics of escape comes through by way of the sonic. In other words, escape is heard in the textures opened up in the utterance. Invoking Eve Kosofsky Sedgwick's idea of texture as involving more senses than just touch, so that "we hear the brush-brush of corduroy trousers or the crunch of extra-crispy chicken," the sound of Hayes's performance demonstrates different strategies for texturing the story of escape.[13] Exploring the story of

Hearst's escape, or rather, its refusal, and Hayes's amplification of Hearst's refusal of escape, I engage the limits and possibilities of white appropriation, or uptake, of Black radicalism. I explore the racialization of genre in the way this story is heard, seen, and felt. In this infelicitous alignment between voice and body, Hearst and Hayes sound out an escape narrative—a narrative genre that, as I have previously mentioned, has its roots in American Black radicalism and fugitivity. Focusing in on the failed radicality of the SLA, their ventriloquism of Hearst, and Sharon Hayes's own respeaking performance of an ambivalent scene of political activism, I limn the relationality of escape and its racialized structuring politics.

The Symbionese Liberation Army

The SLA emerged at the end of the "New Left" movement that had begun a decade earlier with the Students for a Democratic Society (SDS) in Michigan and the signing of the Port Huron Statement. Riding on the heels of a wave of student protest movements and in the aftermath of the mixed success of the civil rights movement culminating in the death of Martin Luther King Jr. in 1968, the SLA was born during the decline of collective radical oppositional politics. Influenced by the writings of George Jackson, Argentinean revolutionary Che Guevera, and the Tupamaros of Uruguay, the SLA aspired to continue the radical reform that had begun a decade earlier through violent guerilla tactics and media manipulation. Patty Hearst—great-granddaughter of William Randolph Hearst and heiress to the Hearst Corporation—seemed an appropriate target for this nascent organization seeking to realign the country back onto a course for radical change. The SLA responded to social, racial, and political inequality through their own form of protective and reactive violence that played out through the highly mediatized kidnapping and "brainwashing" of Patty Hearst spanning from February 4, 1974, to her arrest on September 18, 1975, some twenty months later.

The SLA was formed when William Wolfe, an undergraduate at the University of California, Berkeley, and Russ Little began volunteering at Vacaville state prison as student tutors through the Black Cultural Association. At Vacaville, they became close with inmate Donald Defreeze, who would later go by the SLA name Cinque Mtume. The SLA began to take shape after Cinque's escape from prison, and with fellow members Patricia "Mizmoon" Soltysik (Zoya), Camilla Hall (Gabi), Emily Harris (Yolanda), Bill Harris (Teko), Nancy Ling Perry (Fahizah), and Angela Atwood (Gelina) joining the ranks of the "people's army."[14] The radical army of mostly white twenty-somethings emerged as an organization that was, as Bill Harris later claimed, "a means to achieve popular freedom to build a society that was free from racism, sexism and classism; a society where there were no elites, no oppressive bureaucracy."[15] Despite their study of Maoism, Marxism, and the writings of George Jackson, the SLA still had little focus or insight in how to make a revolution happen or connect their work to that of other radicals and social organizations at the time. They believed in "Third World leadership" and that "only black and other oppressed people could lead the struggle for freedom"; yet the SLA remained a majority white organization.[16] Instead of organizing for education like the Black Panthers, the SLA wished to be the spark that lit the revolutionary flame.

On February 4, 1974, they kidnapped Patty Hearst at her home in Berkeley. The incident of Hearst's kidnapping by the SLA was heavily covered by the media, and after her arrest, the trial itself became a media sensation. Everyone surrounding Hearst seemed to have bought into the sale and circulation of their own version of Hearst's story. First, Hearst's defense attorney F. Lee Bailey negotiated for exclusive publishing rights on the trial, while the remaining SLA members Bill and Emily Harris had begun to chronicle their own story with Hearst in *The Tania Interview*, a document which was then used against Hearst in her court trial. Even Hearst's former fiancé, Steven Weed, published an account of Hearst's abduction, *My Search for Patty Hearst* (1976). In the past fifty years, a number of books have been published on Hearst and the SLA ranging from Patty Hearst's own autobiography *Every Secret Thing* (1982) to novels inspired by Hearst such as *American Woman* (2003) by Susan Choi and *Trance* (2006) by Christopher Sorrentino.[17] The Patty Hearst story continues to live on in Jeffery Toobin's *American Heiress: The Wild Saga of the Kidnapping, Crime, and Trial of Patty Hearst* (2016), which was then adapted into a CNN movie, *The Radical Story of Patty Hearst* (2018). Taking my cue from Sharon Hayes's own resounding of the Hearst story, I focus my reading on the audio communiqués that featured various SLA members speaking to the public, reading demands, and explaining the logic behind the organization. Hearst herself made five such audio communiqués, four of which Hayes respeaks in her performance. These audiotapes were sent to public radio stations, and, as part of the ransom demands, all the SLA communiqués were made to be played over the radio. The audio began with the quivering, hesitant, and disaffected voice of Hearst, saying "Mom, Dad, I'm okay." These now iconic words, broadcast through the radio airwaves and replayed over the years, call forth the fall of the New Left in the form of the SLA's misguided militarism and foreshadow Hearst's brilliant camp performances in a number of John Waters films from *Crybaby* (1990) to *A Dirty Shame* (2004). The voice of Hearst—characterized in early media accounts as a young innocent girl, calling out to her mother and father—resounds across the years.

In the first of the communiqués, *Screed #13*, Hearst explained that she was "not being starved or beaten or unnecessarily frightened" and was doing just fine. Throughout the tape there are many stops and starts, where the stop button was pushed to arrest the flow and buy the speaker time. As Robert Pearsall writes in his 1974 book analyzing the SLA's written and audio communications, "Her voice was thin and strained, and it was immediately conjectured that she spoke under the influence of medical sedation or street drugs. Her discourse was also chopped into short sections by starting and stopping the tape recorder."[18] In Pearsall's effort to contextualize Hearst's message, we can see the confusion that he imagines she must have felt, the projection of chemical interference in Hearst's person that he finds evidenced in the sound of her voice. This interpretation illustrates the need to project the role of victim onto Hearst. Pearsall characterizes her as disjointed and unable to fight back (through the infliction of force, drugs, etc.) and unable to access her own voice as a hostage.

In the recording, Hearst continues to explain that she is "with a combat unit" who "aren't just a bunch of nuts." She continues, "I've been stopping and starting this tape myself, so that I can collect my thoughts. That's why there are so many stops in it. I am not being forced to say this." Hearst's recorded claim that the stops in the audiotape are meant for her to collect her thoughts leads to a reading of this tape as fallacious, full of what initially appear to be half-truths. The listener believes that they know more about the reality of the situation and the speaker than she does. Here, the at-home audience plays the psychoanalyst, doctor, and lawyer who knows Hearst's will, who can diagnose and find her truth and fidelity to the genre.

The will to confess the private "interiorized subject" produces self-narratives oriented toward describing the innermost feelings, desires, and thoughts to an audience. As Dipesh Chakrabarty reminds us, "the bourgeois individual is not born until one discovers the pleasures of privacy." He continues, "But this is a very special kind of 'private self'—it is, in fact, a deferred 'public' self, for this bourgeois private self, as Jurgen Habermas has reminded us, is 'always already oriented to an audience.'"[19] The private self, in Chakrabarty's estimation, becomes known even to itself through the idea of an eventual and deferred public to structure its narrative. This private truth of the bourgeois subject requires an audience, a theater of confession, to produce the bourgeois individual subject at the heart of autobiographical and narrative forms. In other words, one is recognized as, and becomes a modern liberal subject through, the continual outpouring of the interior private self. Recalling Hayes's performance with which I began this chapter, Hearst's audio screeds demonstrate the ways in which the deferred audience can vehemently refuse the authenticity and authority of the private self. Like a bad theater piece, the audience might boo at any given self-presentation as inappropriate, untrue, or infelicitous. The private self, exemplified through Hearst's voice, can only be received as genuinely reflecting the private self if it matches the public audience's expectations in form and appearance.

Most of Hearst's words, especially in this first audiotape, are like the lines delivered by a bad actor. They are not theatrical and overdone, yet there seems to be a lie or a half-truth in all of them. The quality of her voice sounds flat, exhausted, and confused. It recalls the voice of a child before bedtime, only half present under the sheer weight of exhaustion. Or perhaps this is simply the voice of someone kept against her will and potentially experiencing physical and or sexual trauma. Even as it is difficult to pinpoint the source of infelicity, the words don't sound quite right; they falter and fall flat. As Christopher Castiglia, Nancy Isenberg, and Shana Alexander have argued, the words and their delivery prop Hearst up as a screen upon which to project national fears, personal anxieties, and social expectations of race, class, and gender. As William Graebner claims, "Because Patty's motives and intentions were, from the beginning, unclear, her case allowed Americans—her parents, the lawyers, journalists, the jury, ordinary folks of all persuasions and from all walks of life—to project their values, ideals and concerns onto the persona of Patty Hearst and to interpret her conduct as they saw fit."[20] The demand for a motive and the lack of a clear sense of Hearst—whitewashed as a "normal" (i.e., a white, wealthy, educated young woman) and therefore blank—left her available for possession and inhabitation from outside. In the public's eye, Hearst was responsible for the sound of her voice and the words that they conveyed, and yet she was simultaneously divorced from their meaning and authorship.

One of the ways in which SLA's theater of abduction activated the social and national imaginary was through the specter of race. Hearst's kidnapping was racialized from the beginning; her body and her image had been stolen from their rightful owners—her father, white America—and now were in the possession of what Christopher Castiglia terms "the poor, the black, the sexually 'liberated.'"[21] The story began as one of horror, racialized encounter, and sexual titillation. Towards the end of the first tape, Hearst claims that

SLA members Remiro and Little are being wrongfully held by the US government as prisoners of war for their shooting of Oakland's first Black superintendent, Marcus Foster. Hearst relays in her communiqué that "witnesses to the shooting . . . saw Black men. And two white men have been arrested for this."[22] Hearst announces Remiro and Little's innocence by placing the blame on two Black men reported to have been at the scene of the crime. This is an all too familiar claim, Blackness-as-criminality. Defreeze, aka Cinque, was by most accounts the only Black member of the SLA. At one point, the SLA had help from a fellow ex-prisoner and Black radical named Thero Wheeler, but there are conflicting stories about when exactly Wheeler left the organization, and by most accounts, he had gone before the shooting of Foster.[23] Since Cinque was the only Black man actively involved in the SLA, the two Black men that Hearst refers to *might* be Cinque and Wheeler. Other sources, such as Paul Schrader's 1988 film—which Hearst consulted on—and Pearsall's documentation of the SLA communiqués, claim that white members of the SLA often dressed in racial drag. Indeed, this would explain the "two black men" who were reported to have kidnapped Hearst on February 4. Pearsall writes that in the SLA audio communiqués, members would adopt markedly Black vocal inflections and language which he claimed were indicative of the SLA's "play-school tactic of 'let's pretend.'"[24] Elsewhere he called these vocal performances by members such as Teko and Gelina "conscious projection[s] of emotional tones [through] counterfeited Black accents."[25] Indeed, Angela Atwood (Gelina), a former theater student at Indiana University, was often credited as the theatrical instigator of the SLA's media-savvy moves.[26] Pearsall interprets the SLA tactics as something akin to sonic blackface, an imitation toward deception, an ingestion and re-sounding of Black politics in the style of George Jackson, or an echoing of the Tupameros' urban guerilla programs of food redistribution. Suturing race and criminality by way of Hearst and the SLA's insistence on the white innocence of Remiro and Little appears to conflict with the ideological message that the SLA was attempting to advance.

Describing the shooting of Marcus Foster, Jeffery Toobin writes in his 2016 book that "Nancy Ling fired first [and] Donald Defreeze stepped forward next and fired two blasts. [And then Mizmoon] fired a final shot into the back of [Foster's] neck, severing his spinal cord."[27] Toobin names Nancy, Cinque, and Mizmoon as the shooters of Foster, with no allusion to the potential of either Nancy or Mizmoon being in blackface. I want to linger, however, on Pearsall's interpretation of the SLA's "counterfeited black accents," as it seems key to an understanding of the racial politics of the Hearst's kidnapping story. As Jennifer Stoever-Ackerman writes, "We hear race in addition to seeing it. Sonic phenomena like vocal timbre, accents, and musical tones are racially coded, like skin color, hair texture, and clothing choices."²⁸ She continues, "As the dominant 'listening ear' is disciplined to process white male ways of sounding as default—natural, normal, and desirable—alternate ways of listening and sounding are deemed aberrant and, depending upon the historical context, as excessively sensitive, strikingly deficient, or impossibly both."²⁹ While Stoever-Ackerman is discussing the sonic color line and the racialization of the voice, what she brings our attention to is the way in which the dominant listening ear is trained to process "white male ways of sounding as default." In Pearsall's reading of the tapes, he heard voices that did not sound white. In other words, they lacked the transparency of white sound, they held a racialized sonic texture. If we are to follow along with Pearsall and credit the SLA with "counterfeited black accents," such a move would fit well within the history of white appropriation of Black sound, of Blackness as a means of accessing a fantasy of emotionality, desire, or politics. As Michael Rogin observes, in Al Jolson's *The Jazz Singer*, "black sound becomes the primary element of the performance of blackface, and thus less important than the visual which is already known to be artifice."³⁰ The emphasis on the optics of blackface by the time of Jolson's 1927 film was less important than sounding the part of the white minstrel performers' fantasy projection of Blackness.

Influenced by George Jackson's call for revolutionary change, the SLA used Hearst as a microphone to demand 400 million dollars' worth of food redistribution to Californians and the release of SLA "prisoners of war" Remiro and Little, who were being held at San Quentin Prison. Discussing the history of minstrel performance, Eric Lott observes that "the very form of blackface acts—an investiture in back bodies—seems a manifestation of the particular desire to try on the accents of 'blackness' and demonstrates the permeability of the colorline."³¹ For Lott, sound and voice signal the permeability of the color line perhaps in the way it marks a white fantasy and desire for a material Blackness. He continues, "Blackface minstrelsy is less a sign of absolute white power and control than of panic, anxiety, terror, and pleasure."³² It would seem that there is anxiety and pleasure in the Blackness mobilized by the SLA. While the organization begins with the escape of Cinque from Vacaville prison, SLA members do not continue to focus on Cinque's own story or the abolition of prisons more generally, even as they mobilize an underarticulated critique of the emergence of what would become known as the prison industrial complex and mass incarceration. Instead, the SLA's largely white membership marks a white desire to do good, to be radical, to spark an armed revolution. To my ear, this style of rhetoric that both hinges on and obscures Black life and politics again recalls Saidiya Hartman's reading of white abolitionist John Rankin's 1837 epistle. Hartman writes that:

> the effort to counteract the commonplace callousness to black suffering requires that the white body be positioned in the place of the black body in order to make this suffering visible and intelligible. . . . The ambivalent character of empathy—more exactly, the repressive effects of empathy—as Jonathan Boyarin notes, can be located in the "obliteration of otherness" or the facile intimacy that enable identification with the other only as we "feel ourselves into those we imagine as ourselves."[33]

Empathy, far from a benign mode of white relation, marks an evacuation of Black sentience and identifies Black pain as only comprehensible if it is relatable to white feeling. Hartman further asks why Black suffering is the site through which the white abolitionist seeks to empathize. She continues, "The elusiveness of black suffering can be attributed to a racist optics in which black flesh is itself identified as the source of opacity, the denial of black humanity, and the effacement of sentience integral to the wanton use of the captive body."[34] The "racist optics" marks "black flesh . . . as the source of opacity" and the "white or near-white body" as the site of visibility and legibility. Empathy, then, signifies a kind of white identificatory mobility, an affective tourism or wandering into the zones of radicality.

The SLA was an organization claiming to consist of "forces . . . from every walk of life, from every religion, and of every race" who unite under the "common goal for freedom from the chains of capitalism."[35] Hearst's voice in the audio communiqué and the words behind it make the SLA sound like a markedly white organization half-heartedly adopting the rhetoric—and potentially mannerisms and vocal inflections—of radicals such as the Black Panthers, the Tupamaros, or the Soledad Brothers. Members of the SLA were treated like actors reflecting a failed synchronicity between outward presentation and inner self.

Hearst's autobiography and public kidnapping follow in the tradition of many American captivity narratives. The allegedly mixed-race SLA "captors" in the public imagination are figured as racial others terrorizing the innocence of white femininity and youth in the figure of a naive Hearst. As Cristopher Castiglia explains in *Bound & Determined*, American captivity narratives originally circulated as settler colonial justification of Indigenous extermination, protecting the specter of the virginal white Christian femininity, while at the same time providing a narrative adventure story in the wilds of racial difference. Captivity narratives are stories of abduction with the white individual pitted against the racialized Native. Like slave narratives and other American narrative genres, the captivity narrative was popular not just because it served to reaffirm the difference between civilization and savagery, between "us" and "them," but because the emotional interior of the novel allowed for an eroticized contact with the other that could be arrested by merely putting the book down.

Captivity narratives, at first glance, illustrate the opposite of an escape as they signal capture and control, not freedom and release. In their continuation over the past three hundred years, captivity narratives have developed into a symbolic geography "offer[ing] American women a female picaresque, an adventure story set, unlike most early American literature, outside the home."[36] Poised "post-Vietnam, post-Watergate [in] a climate of malaise," Hearst's captivity narrative as it is recounted by her in *Every Secret Thing*, and the SLA's manipulation of the media, tells the story of a white woman toying with radical guerilla warfare and free love before returning home to safety and wealth. Yet Hearst's return, as Castiglia reminds us, is incomplete. She had been infected and corrupted; her reactions were inappropriate, embarrassing, and unnerving to the political, social, and economic body of the United States. Perhaps her time with the SLA illustrated something about the instability of whiteness itself where Hearst became a race traitor. Why else was she tried in court before any of the other remaining SLA members? It would seem that there is something that Hearst does to the genre of captivity narrative that is unacceptable to her American public audience. She does not verify the purity of the nation and whiteness against the corruption of the racialized other.

In "Runaway Tongues," poet and theorist Harryette Mullen discusses the literary genre established by Harriet Beecher Stowe's *Uncle Tom's Cabin*. Mullen writes that Stowe's novel demonstrates a "grafting of the sentimental novel, a literary genre associated with white women and the ideology of female domestication, onto the slave narrative, a genre associated with the literary production of black men and linking literacy with freedom and manhood . . . . Stowe uses the slave narrative as a reservoir of fact, experience, and realism, while constructing black characters as objects of sentimentality in order to augment the emotive power and political significance of her text."[37] The popularity of *Uncle Tom's Cabin*, not to mention the wild success of its adaptation into a stage play, illustrates an investment in this genre mix of white feminine melodramatic sentimentalism with a backdrop, or "reservoir," of Black realist masculinist self-making. Having emerged in eighteenth-century England, the sentimental novel was meant to elicit sympathy and promote a refined emotional response in its readers. For the sentimental novel, feeling was enough—one need not ever act on their identification with an other. Mixed with the realist autobiography of facts that characterized the (anti)slave escape narrative, Stowe's text seemed to prioritize a white sentimentalism and Black elasticity made comprehensible by white inhabitation. The white sentimentality of the captivity narrative likewise pulls upon the emotive heartstrings of the reader, as did Hearst's own initial story as it was broadcast widely across the television and airwaves. However, the reservoir of realism that props up Hearst's story quickly shifts from that of the classic captivity narrative, a white woman stolen away by racialized (white) radicals, to a white woman gone awry. Confession and self-disclosure go wrong here.

The Sounds of the SLA Screeds

The SLA's first eleven communiqués were written documents sent to major newspapers for print. *Communiqué #12* was the first audio message that the SLA prerecorded for public broadcast. The tape introduced the organization to the public, taking full advantage of the media frenzy around the kidnapping of Hearst.[38] But it was not until *Communiqué #13*, received by KPFA on February 12, 1974, over a week after Hearst's disappearance, that the public first heard her speak. She was portrayed by the media and the public as a voice without a voice of her own, as "the SLA's amanuensis."[39] The sound was right and the phrasing was right; the actual fingerprint of Hearst's voice was identifiable. But the interior identity reflected on the tape was not representative of what the public wanted to hear. The recording was widely believed to be the words of the SLA, projected through Hearst as though she were merely an amplification device, a loudspeaker through which to send out their message. On the tape she explained, "I'm kept blindfolded usually so that I can't identify anyone. My hands are often tied, but generally they're not. I'm not gagged or anything, and I'm comfortable. And I think you can tell that I'm not really terrified or anything and that I'm okay."[40] After her violent abduction and inevitably traumatic confinement in a closet for nearly two months, it is impossible to tell which parts of the recorded message contain "the truth," contain the "real" feelings of Hearst, and genuinely reflect her well-being. Troubling this confluence of voice and truth, Mladen Dolar—by way of Derrida and Saussure—reminds us that the voice is separated from other "noise" because the voice is a sound that is imagined to have "meaning." It is endowed "with the will to 'say something,' with an inner intentionality."[41] Although the voice seems to flow from nowhere in particular, vaguely originating somewhere in the throat or the mouth, it is imagined to be indelibly attached to the core of the body and mind and even to bridge the two. The voice reflects the subject at the center of the body, the inner being; it is "the hidden bodily treasure beyond the visible envelope."[42] When this already intimate and revealing voice is removed from the body—as in the case of Hearst's audiotapes—it further adds to the sense of meaning behind the voice. Such recordings contribute an air of omnipotence to the voice that, no longer bound by the body, can travel anywhere and do anything, haunting us like the acousmatic voice of God himself. The timbre, the character, the intonation of the voice also contain information, as we see in the inevitable state interpretations of Hearst's voice as "tired" or "drugged." The quality of the voice—unlike its linguistic signifiers—possesses a meaning that is open to interpretation. The shading of the voice does not add to signification, but is instead the nonlinguistic element of the voice, its material "ancillary."[43] These extralinguistic elements of the voice—"the accent, the intonation, the timbre"—tell us something else that cannot quite be measured.[44] It is this character of Hearst's voice that the FBI and media paid attention to. Yet, instead of this attention to the quality of her voice opening up the potential to listen to her words for a variety of meanings, for their veering trajectories, the analysts of Hearst's audio read the sound of her voice through the legitimating lenses of medical and psychoanalytic diagnostics. What the "tape experts" do not notice, or rather, cannot hear, is the potential for contradictory or ambivalent meanings that are carried through the timbre and accent of Hearst's voice.[45] To read Hearst's voice in this first tape as reflecting a drugged and traumatized young woman is only part of the story. The words used to describe her voice rely on the language of interiority and intention which make it difficult to describe Hearst's voice without falling back on diagnostic words like "dissociative," "meek," or "lost."

Hearst's second audiotape—*Screed #16*—was delivered to KPFA on February 16 and it followed the format of the first tape. Her voice sounded a little more sure and less confused, as if she had gotten used to the recording process and what was expected of her. There is more energy or focus in her delivery and performance; she sounds awake. At one point she even narrates herself looking at writing as a guide, saying, "[Let me] turn over my notes here." Yet, for most of the tape, Hearst still sounds a little confused, like she isn't quite clear what words will come next. She takes big breaths, sighs between phrases, which has the effect of pulling the focus from the direct confidence of each line. The section of the tape where she sounds most committed to the words, most physically present behind them, is when she tells her parents she is okay.

"Also, I would like to emphasize that *I am alive* and that *I am well*, and that in spite of what certain tape experts seem to think. I mean, *I'm fine*. It's really depressing to hear people talk about me like I'm dead. I can't explain what it's like."[46] Fighting the idea of her immanent death, Hearst reinforces an individual bodily perseverance. When she speaks in first person, which she returns to again later in the tape, she does so with a certain emphasis behind the individual words, as though she is really trying to convince the listener. Later she explains, "I am *not left alone* and I am not just shoved off, I mean, *I am fine*. I am *not being starved* and I am *not being beaten or tortured. Really*."[47] She sounds almost exasperated, frustrated by being forced to repeat herself and insist on her bodily integrity. The voice, Hearst's voice, becomes the promise that her body is still alive. Reinforcing the self through a repetition of "I," her voice marks the absence of the body and an insistence on its future return.

At the end of the tape, her voice changes again to an almost listless searching. It is as if she is listening for a way to say the words that she is not allowed to say. As she tells her parents to "take care of Steve" it sounds like she wants to tell them to do other things too, to send a message through to them without jeopardizing her own safety. In her autobiography Hearst reflects on the first audio recording:

> The first part of the tape went simply enough. I could understand what Cinque was trying to get across and out into words. But as we went on, it became more and more difficult for me. I had to exert all of my determination to keep from breaking down and crying as I told lie after lie about how well I was being treated and especially when I expressed the hope of getting back to my family and to Steve. The truth was: I was so scared but still resented that I was being used to disseminate their lies.[48]

In her court case, Hearst's own statements of "truth" were highly criticized and questioned because, in the aftermath of her audio recordings with the SLA, she was no longer considered to be a credible source. The jury—after viewing the surveillance tape from the Hibernia Bank robbery depicting Hearst shouting and wielding a shotgun—would no longer believe the defense's argument that Hearst was a victim. I am likewise reluctant to see her confession in court or her autobiography as truth because of the ways in which Hearst was required, by the federal law during her trial, to repent for her sins, to relinquish any potentially lingering affinity with the SLA and its members, and to pledge allegiance to the United States government. We can mine this statement for other modes of meaning; for instance, Hearst paints a picture of the circumstance of these recordings, and one that seems fairly believable. In her re-creation of the scene of this first tape recording, Hearst explains, "when I finished each point, I was to click off the tape recorder and he would tell me what next to say, one point at a time. I was so happy to cooperate in this; I would do anything, I thought, to get a message home."[49] According to Hearst, the content of the message was less important than its transmission and the virtual contact that it engendered between her and her family. The material of the voice itself—its fingerprint, presence, and circulation—is the message that Hearst wants to send home with little regard for the actual words being uttered.

Hearst's third tape, *Screed #20*, came three weeks later, on March 9, day thirty-four of her captivity. In this tape, her voice is much stronger, and she speaks her words in a direct manner, each word following neatly after the last. Because of the articulate language and relative speed of her voice, it would seem that either Hearst or one of the SLA members had written out her statement and she had practiced its recitation. It is around this third tape where Hearst stops pleading to her parents, stops sounding confused and mournful, and begins to vocally engage the lines in a different manner when the press and public begin to suspect Hearst's motives and character. Instead of her usual beseeching rhetoric and tone, Hearst's audio directly accuses her parents of indifference. About a minute into the recording, she says, "I don't believe you're doing everything you can, everything in your power. I don't believe that you're doing anything at all. You said it was out of your hands; what you should have said was that you wash your hands of it. . . . I don't know who influenced you not to comply with the good faith gesture."[50] She accuses her parents of negligence and a disregard for both her safety and the well-being of California's poor. In this audio, Hearst's voice adopts the tone and style of SLA communiqués previously spoken by Cinque or Gelina as she holds individuals responsible for larger political and corporate decisions. Hearst's words gesture toward the precarious production of the "truth" and the impossible promise of self and interiority that is at the heart of this notion of personal truth, individual intent, and the suturing of meaning to vocal inflection.

Writing in *Every Secret Thing*, Hearst notes, "I really did not care what I said at this point. I was ready to do anything the SLA asked of me, for my life was in their hands. They were delighted with my performance."[51] Hearst explains that the screed had been written by Gelina, who, prior to joining the SLA, was "an actress in amateur theatricals."[52] From the now iconic photograph of Hearst wielding a shotgun in front of the SLA cobra flag to the disguises the SLA wore to the scripts and vocal performance of their communiqués, there was something undeniably theatrical about their oppositional guerilla tactics. In her autobiography, Hearst emphasizes the rehearsals and dress of the SLA soldiers, crediting Gelina as the Broadway mastermind behind their work. According to her, the SLA willingly chose to be a spectacle so that they might garner more media attention and thus more support for their cause. Hearst had directors and coaches demonstrating and performing alongside her in the style and tone that she was meant to adopt. In the SLA, Hearst was part of a group performance, one seemingly committed as much to guerilla theater as to its political outcome. Because the SLA's radical drama played out in the public eye, their political acts, much like contemporary Republicans Ronald Reagan and Richard Nixon, were oriented towards an audience who preferred the live to the written.

Hearst goes on in this third screed to say, "The media, with cooperation from my parents, has created a public image of me as a helpless innocent girl who was supposedly abducted by two terrible Blacks, escaped convicts. I'm a strong woman and I resent being used in this way."[53] Blackness returns here as "escaped" criminality. Hearst's "re-education" by the SLA women included an awareness of the emerging feminist movement of the early 1970s—from the reintroduction of the Equal Rights Amendment into Congress (1972), the birth of *Ms.* magazine (1972), and legalization of abortion in *Roe v. Wade* (1973). As Castiglia argues, Hearst's story was always a sexual story, a battle over the ideological and sexual possession of her white body. From her early adoption of the feminism of her SLA "sisters" to her articulation that her fiancé Steven Weed's treatment of her was "chauvinistic, sexist, and bourgeois" to her performances in John Waters films celebrating the oppositional and perverse, feminist politics seems to be the one thing that came easy to Hearst and which she retained even after the kidnapping and release.[54]

At one point in her autobiography, Hearst even critiques the other women for following the rule of the SLA men: "It was ironic that all of the SLA sisters believed in the liberation of women, and yet the men in this cell acted as though the women were there to serve them sexually. It was even more peculiar that none of the other women appeared able to see what I could see."[55] For the FBI, Hearst was only a rescuable victim as long as she was vulnerable and voiceless. There is undoubtedly a sexualization of Patty's captivity—from the FBI code name for her rescue "HERSNATCH" to the reports of sexual abuse while with the SLA to the prosecution's accusation that Hearst was "in love" with Cujo—as well as of her projected rescue by the FBI.[56] Hearst was not passive enough for the government to reclaim her, nor was she heroic enough for them to be proud of her willful resistance to the SLA radicals. In her FBI trial, Hearst was made into an example; she was a bad subject, a bad citizen, neither weak enough nor strong enough to be acquitted.

On April 3, in *Screed #28*—day fifty-nine of Hearst's kidnapping—Patty came out to the public as Tania. In this tape, Hearst's voice is calm and evenly paced even as she retains what we might call a distant wealthy white affect. Hearst sounds slightly disdainful and righteous and yet does not appear particularly committed to her words. By the fourth tape, Hearst has become a convincing actor, if not a particularly compelling one. Put differently, the sounds of the words matched their delivery. She explains, "I have been given the choice of (one) being released in a safe area, or (two), joining the forces of the Symbionese Liberation Army and fighting for my freedom and the freedom of all oppressed people. I have chosen to stay and fight."[57] Employing the rhetoric of choice, Hearst's words explain that she has chosen both personal freedom and "the freedom of all oppressed people." This statement brings to light the multiple definitions at play here concerning both freedom and its radical and shameful avenue of attainment, escape. Hearst's usage of the word "freedom" in this instance follows the logic set forth by the SLA, indicating freedom as the way out of capitalist systems of exploitation, a release from economic and social systems that privilege and protect the lives of those with money or white skin. The SLA believed that through their kidnapping of Hearst, they had provided her with just such a freedom and enabled her escape out of social and economic privilege and indifference. Yet Hearst's definition of freedom in *Screed #28* goes against the definition in use in the public during the time of her capture. The media, the FBI, and Patty's own parents wanted her to escape, either to be the good little girl in need of liberation, or to instead liberate herself from the constraints of the SLA—its closet, its "consciousness-raising" rhetoric, and its ever-present threat of violent "terrorism." These two directly competing definitions of freedom are at the center of the scandal that was Hearst's kidnapping and the sensational reaction to her capture. The SLA saw freedom in opposition to economically driven and selective social protection by the state, while the Hearst family and the FBI saw freedom as a return to the state and its warm embrace for those benefiting from its social policies.

Hearst prefaces this last communiqué, presumably having learned that her tapes were being discredited in the media as false, with an authenticating statement. Emphasizing her intent, free will, and individual authorship of the words, she explains: "It's what I feel. I have never been forced to say anything on tape. Nor have I been brainwashed, drugged, tortured, hypnotized or in any way confused."[58] It would be safe to say that Hearst's kidnapping and the chain of events that followed would likely inspire a range of emotions. Yet, statements like the one above inspire in the listener the very disbelief and questions that they are meant to foreclose. Hearst's final transformation from good girl to bad comes in her now famous statement and sound bite; "I have been given the name Tania after a comrade who fought alongside Che (Guevara) in Bolivia for the people of Bolivia. I embrace the name with the determination to continue fighting with her spirit. There is no victory in half-assed attempts at revolution."[59] She promises to continue to fight with "total dedication" in "the oppressed American people's revolution."[60] Hearst's statement shocked the public, inviting immediate character attacks, discounting any innocence that she may have ever possessed in regard to her capture, or any power she had over her own voice, body, or words. This message solidified her guilt, corruption, and overall weak character and constitution. The media speculated that she had been colluding with the SLA all along, perhaps even heading the violent organization herself. Hearst was a POW who had transformed into a guerilla. She altered the direction of freedom, as if changing the location on a map and altering the territory previously marked as "free" as now the space of capture and corruption. Such radical cartography allows for a reexamination of the limits of escape.

Patty Hearst's kidnapping has become an iconic example of Stockholm syndrome, of the innocent young girl brainwashed into identifying with her captors and eventually transforming into a radical vigilante. In the eyes of the media and FBI, Hearst went from fragile young lady to psychologically penetrated social exile. The primary argument used by the defense in Hearst's trial for her participation in the Hibernia Bank robbery was that of brainwashing, or what the defense labeled "coercive persuasion."[61] As reflected in her audio communiqués, Hearst and the SLA were aware that her words were being dismissed as false. Her failure to surface after the shootout and fire at the Los Angeles "safehouse" on May 17, 1974—killing all other SLA members but Hearst and the Harrises—or during what is referred to as "the missing year" that Bill and Emily Harris took her into hiding only furthered the public opinion that she had lost control of her own will and mind. The brainwashing explanation was the only way the public could rationally understand the duration of Hearst's absence and her perceived wealth of escape opportunities. Why hadn't Hearst escaped from Bill and Emily Harris? Why had she even gone so far as to defended the Harrises with a gun during the May 16 confrontation at Mel's Sporting Goods when she could have just as easily shot them or run away? The brainwashing defense reconciled the pre-SLA image of Patty with the post-SLA guerilla Tania without discounting the original imagined character of Patty as representative of a white, trustworthy, and infallible America. Graebner sums it up in saying that "Patty's sin of omission was no less serious than those she had committed: she had not tried to escape."[62] What seems to be at stake in this brainwashing defense is the verdict on whether Patty was a victim or a criminal, innocent or guilty, patriot or terrorist, radical or theatrical. The brainwashing defense as well as the social commentaries at the time—describing Patty as a "spoiled rich kid" or a "crazy little girl"—simply served "to separate Patty from whatever serious political or social motives she may have had for joining and remaining a member of the SLA."[63]

Whereas it is possible that the SLA offered Hearst a break from the legacy of the Hearst castle, it seems safe to say that the organization changed her. The logic behind brainwashing sets up an "us" versus "them" dynamic, you're either with us, your truth is as an "us," or you have been subjected to mind control and thus alienated from your own self and your natural allegiances. One need only look at the plethora of films at the time, from *Invasion of the Body Snatchers* (1956) to *Manchurian Candidate* (1962), to see examples of this national fear of mind control. Yet, in Hearst's time with the SLA, she became part of the "them" of the SLA; she now belonged to a radically different community than the one she was born into. Her entry into the ranks of the SLA—in addition to providing her with endless traumatic hours locked in a closet and not knowing if she would live or die—also enabled her to try on different forms of collective, feminist, and militant identities that she had not previously had access to in her life as a Hearst.[64]

The term *brainwashing* came about by way of the Korean War—a war characterized in the American imagination through captivity and torture "over there" at the hands of communists. The term originates in English in the 1950s around the fear that communist infiltration of both the national body and the individual mind pervaded the country. This was a fear of aliens lurking among "us" and passing as loyal Americans; this political fear would culminate in McCarthyism and the execution of Julius and Ethel Rosenberg. As historian Charles Young writes, "Brainwashing explained the inexplicable. It was colloquially understood as preternatural control of thought; it spread as urban myth as much as in news reports."[65] During the Korean War in particular, the idea was that POWs, throughout their capture, reeducation, and torture, had been subjected to the science fiction of mind control; communists had snuck into the boundaries of the body and mind in order to corrupt the national social fabric from within. Young continues, "American POWs reading confessions or letters home were a regular feature on Radio Peking shortwave broadcasts. Typical was 'This is Sergeant First Class Richard K. Artesani, 3rd Battalion, Eight Army Regiment. Dear Folks... The food is very good... GI's not interested in war 5,000 miles away... love to all, avoid another world war.' Such statements disturbed people at home and formed a bank of evidence for disciplinary proceedings after the war."[66] It would seem that part of the myth and fear of brainwashing was not simply about the fear of the susceptibility of the mind, but that brainwashing also contained a confessional element that had become so intrinsic to Western identity formation.

The Peking Radio broadcasts and the SLA audio communiqués both rely on the voice to relay the inner psychological truths of the mind. These aural missives reflected the ability of the enemy to make Americans into foreigners; this was a form of psychic capture that occluded the possibility of escape and that prevented the soldiers from even realizing that they wanted to escape, or rather, that they *should* want to escape. This shift toward the rhetoric of brainwashing marks captivity and freedom as a psychic problem with national ramifications beyond the confines of the individual mind. "With Korea, the encounter with communism became an unusually personal and intimate battle with demons of thought.... Captivity became an inner trial, not an escape fable."[67] If we trace the etymology of the word "brainwashing," then its emergence in the 1950s in tandem with the Korean War might suggest that the nature of captivity and escape changes to include distinctly psychological features and fears. The birth of the concept of "brainwashing" does not reflect a new set of psychological traumas, but rather, it demonstrates the manner in which these traumas are used to shore up a certain sense of the sanctity of individual identity, national power, national security, race, and gender.

Brainwashing also occurs in tandem with the threat of violence, with the fear for one's life. Her autobiography explains in the very title that Hearst will tell "every secret thing" that there is to know. She will give us the real deal behind her kidnapping and expose the inner secrets which emanate from inside her mind. As I mentioned earlier, Hearst is compelled to perform an ideal mix of victimization and internal coherence in her autobiographical confession and in her jury statement during the trial. Caught in the language of sentimental fiction, autobiography, second-wave feminism, and political manifestos, Hearst performs to—and in excess of—a certain genre of literature. Her voice becomes known to herself and the public through these genre markers and confessional cultural frames that situate and legitimate her ability to create the truth. Thinking with Pamela Haag, second-wave feminism places emphasis on "therapeutically inspired axioms [such as] 'empathy,' 'closure,' and 'raw experience' as opposed to critique [or] analysis."[68] For some strands of feminism, sexual violence becomes the epitome of violation through the wounding of a woman's core, the utmost private domain, her sex. To heal from such sexual wounding, this "economy of sentimentalism" has taught women that they need to perform this victimization, to "cry amply, unfurl physical bruises, and appear sufficiently raw and distraught—minds inhabiting shattered bodies—because if they do not their victimization is too subtle to register in courts of law or public opinion."[69] According to this prevalent model set up by both the legal system and feminist axioms, to garner innocence or redemption one is required to convincingly perform their undoing, and vulnerability.

Turning to Sándor Ferenczi's 1931 essay, *Confusion of Tongues between Adults and the Child*, which outlines the psychological reasons for what Ferenczi calls "identification with the aggressor," we can trace some of the theories that would seem to predate the emergence of both brainwashing or Stockholm syndrome. Identification with the aggressor is what happens when one perceives the situation in which they find themself to be inescapable. The escape mechanisms of self-perseverance are not accessible and so the self disappears into the intrapsychic realm through the introjection of the aggressor. Jay Frankel elaborates on Ferenczi, explaining that "like chameleons, we blend into the world around us, into the very thing that threatens us, in order to protect ourselves. We stop being ourselves and transform ourselves into someone else's *image* of us. This happens automatically."[70] Identification with the aggressor, in these terms, is not part of an escape fable or grand captivity narrative but is instead part and parcel of the everyday. Furthermore, it is described as seeing, as another person's image of you that comes to stand in for your own self-image.

We might say that Hearst's real crime was her failed performance in the courtroom. The jury found Hearst to be much more convincing as a militant guerrilla then as a kidnap victim and survivor. As Haag explains, "The victim and the individual, insofar as both demand full abjection or full self-determination, respectively, are both distortive models of subjectivity and social roles." The trap of sexual subjectivity in second-wave feminism demands either a victim or a survivor: someone who cannot fend for herself, or a "rugged" individual who is created by way of the refusal of even the possibility of victimization.[71] To demand that a victim of violence remake herself as a subject requires a reexamination of the models of subjectivity, of self-ness, as well as the way in which we achieve it. The ownership of the self, the cohesive, strong-willed, un-budging self is part of the white masculinist domain which white popular feminism sought to recuperate. Women are allocated to the emotional arena of self-doubt, insecurity, humility, and the voiceless. Much like Rey Chow's concept of "coercive mimeticism," in which one is both consciously and unconsciously compelled to perform faithfully to the stereotype of their ethnic identity, Hearst's only avenue for legal acquittal was through explaining herself in the precise and stringent terms of gendered victim.[72] Even in the language of women's liberation, it was not possible to see Hearst as both victim and self-possessed individual. Having already seen her in the role of the powerful and violent guerilla espousing the confident and direct language of the SLA and cohabiting with radicals, Black men, and the poor, the jury did not buy her performance of repentant survivor and injured woman.

Sharon Hayes's *Symbionese Liberation Army Screeds*

Sharon Hayes presents Patty Hearst's SLA audio recordings as a disobedient scene of subject formation. By respeaking, or performing what artist Wu Tsang calls "full body quotation," Hayes amplifies Hearst's original disobedience from the captivity narrative and a static understanding of self. From respeaking public documents, such as the Guantánamo Bay prison tribunals in *Combatant Status Review Tribunals, pp. 002954-003064: A Public Reading* and Ronald Reagan's official "Address to the Nation" speeches in *My Fellow Americans: 1981-1988*, to her performance of political protest slogans on the streets of Manhattan titled *In the Near Future*, Hayes's performances, installations, and videos explore the manner in which language, politics, and histories tend to, in her words, "find a home in the body."[73] Her work is performance based, expanding across video, painting, lithography, and sound installation, and often has an initially "public" moment on the street featuring unknowable open audiences. Afterward, the performance script, audio recording, or video documentation of that action is reframed and presented in the space of the gallery. Through the various audiences and moments created in her choreography of media, Hayes engages questions of public address to explore the power of recitation in the body and on the tongue. Coming of age and coming into art in the New York City of the early '90s, Hayes is deeply attached to the specificity of space and context, to the performance situation in which art comes to be and comes to be seen. Emerging into a political queer performance scene in 1991 in NYC—from ACT UP to Queer Nation to the Lesbian Avengers—she explains, "We became political, we became artists in deep relation to precise historical conditions and these singularities, these precisions linger with us;

they're carried along with us in our bodies."⁷⁴ Reminding us of the political scenes that shape us in Hayes's historical stuttering repetitions, she shows us how our stories, our narratives of self, are never strictly autobiographical, but are instead reflective of a time and a space in which we were mutually constituted by what she calls the "singularity" of experience.⁷⁵ Hayes likewise turns from the reign of the visual and returns us to the scene of collective speech and voice, to the textured plane of utterance.⁷⁶

Veering from this approximation of voice as true word, Sharon Hayes's four-channel respeaking starts with *Screed #13*, Hearst's first communication with the public. The video begins with a tight headshot of Hayes staring directly into and through the camera lens, as though she were speaking to both the large glassy eye of the camera and the audience beyond. The studio background is white and Hayes is well lit, drawing our attention away from formal and aesthetic elements of the shot to Hayes herself, her face, her curly hair, and her voice. Staring blankly into the camera, Hayes reveals little about who she is or what she feels. She begins speaking, "Mom, Dad, I'm okay." Hayes remembers this line without faltering; her affect is nervous and her voice sounds a little bit shaky. Hayes seems to know her lines as she speaks for twenty to thirty minutes in each video without forgetting whole paragraphs or pages; she only ever requires a prompt when she has lost her footing or is seeking reassurance from the audience. However, Hayes is not actually performing the SLA communiqués in any theatrical or convincing sense. Instead, her words sound empty, or rather, it seems as if she has no personal connection to them.

Hayes performs what J. L. Austin calls a "misfire."⁷⁷ The performative utterance does not carry the weight of either convention or ritual. The external vocalization does not appear to have any relationship to the inward performance of feeling or information that the words are meant to convey. As Shoshana Felman suggests, the performative utterance has a tendency to fail; it is defined in part by its very openness to failure. When a speech act has misfired, it is "not because something is missing, but because something else is done."⁷⁸ For Felman, a misfire is a moment of potential. As José Esteban Muñoz elaborates, "The misfire, this failure, is intrinsic to how the performative illustrates the ways different courses are traveled in contrast to what heteronormativity [or *straight time*] demands."⁷⁹ In other words, the misfire produces generative meanings that are not already mapped by dominant organizing temporal or spatial structures. Hayes's misfires are reminiscent of Hearst's perceived infidelity, as her captured voice, its rhetorical whiteness and potential approximate Blackness, does something else. What is more,

Hayes speaks in the context of a stage, and for Austin, the space of the theater invalidates the force of speech all together. As Sedgwick and Parker note, Austin's degradation of the theatrical utterance disqualifies it, claiming that it no longer *does* anything and linking it to "the perverted, the artificial, the unnatural, the abnormal, the decadent, the effete, the diseased."[80] In short, language in the theater is always already queer in its misalignment. Watching Hayes, I am more aware of the relationship between memory, the body, and her public than I am of the information or content of Hearst's words. Hearing the audience correct Hayes and watching her recall the lines as she asks her live audience, "I'm sorry, the whole line?" brings my attention to the citation process itself—from theatrical lines to the normative gendered and racialized presentations we are expected to recite perfectly.

It isn't until about four minutes into *SLA Screed #13* that the audience begins to feel comfortable chiming in and correcting Hayes. Initially, solitary voices correct her sparingly, but as the performance goes on, the audience gets braver. At first there is a lone voice feeding Hayes the lines, but as the audience becomes more confident in their role as linguistic correction officers, they speak out in cacophonous chorus, and, through the monitor of the playback screen, it becomes hard to hear precisely what they are saying. Hayes's eyes move to different faces, not grazing the audience's, but departing from the camera to look directly at different voices. She searches for her cue, trying to visually register the words that she has gotten wrong and understand which were the right words. She asks the audience "Cuz? Cuz?" before understanding what they are saying and then correcting herself, stating "*because*." Hayes's textured utterances are respoken statements coming from a woman under duress and a series of utterances driven by an audience calling her into line. Her performance is one of liminality, vulnerability, and contradiction. Hearst has been called "a cipher" and an exemplary postmodern legal subject for being unremarkable beyond the words that the SLA projected through her.[81] Sharon Hayes, however, takes a different performative approach, mining the tapes for sounds that were foreclosed in the SLA recordings. Thinking with Gayatri Chakravorty Spivak's foundational essay "Can the Subaltern Speak?," how might we be able to listen to voices that are not immediately legitimized through legal and ideological traditions?[82]

Originally produced as an unlimited edition, Hayes's four screeds appeared in VHS format, stacked against the wall of the gallery. Hayes meant for the tapes to be taken by the viewers and watched at home with the viewer stopping and starting the tape at will. Mirroring the original distribution of the SLA communiqués which the SLA would drop off at remote locations,

The Optics of Escape   121

only to later anonymously inform the press of the tape's whereabouts, Hayes's video screeds are similarly messages sent into the darkness. The *SLA Screeds* move with a performative dependence on both previous and forthcoming media—both on Hearst's audio utterances broadcast over the public radio airwaves and on the viewership and circulation of her performance that takes place not in the live moment but in the works' circulation and repetition to come. The intended public is the mediated one, reached through the technological repetition of voice and image.

While Hayes "partially memorized" the lines of each of the screeds, as she explains, she did not fully commit them to memory on a bodily register.[83] The language that Hayes recalls is somewhere between embodied language and short-term recitation, a knowledge of the script without the attendant feelings or emotional commitment wherein the words find a home within your body. If the voice, according to Dolar, is "the hidden bodily treasure beyond the visible envelope," neither Hayes's nor Hearst's voices read as such.[84] Instead, their voices question the very relationship between the body and the vocal presentation of intentionality and self. Hayes brings our attention to the slippery matter that is language, its iterative force, and the manner in

3.2 Sharon Hayes, *Symbionese Liberation Army (SLA) Screeds #13, 16, 20 & 29*, installation shot, 2003.

which it becomes stitched into the body of the subject somewhere between "free will" and "acculturation." The citational utterances which Hayes voices in *Screeds* endow Hearst with force, with the demand to be taken seriously, and this recitation further allows Hayes to do her own perversely sober reading of Hearst beyond the ones socially scripted for Hearst by her boyfriend, her family legacy, the SLA, and the FBI.

Hayes performs a "full body quotation"—a term used by her friend and sometimes-collaborator Wu Tsang—"to question [the] authenticity and intention of the speaker, and understand content differently, out of its original context."[85] Such a method acknowledges the embodied elements performed in a version of reenactment, but one that focuses on the political ambivalence associated with the idea of putting another's language into one's own mouth. Tsang explains, "The full body quotation technique is a way to perform our ambivalence." What Hayes refers to as "respeaking" is "about a kind of oral-to-oral translation. It's moving from voice to voice, moving from one address that was made at a particular time and in a particular place, and shifting that time and place, readdressing a different moment in time and space."[86] Similar to full body quotation, respeaking lets us hear how the content of the language moves differently when voice unstitches itself from a body. As Summer Kim Lee writes, "Tsang's full body quotation shapes scenes of study that are hard and uncomfortable as much as they are careful and loving. It seeks out difficult forms of relation that are a necessary part of giving an account of oneself, since that account is always grounded in the self's need for others, in how the self is complicit with a collectivity larger than oneself."[87] Full body quotation is not an attempt to become another across difference, to appear identical, but is instead invested in amplifying certain bodily gestures and tones. The self becomes the self in its relationship to others, formed in conversation and collectivity. As Julia Bryan-Wilson writes, Hayes's citational style comes about by way of "Bertolt Brecht's idea of demonstration, as an operation that points at something rather than pretends to be it."[88] Hayes brings our attention to Brecht's refusal of illusion, a refusal of the what Roger Grant calls the "Enlightenment aesthetic doctrine of mimesis."[89] Hayes shows us an actor who does not become one with the character, a speaker who does not become one with her speech. The discomfort of the full body quotation that "points at something rather than pretend[ing] to be it" shows the dissonance inherent in relationally constituted selves.

Discussing Hayes's audio performances and the technologies of amplification they employ, Craig Willse writes that "the microphone projects you outward, but only if you offer it your voice, and only along the airwaves it directs. . . . It enables and forecloses inclusion and, more importantly, upholds false promises of inclusion, inviting us in—into the official chambers of legitimated public address, in from outside."⁹⁰ While Willse is writing in relation to Hayes's public protest performances such as *I March in the Parade of Liberty but as Long as I Love You I Am Not Free* (2008) and *Revolutionary Love: I Am Your Worst Fear, I Am Your Fantasy* (2008), his invocation of the microphone—a mediation device employed by both Hearst and Hayes in their recordings—reminds us that the technologically mediated voice is processed through an echo chamber. The microphone, even in the "live" moment of address, creates a form of "legitimated public address" which is able to amplify only one voice at a time. The din of the multiple voices, of collective consensus, cannot be heard making noise around the "official chambers" of address. The SLA stole the microphone of 1970s media channels, commandeering a way to address the public that had previously been unavailable to them; they needed the microphone in order to be heard. Using Hearst's voice as the SLA's own microphone, their own amplification device, they gain an attentive audience of address. In *Symbionese Liberation Army Screeds*, Hayes makes her voice into the microphone, amplifying, distorting, and respeaking Hearst's SLA manifestos and pleas.

Even as Hearst's first audio recording was made from within the enclosed space of the SLA safe house closet in which she was kept, Hayes chooses to focus on the optical in her re-sounding of what was once only auditory. The sound of Hearst's voice is now dominated by the visual of Hayes's face. Instead of listening in the darkness over the radio waves, Hayes-as-Hearst turns into a deer in headlights; it's almost as if the whiteness of her own face reflects the racialized fear and desire of the SLA. I read the staggering whiteness of this image as key to the public understanding of Hearst as a narrative anomaly, as a white heiress who chose to think with philosophies that registered as Black to the listening white American public. The public imagined Hearst's captors as Black in part due to the racialized "third world" ideology the SLA mimed in their language and vocal intonations. Consequently, to look upon Hayes is to hear the narrative framing mechanisms of Hearst's story, depicting her as a failed radical, a silly rich girl, and a ventriloquist's dummy. We see Hayes's face in order to visualize the game being played out between her and the invisible audience, to understand the stops and starts on the audiotape as narrative interruptions that lead to neither capture nor survival. Whereas Hearst was rendered as a voice, a wounded victim taken from her own body by imagined Black captors, Hayes's face becomes a sonic texture that has everything to do with the color and shape of these audio communiqués. It is almost as if, in her transition away from the framing of her wealthy white home of origin, Hearst was infiltrated by a Blackness-as-radical polemic and became a proponent of rhetorical miscegenation. Hearst was accused of serving as a ventriloquist's dummy for the SLA; her political challenges to the state, to the privatization of wealth, to the prison system were discredited because she was not taken seriously as an authoritative voice. This is in part what Hayes stages when she asks her audience to put the right words into her mouth. As Sarah Kessler explains, with the help of Trinh Minh-ha, "The split subjective voice of ventriloquism supports existing arguments that subjectivity is not static or synchronous but divided, active, and relational—as the back-and-forth of a ventriloquist's banter with her dummy aptly demonstrates."[91] Akin to what Minh-ha calls "speaking nearby," Kessler brings our attention to the bifurcation of the speaking voice in ventriloquism, an understanding of that the voice as relationally constituted.

Returning to my earlier discussion of the racialization of the voice, there is something to be said about the presumed white transparency of Hearst's speech. This is, in part, what Hayes allows us to see in contrast to the "counterfeited black accents." Hayes stages the relationship between voice and body, between self and collective, by shifting our focus to the conditions in which subject formation is wrought. It would seem that the radical voices which Hearst ventriloquizes are to be kept in the realm of the particular and thus prevented from bearing on larger questions of the human. This slippage registers Hearst as the anomaly, as disobedient, as never able to return from the "madness" of captivity itself. Writing about her practice, Hayes explains: "I am constantly informed, obviously, by many other people in a thousand other different worlds and positions in that same sort of multiplicity. But all these systems that hold our work, whether it's as political activists or artists or filmmakers or film actors, are constantly valorizing and privileging individual output. In a way, it's a great and constantly vexing problem to have. How do you document a practice that is indebted to thousands of other people?"[92] Where confessional and autobiographic styles tend to imagine a single voice telling the truth of the story, Hayes underscores that many voices inform her work, her practice, her textured voice upon voice. The captivity narrative is no different as it imagines a singular white voice in a sea of racialized Indigenous capturers. Hayes offers a critique of propertied personhood precisely by way of an interrogation of the voice's alignment with flesh and the infelicitous.

I am drawn to Hearst's story and its camp comedic rhyme precisely because it provides a complicated space in the traditional history of radical politics. Revisiting Hearst's kidnapping as a space of generative contemplation, as "an arresting image" to which both Sharon Hayes and the nation have cathected, Hayes explains, "through these relationships we accumulate a field of events to which we are witnesses, not passive observers of a thing that has past, but watchers with collective and individual spectatorial responsibility in the present moment."[93] How Hearst's voice was heard in her 1976 trial has everything to do with the singularity of the historical moment and Hearst's location.[94] We might ask, had she been tried in 2003, at the time of Hayes's performance—post-9/11, in the George W. Bush era, during massive Iraq War protests, at the birth of the legalization of gay marriage—what might have been different? Or, in a different speculative scenario, would Hearst have been taken more seriously in the #MeToo era and valued as a survivor of sexual abuse and torture? Do Hearst and the SLA's misguided action and serious political aspiration merely get read as camp today, where serious becomes frivolous, as in Kristen Wiig's 2013 *Drunk History* reenactment of Hearst's kidnapping? In the popular Comedy Central television show where comedians get drunk only to recount historical events, Wiig plays the ventriloquist's dummy actor mouthing the lines given to her where, upon emerging from the closet, she exclaims, "Oh my god, you're so beautiful! Oh, who are these people...? You guys, like, you're my mommy!" The character of Hearst forgets herself in her scene of capture and "identifi[es] with the aggressor." All the while, the *Drunk History* narrator succinctly states that "this is Stockholm Syndrome."

I suggest that the radio and television circulation, and the resurgence of Hearst's story in the public—to return to Muñoz and Felman—does something else in its performative misfire. This is not just a story of the theatricality of failed 1970s radical political projects, of what Jeffery Toobin calls the "junior varsity" version of George Jackson's activist writings. Instead, this style of political theater resurfaces in Hayes's queer aesthetics of political demonstrations, videos, and performances. Part of what keeps Patty Hearst alive in the public imagination is that her story veers from the prescribed course of captivity and escape. She made the peculiar move toward identifying with her racialized white captors. She becomes a joke due to the naivete of the SLA's political demands and the public's inability to believe Hearst, to accept that her inward performance matched her outward one. And this joke is funny precisely because it alters the rules of the game. Patty-turned-Tania rejects the national captivity narrative placed upon her, but by the time the FBI figures this out, Hearst is already a media sensation that needs to be managed. In her *SLA Screeds* performance recording, Hayes plays on the mass media's demand that Hearst be visible and legible—that her story be comprehensible through the logics of capital, femininity, and whiteness. She restages the hypervisible erasure of Hearst, which is always an erasure of her own sexual trauma and play into the racially mixed and "sexually liberated" SLA. Hayes's recitation in the gallery setting as installation, as relational aesthetics, illustrates the trap of visibility and re-sounds escape as a practice of sidestepping the regulation of narrative. Reading Hayes, it becomes clear that Hearst's escape was not from the SLA back to the warm embrace of the FBI and the Hearst castle, but more nearly, it was an escape from a representational demand that would fix Hearst's body and political affiliation through allegory and narrative gender conventions. Instead, we are reminded that identity is relationally constituted. The escape strategy that Hayes demonstrates has everything to do with a failure and infelicity in the time and space of the utterance, an escape manifest in the interval of circulating VHS headshots, a textured utterance that illustrates narrative survival, full of fake stops and starts.

We walk into an LA gallery in 2003 and collect a VHS tape of Hayes's *SLA Screeds* to watch at home. The tape will fall apart and degrade; it will leave a fuzzy trace across its middle; it will move like a bootleg video. Or in 2012, with VHS long dead, we walk into a black box in the open floor space of the Whitney Museum to gaze upon Hayes's head projected large in the dark. She is anxiously captured again in white, reciting the lines. The gallery floor is filled with Hayes's other speech acts, some on protest signs in a mock front yard, some spoken from speakers facing each other in a square, and some woven into a large banner the length of the gallery wall. The way out is found in the microforms of "survivance" that such repetitions suggest—against conceptions of captivity and freedom, against the demand to survive when to survive is to be swallowed in narrative and produced by the linearity of a fixed genre.[95] Instead of a grand trajectory of escape that ends in liberation and freedom, the veering strategies of escape offered by Hayes are made through repetition, infelicity, and constant audiovisual capture. Escape does not represent a scene of rescue, but provides a narrative flicker of another kind of relationship with radical aesthetics. Hayes recites the joke that was made of Hearst, the joke of Hearst's failed performances as either a victim or a revolutionary, the joke that there is no self in Hearst's audiovisual projections. Yet, as we know, subject formation isn't that simple, and Hearst's story has been straightened out in our retrospective popular retellings of what counts as radical politics that are worth repeating. Escape, in this instance, provides a way of critiquing the structures of subjectivity and humanity as they collide in an American public's desire for the kidnap narrative. As a genre of change, escape here names a narrative space of plurality and discomfort. It places pressure on the American ideals of freedom and subjectivity. In the textured utterance that is the *SLA Screeds*, I hear radical thought that cannot be contained by discrete narratives but is instead formed by collective, imperfect, and uncomfortable speech. Hayes's narrative rhyme flickers with a trajectory of radical thought, staged for us by way of its messy inability to be heard just once, just right.

THIS FACE IS NOT FOR US
Grounding Pleasure

A long fire-red braid flows over the shoulder of a figure kneeling in a cornfield. The shadow of a late season flowering weed appears in silhouette against the skin of her inner thigh. Wearing a space helmet with its soft white enclosure strapped below her chin and dressed in white, she is decidedly from the future. A silver metal band blocks her eyes from the viewer and her nipple peeks through her sheer bra. With royal blue–tipped fingers she clutches onto the corn with both hands facing the camera. Corn is monoecious: it contains tassel and ear, it has two genders with separate structures on the same plant. Titled *Violet Copper* after the rich-purple-and-orange butterfly, the photo is part of a series by the artist Tourmaline. The images depict a nonbinary trans woman outside in a pleasure garden, a friend to the flowers and earthly plants in which she rests. Pulling the two stalks of corn apart she looks at us, at the camera, tentative and direct.

Mounted in late 2020 at Chapter NY gallery, *Pleasure Garden* features a series of five 30×30-inch photographic self-portraits of the artist in open spaces, unbound gardens, and farmlands. Each image is named after a butterfly, some of them pollinators, all of them humble, flower-loving beauties. The photos are not sexual, per se, but they are erotic and blissful. I begin the chapter with this image from *Pleasure Garden* as a return to the question of pleasure and desire woven into the story of escape. Focusing on the architectures of en-

4.1 Tourmaline, *Violet Copper*, 2021.

closure, which in its very openness, *Pleasure Garden* refuses, this chapter engages the erotics of the escape story through an analysis of queer visual film and photography. The story of escape is always about pleasure that unevenly accrues across its tellings; in this chapter, I turn instead to a consideration of the relationship between sexuality, erotics, and the images that envision the sexual encounter apart from the walled enclosures of the subject.

As I have discussed, genres are discrete bodies that set expectations; they provide codes through which we come to know ourselves and each other. The box, the book, and the radio are forms bound by physical, literary, and sonic bodies, respectively. And yet, genres meet. They brush up against each other. They mix and mingle. They behave promiscuously. We call genres monstrous in order to mark the places where genre, gender, and racialization refuse the alignment of their normative protocols. In each chapter thus far, I have discussed the energetic capacities of stories that circulate around escape—what they do to form and genre. In this final chapter, I move to consider the architectures of enclosure, the spaces and genres that hold stories together, as well as the holes that are poked in the normative forces of escape.

This chapter arises from a place that many academic inquiries likely do: with a question I could not put down. It began with another series of images by photographer Eve Fowler entitled *Gloria Hole* (2008). The pictures document a sexual performance of sorts, white hands, mounds of brunette hair, and fingers emerge through the space of a large wooden hole. On the camera side of the hole, a torso engages the shy genital mounds with inquiring fingers or, conversely, brushes the long hair that is placed in and through the hole. From both the architectural proposition and the title, it is clear that the hole itself is a glory hole, a classically gay male space for anonymous sexual encounter. Fowler's take on the glory hole, in collaboration with artist Math Bass, proposed a set of questions which deeply intrigued me. The work asked: Who is the glory hole a fantasy space for, how is it available, and what sort of ambiguous escape does it envision? It places pressure on the spatialization and architectures of pleasure and its containment. Fowler's photographs operate as a surprising critique of the ways in which white queer pleasure is theorized in the sexual encounter. It is from this starting point—admittedly my own line of inquiry that I could not let go of, worrying some question at its core—that I enter into this chapter-long consideration of the sexualized structures of escape. Having previously engaged the white pleasures that accrue around the stories of escape, from Dickinson to Hearst, this chapter extends the engagement with the pleasure found in the escape story by landing squarely in the sexualized erotics of escape.

How does escape illuminate the queer architectures of enclosure and the holes poked in them, holes like the camera obscura, holes that let in enough light to create entire worlds? It is my argument that the glory hole brings our attention to covert moments of pleasure and their perpetual threat of violent subjugation. An interstitial and liminal space, it is a hole outside of the body. The glory hole recalls the camera obscura, a structure of seeing and capture of the image, a theater of what is beyond the closed architecture of the dark room. Iconic glory holes depict predominantly white truckers or sailors. Men cruising the WPA public restrooms in the 1920s come to mind. The 16 mm porn film, *El Paso Wrecking Corp* (dir. Joe Cage, 1978), shows white men in tight jeans somewhere between Kansas City, Texas, and California at a truck stop with one or two glory holes in each stall. Glory holes appear in porn films, in oral histories, in tearooms. In the gay German film *Taxi zum Klo* (1981), which translates to "Taxi to the Toilet," the main character negotiates his role as a Berlin schoolteacher and his "private" life as a queer man cruising for sex. He watches men jerk off through the glory hole while grading student papers. The "glory hole" most often refers to a waist-high hole in the wall of a men's toilet stall, bathhouse, or video arcade used for anonymous gay sex. In his 1970 study of male sexual encounters in public restrooms sociologist Laud Humphreys observed that "the glory hole has three functions . . . : as a peep hole for observation, as a signaling device, and as a place of entry for the penis into the insertee's wall."[1] Such holes, as one might imagine, are spaces of "glorious" activity as they promote blowjobs, voyeurism, and other anonymous sex acts at a distance, between two adjoining spaces. Sociologist Edward Delph, in his 1978 book on public sex in New York City titled *The Silent Community*, wrote: "The glory hole is an example of social interaction in total anonymity on the one hand, and extreme ideal typifications of erotic identities on the other. Interaction depends on two or at most three parts of the body: the penis and the mouth or anus. A wall separates interactants, completely isolating them from each other except for contact between penis and mouth or anus."[2] Delph focuses on the simultaneous public and covert acting out of desire in what he terms *closed*, *semi-closed*, and *open* settings. The glory hole is a space of social interaction in which one remains separated from the other person typically by a toilet wall divider. Fantasy is key in this interaction, and ambiguity enables a fantasy projection of a body connected to the penis, mouth, or anus. Delph continues, "The aperture of the glory hole and the small, constrained visual range of the other side of the hole become the focal point of all sociation [sic]. Because of the restricted vision, the genitals on the opposite side of [the] aperture could belong to the self's most fantastic sexual ideal."[3] Like the aperture of the camera, the glory hole creates a field of vision, a focus on only one part of the body, one space of social interaction.

Escape up to this point has been used to describe the sometimes-ambivalent movements both toward and away from collective liberationist projects. Pleasure has heretofore appeared as part of the spectacle of escape and its white enjoyment. In this last chapter, I turn to sex as a site in which escape is imagined as a space for ecstasis, getting out of oneself. Sex is constantly mobilized in social and political discourses on humanity, property, and freedom, and consequently provides an interesting site from which to think escape. I explore the queer pleasure of escape, how Black and non-Black pleasures and visual strategies necessarily differ, and what we might learn about queer visual culture's relationship with the architectures of escape and enclosure. I shift my focus from the narrative, affective, and sonic scenes of escape explored in previous chapters to outline the relationship between escape and pleasure, anonymity and public performance. Moving through a discussion of the glory hole as emblematic of a certain strand of queer theory that imagines an escape from subjectivity, I trace the unexamined whiteness of much thought on sexual liberation. In conclusion, I turn to the photographic series *Pleasure Garden* by the artist and filmmaker Tourmaline in an attempt to explore pleasure not predicated on white escape from representation and subjectivity but by way of convivial acts of portraiture, glamour, and open-air futurity. In this chapter, I focus on the glory hole as emblematic of queer public sex discourse and white queer visual radical imaginings. While the glory hole imagines an anonymous escape from representation and subjectivity, it provides a key conceptual framework through which to articulate the problems of queer theory's flirtation with enclosure. Exposing the logic of white queer sexual exceptionalism, I explore escape as it arises in the language around public sex and queer visual pleasure.

Grounding my reading of queer sexualized escape in Black Studies, I foreground the understanding that, as Darieck Scott names, "the history that produced blackness is a sexual history, that is, a history of state sanctioned population-level manipulation of sex's reproductive and pleasure-producing capacities."[4] As Sharon P. Holland further reminds us, "the transatlantic trade altered the very shape of sexuality in the Americas for everyone." Anti-Black and settler colonial histories define sexuality in the Americas, which is to say that white sexuality, as the de facto of modern sexuality, is constantly

4.2 Still from *Taxi zum Klo*, Frank Ripploh, dir., 1981.

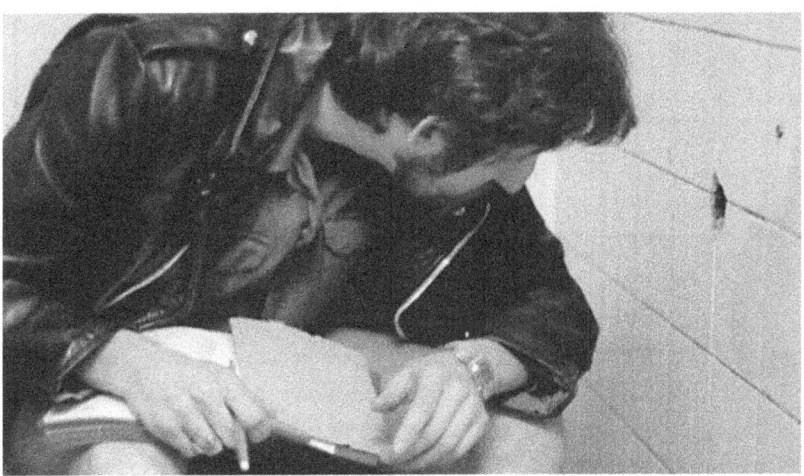

figuring itself in relation to histories of white supremacy and genocide. So, what does it mean to consider the sensuality, or ecstasy, of escape in contemporary art? In Black Studies, escape is a pedagogical narrative of agency, possibility, and futurity even as it is shaped by its paradigmatic impossibility. Where queer modernity is shaped by both the histories of settler colonialism and white supremacy, the white desire for stories of escape cannot be thought apart from a pornotroping desire for the conceptual and visual possession of Black bodies. Introduced by Hortense Spillers, pornotroping describes the violent process of objectification which turns people into objects, into commodities, "while simultaneously rendering them sexually available."[5] In what follows, I try to give some provisional answers to the question: How do we understand the white erotics of the sexual desire for escape? Furthermore, how do such desires get taken up as recurring tropes in queer visual work?

Moving away from the literary and performative stories of escape, I consider what Jennifer Nash calls "sexual-spatial" formations. I use the glory hole as a framework for tracing current discourses of queer pleasure and their conceptual limits. The term "glory hole" originated in the nineteenth century—before the glory hole of the 1940s truck stop emerged—to describe the space of punishment for misbehaving children or seamen. The glory hole referred to the lower compartment of a ship, cargo hold, or sleeping quarters for stewards that—related to the Scottish word "glaury"—were most often filthy and disgusting spaces "without any attempt at order or tidiness."[6] Described in T. Cooper's 1845 *Purgatory of Suicides*, "a filthy cell to which prisoners are brought from the gaol [jail] on the day of trial, and which, in the language of the degraded beings who usually occupy it, is called a glory hole."[7] The term emerges not only to describe the dirty and slimy tiny space of a room, jail, or closet, but the phrase "glory hole" itself is uttered by the mouths of "human filth" who are themselves confined to such spaces. Tracing the etymology of the glory hole becomes interesting as the term not only represented the negative space of the hole, but also describes a site of containment, an enclosure for the deviant. Such a history encourages us to think about the rich space of the hole itself. This hole is not simply a passage elsewhere, but a space that holds those who must be punished, those who must be kept apart from the clean and well-behaved population.

The explicitly homosexual glory hole emerged at a time when homosexuality was overtly criminalized in the public sphere; consequently, the semiprivate cubicle of the anonymous bathroom became a space for this illegal sexual behavior to covertly occur.[8] We might date such American glory holes—what John Stranack in *Christopher Street Magazine* calls "our own gay sexual version of the catholic confessional"—back further to the 1920s when we begin to see documented arrests based on homosexual acts carried out in lavatories.[9] Laud Humphreys dates the birth of the "tearoom trade," anonymous sexual encounters in men's public restrooms, back to the Great Depression and the arrival of the WPA (Works Progress Administration) in the late 1930s. One of Humphrey's interviewees explains: "But the real fun began during the depression. There were all those new buildings, easy to reach, and the automobile was really getting popular about then.... Suddenly, it just seemed like half the men in town met in the tearooms."[10] Mobility in less urban spaces seems to encourage a newfound anonymity, away from the small town. Such anonymous bathroom sex has been common practice in the United States as long as public restrooms have been around, and although glory holes and anonymous bathroom sex are not synonymous, they encourage a similar kind of contact.[11]

Part of the difficulty in historicizing glory holes may have to do with the fact that they are not themselves permanent fixtures; when their presence in a bathroom stall is discovered, glory holes are often closed or boarded up. Instead of being seen as a sexual structure, they are read as glitches in the physical infrastructure, mistakes in the individualized privacy afforded by the bathroom toilet stall. Although the prevalence of the glory hole has subsided in recent years with the onset of the HIV/AIDS public health crisis and due to the relative tolerance of (white) homosexuals and the public desexualization of gay practices, the glory hole persists in gay male clubs, bathhouses, cinemas, and other establishments that actively encourage sexual activities.[12] Homosexual-identified men, as well as those who are married or straight, employ what Stranack refers to as the "the anonymous orifice."[13] Today, in the age of cruising apps and gay clubs, the glory hole comes to represent the persistence of, and fantasy for, queer anonymous and public sexual encounters at the same time that it demonstrates a historical nostalgia for encounters mediated by anonymity and the wall of a bathroom stall instead of a mobile phone.[14]

The magic act of escape often suggests a figurative or metaphorical escape, a loophole or a trapdoor in the structuring logic of action that enables a flight from constraint. In their study on "faceless sex" Dave Holmes, Patrick O'Byrne, and Stuart Murray observe that glory hole sex is "animalistic" and "primal" because it is a focused space of sexual energy and "affords an intense, temporary escape from the demands of subjectivity."[15] The stage of sexual pleasure performed through the glory hole is distant from the space of domesticity and the gay progress narratives that culminate in "freedoms" such as gay marriage. In this way, there would appear to be something liberatory about the glory hole by way of its anonymity, its fantasy of a sexual interaction that is free from the constraints of subjectivity. And yet, this fantasy of the anonymous sexual encounter, which is not limited only to the glory hole scenario, but of which the glory hole somehow becomes the epitome, is typically only available to white cis men. The glory hole as "a temporary escape from the demands of subjectivity" necessarily demands a subject to begin with. And, as we know, the subject comes into being as a subject by way of white logics of individualism and self-possession. The rendering of queer liberation in this way presumes an analogy between whiteness and queerness, where to discuss queer history and the formation of queer identity is to assume a whiteness not only in content but also in definitional form, that is, to say queer is all too often to say white queer. It is thus worth considering the way racialization plays out in the queer fantasy of an escape from subjectivity, by way of the "intense," "animalistic," and "primal" space of the glory hole.

The glory hole stages a fantasy sexual encounter that is "faceless." Such facelessness amplifies an already anonymous sexual culture of the tearoom. Like the depiction of "faceless sex" as proposed by Holmes, O'Byrne, and Murray, anonymous sex might describe a face-to-face encounter without ever exchanging any identifying facts. In an anonymous sexual exchange, you might see another person's face, but not know who they are or how to find them again. In contrast, the potential vulnerability of the exposed face is lost in the faceless encounter of the glory hole and, as Tim Dean notes, turns the other into a symbolic nonhuman object or part object. As he writes in *Beyond Sexuality*, "Men having sex through a gloryhole reveals that sexual relationality is as much about the Other and the object *a* as it is about interpersonal connection. Sometimes the gay man relates to his partner not as a person but as an object—and there is something to praise as well as lament in this form of relating."[16] The glory hole exchange does not necessarily recognize the other participant as a person and, as Dean observes, this is both a curious and compelling way to think about sexuality, which is also to think about models of relationality. Dean invokes Lacan's *object petite a* in order to name a kind of destabilizing pleasure in pain or intensity. In this sense, the glory hole has little to do with the other person but names an example of the sense of desire associated with a more fantastic or spectral projection of an other.

Where generic escape describes the trajectory from captivity to freedom, what we might call the queer escape narrative typically takes the form of stories marked by sexual deviance and liberation. Escape usually emerges in the scene of modern sexuality as the coming out story. The homosexual reveal marks the center of canonical queer narratives from the nineteenth and twentieth centuries. Paying attention to the structures of queer narratives in *Feeling Backward*, Heather Love argues that "because of the long-standing link of same sex desire with the impossible, queer experience is characterized by extremes of feeling: the vertiginous joy of an *escape* from social structures; at the same time a despair about the impossibility of existing outside of such structures" (emphasis mine).[17] Here, escape is both the "vertiginous" feeling of being gleefully outside of normative structures and a sensation of vulnerability, despair, and fear. As in speculative fiction, escape describes the feelings of being inside and outside of the normative world. Over the past century, queer stories in literature and film have been organized around the gay progress narrative of the coming out story. In this trajectory, the protagonist is often young and just discovering their same-sex desire; they are in the process of moving from "ignorance" into the light of self-knowledge (which often also looks like an arrival into a couple or a lover's arms). In *Epistemology of the Closet*, Eve Kosofsky Sedgwick argues that at the turn of the twentieth century, the closet became the founding discursive structure for sexual identity. Here, homo- and heterosexual identity revolve around the speech act, the affirmative confessional declaration, "I am a homosexual," or the performative silence of presumed sexual shame and secrecy. Channeling Michel Foucault's *History of Sexuality*, Sedgwick explains that "modern Western culture has placed what it calls sexuality in a more and more distinctively privileged relationship to our most prized constructs of individual identity, truth and knowledge."[18] Sexuality is produced, through the speech act, as a key insight into the self. To feel pride, one must "come out," come into the light and escape the ideological structures that demand hidden homosexual selves. But as Sedgwick counters, ignorance is not "a single Manichean, aboriginal maw of darkness from which the heroics of human cognition can occasionally wrestle facts, insights, freedoms, [and] progress."[19] Sedgwick calls into question the social production of the dyadic pair—knowledge and ignorance—where the performance of a certain sexual silence equates to a "dark" and shameful unknowing.

As the coming out story goes, the darkness of the closet is the confining structure from which the queer, or perverse, sexual subject must escape. In this exit from darkness a great release from social constraints is felt, if only momentarily. Yet, as C. Riley Snorton explains, the fantasy structure of the closet as either hidden safety or exposed freedom and joy does not operate for racialized queers in the same way that it does for white queers. Like Love's observation that the queer experience is characterized, in part, by the "vertiginous joy of an escape," Michael P. Brown describes the dark secrecy of the closet as a scene of capture, which establishes "the potential for movement or escape."[20] Opacity and enclosure become key in considering the structure of the closet. Enclosure, in architectural parlance, describes the envelope or skin of a building that creates two distinct spaces, an outside and an inside. Enclosure names a space for safekeeping and its opposite, an unwilful incarceration or holding and display. Snorton elaborates on the visual scene of the closet, explaining that "the closet emerged to describe a nascent condition of surveillance and regulation; its protective measures—ensured by a person's ability to pass, to be read as something other than his or her identity—guarded against the constitution and criminalization of a new kind of person, 'the homosexual.'"[21] The play on light and dark, knowledge and ignorance, interests Sedgwick and Snorton in the configuration of the closet and the sexual narratives it performatively produces and structurally denies. Snorton argues that the logics embedded in the structure of the closet "are put in crisis in the case of blackness, where darkness is everywhere. In the context of blackness, the closet is not a space of concealment but a site for observation and display."[22] In other words, the space for passing and the safety enabled through the structure of the closet is predicated on whiteness because "there is no cover for blackness just as there is no escape from the colonialist legacies implicit in the closet's metaphoricity."[23] The visual language of the closet is steeped in the metaphors of anti-Blackness, figuring the opaque and the dark as dangerous ignorance in opposition to bright opening of knowledge that gives over to sexual freedom. Thus, the closet cannot be thought outside of the anti-Black structures that produce it as a distinctively white colonial structure.

Modern gay identity, Hiram Pérez argues, is not peripheral but in fact central to US imperialism. He writes that gay (white) cosmopolitan desire for "exotic" bodies is "auxiliary to colonial and neocolonial expansion."[24] Returning to Sedgwick's exploration of the founding texts of gay modernity, Pérez critiques the possessive individualism of the "canonized metaphors" of gay experience. "Coming out promises liberation and celebrates a species of individualism in the form of self-determination. Conceptually and materially, that freedom and self-determination are premised on the property of whiteness."[25] The closet, as a space of privacy and individuality, relies on white notions of possessive individualism. Pérez's observation echoes the work of Scott Lauria Morgenson and his argument that queer modernities are born through the relegation of Indigenous sexuality to the past.[26] The closet not only is steeped in the visual language of anti-Blackness and Enlightenment logics of white self-determination, but it helps establish queer modernity as a critical part of both settler colonialism and neocolonial expansion. Martin Manalansan further interrogates the scene of gay modernity through the metaphor of the closet, asking: "What kind of conceptual space is the closet, that confines people who seem neither highly politicized or self-reflexively 'gay'?"[27] The speech act that brings one out of the closet, that performatively officiates someone's homosexual desires, excludes a whole swath of people with queer desire, relegating them to the politically retrograde and unenlightened space of secrecy. Manalansan continues: "Filipino gay men argue that identities are not just proclaimed verbally, but are 'felt' (pakieamdaman) or initiated as well. The swardspeak expression ladlad ngkapa, which literally means unfurling the cape and has been translated as 'coming out,' reveals gay identity to be something 'worn' and not necessarily 'declared.'"[28] This relay of the swardspeak translation of "coming out" as "unfurling the cape" or otherwise adorning oneself seems fitting. Coming out in this sense is not an escape from the closet, but is instead a fluid fabric to roll out when the mood or desire strikes. The cape of *escappare* unfurls in spectacular adornment, a tactile enunciation, even as it might also shroud or hide the body or face from view. Such a metaphor for self-fashioning moves us away from the western fantasy of enclosure and toward the conceptual space of costuming. Such reimagining of queer identity or desire refuses the imagined safety of containment in favor of gender and sexuality as excess or saturation.

As I discuss in previous chapters, the genre of the human excludes those who fall outside of the violent definitions incised by the colonial west. As Amber Musser argues, "desire consolidates the subject even as it privileges its momentary dissolve."[29] Desire does not exist in opposition to harm, but theorizations of sexuality are often caught up in forms of violence. Thinking with Alexander Weheliye, Musser continues: "The kinship between the processes that underlie the pornotrope—projection and objectification—and those that underlie sexuality—those of possession and desire—illustrate the violence embedded in the concept of sexuality itself."[30] As opposed to serving as a fantastical space free from violence, sexuality is caught up in both Enlightenment questions of the human as well as the problems of possession, private property, and non-consensual use of the other.

In his 1987 essay "Is the Rectum a Grave?" Leo Bersani imagines gay male shame embodied in the anal opening as a radical site of pleasurable unmaking and self-shattering. He writes: "Male homosexuality advertises the risk of the sexual itself as the risk of self-dismissal, of losing sight of the self, and in doing so it proposes and dangerously represents jouissance as a mode of ascesis."[31] This anal annihilation makes an argument for radical negativity—not a recuperative understanding of gay male sex, but an assertion of gay male sex as a site of unmaking. Lee Edelman picks up on this idea in *No Future*, suggesting a queer refusal as an interruption of the reproductive futurity of dominant heterosexual culture. This radical negativity or antirelational theory suggests that a turn away from the political is the site of queer radicality. Bersani's and Edelman's antirelational thesis imagines a purity of the sexual attached to the autonomous liberal subject, and with it, there is a presumed whiteness untouched by the relational. Radical negativity turns sex into a romantic symbolic space detached from the lived politics that play out in intimate relations. As Margot Weiss makes clear in *Techniques of Pleasure*, "sexuality often serves as a symbol of freedom, rebellion or intimacy unbound to—and an escape from—structural social inequalities."[32] In this demand that sexuality serve as a symbolic "escape from . . . structural social inequalities," Weiss brings our attention to a willful desire to see sex as existing outside racialization and the very power dynamics that permeate American culture, namely colonialism, white supremacy, and anti-Blackness.

The fantasy of escape's spectacular sensual pleasure seems foundational for queer theory as well as cis gay male theories on public sex. And yet, as we see with Bersani, Dean, and others, this symbolic imaginary of an escape-from-being through pleasure is a decidedly white fantasy that fails to take into account sexuality as a racialized conceptual landscape. While we might say simply, and with ambivalence, that escape is a sensual act of surpassing and undoing the self, it is also important to qualify the whiteness of such ontological cruising when identity is reduced to parts of the whole. Kadji Amin traces the legacy of what he calls "liberationist negativity" to Guy Hocquenghem's 1972 book *Homosexual Desire*. Hocquenghem argues that sex is a "machinic" function that "undoes social identities and disintegrates subject/object, self/other, active/passive, male/female, oppressor/oppressed binaries."[33] Here, sex is impersonal and functional and it is precisely this fact that gives sex its "corrosive power" to destroy "something otherwise pernicious and intractable about how social power works."[34] Exploring Jean Genet's arabophilia, Amin discusses the white desire for phallic annihilation through receptive anal sex. Amin writes, "The white sexual fantasy of being shattered, by passive anal sex with nonwhite men, into prehistoric time, relies on a slippage from the specific histories of black and/or Arab racialization into the fantasy of race as a figure for the prehistoric inhuman itself."[35] The queer white French men of Front homosexuel d'action révolutionnnaire (FHAR) who, like Genet, credit their political awakening to having submissive sex with Algerian men, imagine an "erotic coalition" by way of a self-shattering momentary escape from being. Indeed, they are shattered into "prehistory time" of a "prehistoric inhuman."[36] Racialization figures into this self-shattering scene by demonstrating the white fantasy of having a sovereign self to shatter. It shows that the sexual nature of this fantasy is always predicated on a sense of the nonwhite "other" through whose "use" the white queer man finds himself momentarily undone. This fantasy of a "subjectivity-destroying" self-shattering, what Musser terms an "Oedipal jouissance," always relies on a conception of sex inextricably linked to racial fantasies of the "use" of the other.[37] While there is something attractive about the idea that sex might shatter the social as we know it, so many of these white queer fantasies cannot account for race, or even see themselves as always already raced. Escape here becomes a way to exit a tedium of being as well as a queer fantasy of momentary erotic self-annihilation through the sexual.

One of the key aspects of the glory hole is its facelessness, its staging of self and not-self in moments of ecstasy. In pondering questions on the white erotics of escape, I keep returning to Andy Warhol's 1964 film *Blowjob*. In the film, Warhol tightly frames the face of a young white man getting a blowjob in 16-mm black and white. The promised action takes place below the frame of the camera, beyond our line of sight. Warhol's unmoving half-hour film is played at one-third of the speed at which it was shot. A face moves slowly in and out of the light, in and out of ecstasy. Nothing happens. For Douglas Crimp, Warhol's film isn't just a witty porno wherein we are promised a blowjob and never really get one. Instead, Crimp writes, "Warhol's camera captures this face and the sensation it registers, but simultaneously *withholds* it from us; and he does this through a simple positioning of the light as if by chance." Crimp continues, "We cannot take sexual possession of him. We can see his face, but we cannot, as it were, have it. This face is not for us."[38] I am taken by this question, this meditation on the (uncredited) face placed in Warhol's film, where Warhol's genius lies in imagining eros that exceeds visual possession. Crimp asks what it means to see, but not possess, to take pleasure in and feel desire outside of the ability to consume. The facial denial of Warhol's subject registers to Crimp as falling beyond the scope of a common understanding of sexuality itself. Thinking about the sexual portrait that Warhol produces for, but does not give over to, us—where Warhol is always also ghosted by the hole Valerie Solanas put *in* him—I wonder about whiteness and possession. For Crimp, the portrait is desired precisely because of its anticipatory refusal of faciality. And we are thus left with the question: For whom is the refusal of faciality a radial act and for whom is it simply an ontological given? Crimp writes that the offscreen blowjob makes the subject

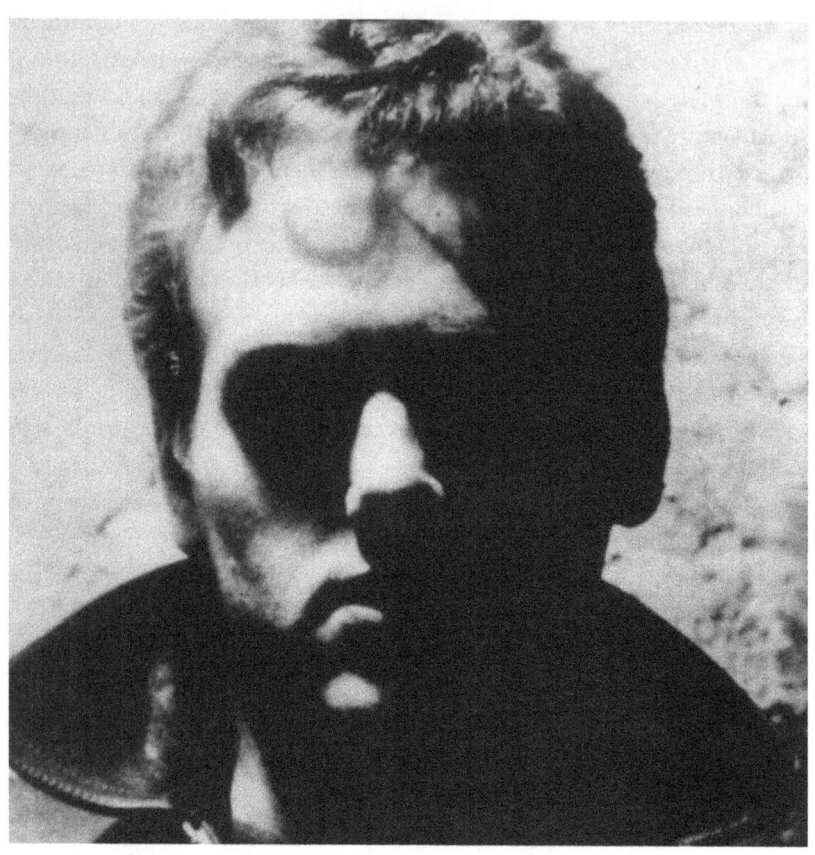

4.3 Still from *Blowjob*, Andy Warhol, dir., 1964.

unaware of the camera, allowing him to let go of a kind of fantasy psychic performance of self for the camera. He proposes that it is the ecstasy of the sexual encounter that Warhol films (but does not show) that makes *Blowjob* such a beautiful portrait. Getting out of oneself and the self-conscious projection of an idealized self-image is precisely what makes this not always facially focused portrait beautiful to Crimp. There is a kind of escape from the demand to be an image for the viewer through a sense of ecstasy.

In his 1995 essay on Black queer photographic archives, Glenn Ligon writes, "I had a dream I was in a box labeled 'Black Men.' It was dark, and the images of men were pressed up against me; we were all a jumble. I couldn't tell where my body ended and another's began. We were indistinguishable. Then I realized we were not in a box at all. We were in a tea room."[39] Ligon describes the dark box of the photographic archive, a box that is vulnerable to the wear of the sun on the thin archival photographic paper. In the associative logic of the dream, the box of photographic bodies pressed against each other turns into a tearoom, a cottage, a bathroom cruising spot for public sex. Inside this tearoom, bodies push up against one another, limbs merge into a jumble of bodies being held together, interchangeable inside the label "Black men." They appear gay by way of their proximity and the final realization that this is a tearoom and not a box. Thinking with Ligon's work at the time on themes of enslavement and captivity, the tearoom also resembles the hold of a ship. In Ligon's writing, I read the "utopian" site of the tearoom as caught up in the white supremacist politics of looking.

Whiteness imagines itself as having no enclosure. Consequently, white queerness dances with the liminality of unfreedom, of enclosure and risk, or what Calvin Warren refers to as a "closeted humanism," which is to say a humanism that "announces its intention to unravel, displace, and discredit the very humanism that sustains it."[40] In considering escape and pleasure, in turning to the insistence on the ego-shattering potential of sex, I am interested in examining white desire as an orienting structure. Putting theories of antiqueer violence in conversation with conceptions of anti-Black violence, Warren writes, "The queer subject is constructed as degenerate and transgressive, but the fundamental distinction between the 'degenerate queer' and the 'derelict black-as-object' is that one possesses a grammar to express unfreedom and the other lacks communicability altogether."[41] In this reasoning, white queer suffering has a grammar through which to articulate violence and trauma, while the "black-as-object" has no possible means of redress or language through which to name the kinds of harm they suffer. For Warren, this is a tension between what Frank Wilderson would call "'an experience of unfreedom' (Queerness) and a structural position of non-ontology (Blackness)."[42] Consequently, the "Black Queer" is a structural impossibility because there is "no grammar outside of humanism to describe the domain of 'pleasure,' 'desire,' 'sexuality,' and 'gender' for the socially dead object."[43] Black (queer) sexuality must be thought beyond Enlightenment structures. White queer theories of escape and freedom that cannot take into account Black queerness are in fact strengthened by anti-Black thought.

It is through the hermetic inward escape that sex can ever retain this fantasy of a pure, uncomplicated sexual encounter. How can queer studies rethink pleasure and the radical sexual encounter not through an understanding of the individual Enlightenment body, but through its entanglement with other bodies and histories? I am not saying one cannot go to a bathroom stall, get off, and never need to think about that person again. Nor am I trying to devalue or discredit the rich space of the queer and stigmatized casual sexual encounter. In fact, I might characterize this writing as a love letter to the persistence of deviant sexual practices, both liberatory and shame-filled. It is worth remembering that the social is always there, whether one wants to be held accountable to it or not. And, echoing others, it seems that a certain strain of queer theory that seeks to examine sex positivity has struggled to account for the fantastical sovereign humanist subject at its center.

The escape of anonymous sex is one avenue (that we don't have to pathologize) in which modern sexuality exists apart from the dictates of cis white heteronormative culture. But instead of infusing such a scene of escape with the individual, how might it shift if we were to consider escape as attached to "fria," to the freedom to be among loved ones? Rerouting the white uptake of queer sexual escape, with an understanding at the same time of its use in a restrictive and phobic culture, encourages alternate ways of understanding what it means to come together in pleasure. If, as I mentioned in the introduction, friend and freedom have the same root, then might we think sex's relationship to the social as neither utopian, nor self-shattering, but as a practice of both freedom and friendship, of entanglement? As carla bergman and Nick Montgomery remind us, "Freedom is the capacity to grapple with some of the toxic habits and relationships fostered by Empire, and to recover other ways of relating."[44] In their wish to recover "other ways of relating," the authors quote Glen Coulthard and Leanne Simpson's idea of "grounded normativity" to describe "the practices and procedures, based on deep reciprocity, that are inherently informed by an intimate relationship to place."[45] These are forms that come before and outside of white supremacy, settler colonialism, and anti-Blackness. To remove the walls and the stalls of the structures of "privacy" and enclosure that exist in the bathrooms would be to remove the demand for escape from the stringent enclosure of the nuclear family and heterosexuality. Put differently, escape emerges when there is an enclosure, and if whiteness knows no enclosure, if whiteness has the ability to choose touch or refuse it, then the shape of white fantasies of escape diverges profoundly from Black and other non-Black minoritarian articulations of escape. Perhaps for whiteness there is a kind of erotic intensity that needs to be invented, an enclosure for which an escape hatch must be produced.

Often glory hole scenes in film have approached these regulatory walls as though they were an erotic joke. In John Waters's camp classic, *Desperate Living* (1977), suburban housewife Peggy Gravel, played by Mink Stole, hides from the police in the low-life town of Mortville. In a scene at the shantytown bar, Gravel is forced to watch lewd entertainment with her degenerate companions. When she visits the toilet to avoid the grotesqueries of the cabaret performances, she is accosted by a double glory hole featuring two large ecstatic and undulating breasts. Gravel cries in horror and begs repeatedly, "Just leave me alone." Such burlesque-adjacent comedic scenes remind us that when turned into breasts, the phallic fetish of the glory hole loses its erotic charge and becomes simply a joke. After all, breasts are always available. The joke, following Paolo Virno, "reveal[s] in a flash a different way of applying the rules of the game."[46] Here, the joke shows the absurdity of sex itself, of the barriers to and inside one's desire.

In another popular representation of the glory hole in the slapstick horror film parody *Scary Movie* (2010), a twenty-something Black man (played by Marlon Wayans) gets stabbed through the head by a white cock. The scene is itself a re-creation of the opening sequence of *Scream 2* (1997), directed by Wes Craven. In *Scream 2*, the inside joke is that the Black characters die first. The character played by Omar Epps hears a whispering children's song in the men's bathroom at a movie theater. And when Epps leans in, smiling to himself, he is knifed through the ear. In *Scream 2*, this appears less as a parody and more of a repetition of the sidelining of Black characters and spectacularizing of Black death; in the next shot Jada Pinkett Smith gets killed against the movie screen as hundreds look on in both glee and horror. In the *Scary Movie* parody, Wayans is in the bathroom when he hears a moaning noise coming from the next stall over. Wayans leans down and puts his ear near the glory hole. A white cock comes out of the hole and tickles his earlobe. He giggles and, we assume, is unaware of the identity of the flirtatious tickler but enjoying the sensation nonetheless. He peers through the hole and says, "Hey who is that?," begging, "Come on, do it again, do it again!" As he presses his ear firmly back against the hole in anticipation of a sensual earlobe caress, the white cock returns stabbing him with a vengeance. A play on the gory horror movie knifing, the cock emerges out of his other ear. While the glory hole is a sexual fantasy available to any body, it prevails as a predominantly white cis male scenario. Written by Shawn Wayans, Marlon Wayans, and four others, *Scary Movie* connects white cocks to Black safety in the space of the absurd and comical glory hole. The Wayans brothers are not wrong in their observation that *Scream 2* already implies a strange homophobic bathroom encounter between Epps's character and the man with a knife hidden under the iconic *Scream* mask and cloak. What they pick up on in the original is the violence implied by men wanting to be in the bathroom with other men, of men who wait for men, or whisper soft things between the stalls. The Wayans brothers seem to literalize Wes Craven's bathroom fear of what men keep inside their pants by drawing out the absurdity of Craven's unconscious horror glory hole surprise as it plays out through the "inside joke" that Black characters die first in horror films.

I return to the structure of the glory hole to consider the way this desire for enclosure and anonymity plays out in visual culture. In Jean Genet's 1950 short film *Un chant d'amour*, two prisoners communicate through a small hole that connects their shared cell wall. They blow smoke through a straw, simulating fellatio, demonstrating Genet's own fantasy of the prison as a space for "the queer by-products of repressive institutions."[47] Other artists who have taken up the glory hole as a "sexual-spatial formation," include Eve Fowler, Suzanne Wright, and Nancy Brooks Brody's *Glory Hole Series*. In these reimaginings the glory hole becomes a pattern and portal. In science fiction parlance, portal narratives describe a doorway to another world or space, a trapdoor, or a loophole. Glory holes appear as queer portals for surprising activity, as in Fowler's *Gloria Hole* photographs which imagine sexual encounters as a kind of queer reach-around. Brody's gray and faintly rainbowed abstract gridded paintings in her *Glory Hole Series* (2008-12), represent the type of circular rainbow known simply as a "glory." Or in Suzanne Wright's work in which she makes *Galactic Glory Holes* (2011-12) as spaceships with circular escape hatches. Perhaps Jeanne Vaccaro best captures a certain strain of lesbian glory hole artwork when she writes, "I am a lesbian, so when it comes to glory holes, I am more talk than action. And like many lesbians I have an aspirational and covetous relationship to the culture of public sex and cruising that's traditionally associated with gay male sexuality."[48] Set apart from the cis gay male culture of glory holes, in queer nonbinary and lesbian imaginings, the portal space of public sex opens up to fantasy. Here, the glory hole represents a kind of frustrated access and deviant sexual desire that falls outside of the normative sexual freeway. In these imaginings, the architectures of the glory hole are variable, the walls themselves are just planks, placed between bodies for the sake of a hole that drips with lubrication, or a grid with light rainbow shades that pull you into its event horizon. The architecture, the physical environment of the sexual scenario, brings the viewer's attention to the envelope of enclosure and the very desire for walls and edges to mediate the erotic.

As may have become clear, to my mind the glory hole is not totally distinct from theorizations of the closet. It is the secrecy of the glory hole paired with its risk of exposure that gives the glory hole its erotic charge and particular place within the queer imaginary. So much of sex is thought of as making or unmaking the social. I want to consider another kind of escape that imagines an unmaking of the social that does not hold the subject at its center as the site of unmaking, but one in which the social is reimagined. The glory hole then becomes conceptually grounded to a space where public sex was once possible for some, in the hope that, somehow, sex can be the site of something more in the future. The glory hole is a curious portal that connects sexuality, enclosure, and freedom. As I have argued, many conceptions of de facto queer sex and its embraced perversion are deeply informed by what Marlon Ross calls "claustrophillia" to describe "a fixation on the closet function as the grounding principle for sexual experience, knowledge, and politics."[49] This reading consequently places pressure on the obsession with the closet as an organizing structure of all modern sexuality. I am arguing that white queer liberationist thought has historically had a difficult time imagining sexuality outside of enclosure, and this is the lens through which modern sexuality is commonly articulated. What might escape *do* if we consider the term as having more to do with the donning of the cape (to think about the cloak of escape), the wearing of one's sexuality like a garment? How might this alter an understanding of sexuality and its relationship to the freedom to gather, to be among loved ones? How might it encourage a sense of physical or haptic intimacy outside the regime of the human? If whiteness has to fabricate an enclosure to feel free, has to mimic and appropriate Black articulations of freedom, the task would be to create a haven from the extractive, naive, and violent force of whiteness.

I want to consider a photograph often not shown but discussed in the work of Fred Moten and Saidiya Hartman. The photograph in question appears in the archive of Thomas Eakins and depicts a young Black girl reclining nude in the style of Manet's *Olympia* (1863). In his reading of the 1882 photograph, titled *African American Girl Nude, Reclining on a Couch*, Fred Moten proposes what he refers to as a troubling escape. Moten traces the history of photography, by way of the forced movement and stillness of Black bodies—of being sent—a question of stillness and movement posed and opposed by the photograph of a little girl. For Moten, "The law of narrative development . . . [is] animated by the interplay of race and teleology."[50] This is to say that the histories of "seriality and aesthetic criminality"—by way of the phenotype, Francis Galton's composite portrait, and Thomas Eakins's own obsession with gross anatomy—contribute to modes of seeing the simultaneous hypervisibilty and the invisibility of the girl. In her portraiture pose, Moten reads a "momentous enactment of escape, . . . a dissonance in the histories to which she is submitted."[51] For Moten, her pose marks a swerve in and out of the scene of capture, a "choreography in confinement, internal to a frame it instantiates and shatters."⁵² As Moten writes, this is momentous choreography of fugitive movement. Here, escape marks a dissonant and improvisatory genre of movement both prescribed by the structures of anti-Black confinement and in anticipation of their failures.

As the white referent for Eakins's posing of this young child, Manet's *Oylmpia* presents modern white sexuality's reliance on Blackness. Manet features a young white woman, the artist and model Victorine Meurent, reclining nude. With a flower in her hair, Meurent confidently stares directly at the painter while behind her, a Black servant wearing a white dress almost blends with the shadows and drop cloths of the set dressing. This woman is named in another of Manet's paintings as "Laure." In *Olympia*, Laure glances down and sideways in a supplicating posture as she holds a bouquet of flowers. Her dark skin is meant to hold the shadows of the painting, to create a shallow depth of field. As Emile Zola wrote to Manet, "You wanted a nude, and you chose Olympia, the first to come along. You wanted bright luminous patches, and you put a bouquet. You wanted black patches and you placed a Negress and a cat in a corner."⁵³ This is the history of the pose, of the shadow of the pose, of white feminine defiance and sexual self-possession and its reliance on Blackness for the bouquet. In the Eakins photo, which Moten reads but does not show, we have the history of the pose of Manet's Meurent ghosted by Laure. This is the image of a young girl, younger than Meurent, posed in the style of *Olympia*. In Eakins's "forensic [albumen] image," we find a young girl forced into a pose of sexual availability.⁵⁴ For Moten, this image, along with Harriet Jacob's *crawl* space and *scrawlspace*, represents instances of escape-in-confinement, which is also to say "constant escape" as he intones, "freedom in unfreedom is flight."⁵⁵ And while this image is, as Hartman writes, "redolent with the auction block, the plantation, and the brothel," the young girl likewise stands in for the chorus of "wayward" young women.⁵⁶ For Hartman, this girl is part of a chorus, a minor figure whose "anonymity enables her to stand in for all the others."⁵⁷ She is one of the many young Black women whom Hartman is searching for, just one of the many who exist in the archive who are attuned to the "hurt and the promise" of living in an anti-Black world.⁵⁸ Such images mark the ongoing "practice of everyday life and *escape subsistence*," a practice that is both stationary and wonderfully imaginative. Hartman writes: "Beautiful experiments in living free, urban plots against the plantation flourished, yet were unsustainable or thwarted or criminalized before they could take root."⁵⁹ Her story is "every story altered and unchanging: How can I live? I want to be free. Hold on."⁶⁰ The repetition of the prayer and the practice is sung by all of the wayward lives: "How can I live? I want to be free. Hold on." Without neglecting the racialized and sexualized violence present in the framing and posing of the little girl, Hartman emphasizes her "plot against the plantation." Like Moten's "constant escape," she imagines "escape subsistence" as the demand—"How can I live?"—where the answer is an improvisatory sustaining collective choreography inside a series of violent containers. Where freedom, as Hartman elsewhere writes, is an "incomplete project," this escape is operational against, and in spite of, the sexual narrative of desire as the will to either possess or be shattered by the other.[61]

In considering the visual history of sexual self-possession and imagining desire and its relationship to the pose, to light and shadow, to possession and entanglement, I return to *Pleasure Garden* by the artist and activist Tourmaline. Having worked as a community organizer, Tourmaline has theorized in many forms the potential of the visual to both abolish systems of confinement and build trans and queer life worlds. She works in the mode of fabulation to imagine the lives and pleasures of Black and trans femmes that were and could be. Tourmaline's films focus on trans activists Marsha P. Johnson in *Happy Birthday, Marsha!* (codirected with Sasha Wortzel, 2018), Miss Major Griffin-Gracy in *The Personal Things* (2016), and Egypt LaBeija in *The Atlantic Is a Sea of Bones* (2017). Her work has often toggled between what she has called being a "somebody" and being a "nobody," the tension between being visible to extractive state logics and institutions and flying under the radar to stay safe among loved ones in collective formation. In the introduction to their edited volume, *Trapdoor: Trans Cultural Production and the Politics of Visibility*, Tourmaline, Eric Stanley, and Johanna Burton explain that where representation is often "said to remedy broader acute social crises ranging from poverty to murder to police violence" for Black bodies, for nonnormatively gendered bodies, this often correlates with an increase in violence against those same bodies.[62] But the authors remind us that representations can also serve as "doors into making new futures possible."[63] Sometimes these doors are traps, and sometimes they are trapdoors, "those clever contraptions that are not entrances or exits but secret passageways that take you someplace else, often someplace as yet unknown."[64] Visual representation does not provide access to healthcare, safety, legal protections, or increased life chances. Yet, Tourmaline, Stanley, and Burton caution us against jettisoning it altogether, proposing instead a trapdoor that, portal-like, takes us to other worlds, or perhaps to other ways of seeing the structures which orient us toward this one.

Pleasure Garden provides a visual engagement with self-portraiture as one such trapdoor, feet off the ground in a speculative leap. In these images, and the accompanying short film *Salacia* (2019), also included in the exhibit, Tourmaline speaks of historical and speculative Black queer havens. In *Morning Cloak*, the artist's top has come undone and she holds her legs wide open as though ready for an embrace. The images are high fashion, glamorous, and elegant; the colors are rich and luscious. The blue-tinged white clouds in this photograph are held up in a horizontal line by the green overgrowth of the fence. She sits alone in front of a densely woven grapevine. Her hair is a deep fuchsia. Her beige-fronted bodice is pulled down below her breasts, and in her right fingers, she sucks on a grape. She stares directly into the camera, revealing nothing discernible in her gaze. Tall, dried grasses surround where she perches, knees wide on a white sheet which blends into her white Victorian-era underskirt as it pools around her ankles and knees. In the title of this photograph, the mourning cloak butterfly has lost its "u;" no longer filled with grief the deep purple butterfly has metamorphosed into a cloak meant

4.4   Tourmaline, *Morning Cloak*, 2020.

to adorn the sunrise. A sap-loving butterfly, the mourning cloak is qualified as a sometimes-pollinator—a nectar-drinking go-between, the butterfly is an important part of the mating ritual of flowers.

In the photograph *Summer Azure*, Tourmaline is mid-air, again in her all-white spacesuit, leaping against the earth's watery blue humid atmosphere. Her pants expose her legs along their vertical sides, along with a sheer mesh bodysuit. The white astronaut's helmet reflects the sun on its small glass window. Her mid-flight pose reminds me of '90s feminist readings of *Thelma and Louise* that insisted we do not see their car descend into the canyon at the end of the film; instead, Thelma and Louise's dream of freedom and sexual liberation perpetually hovers in the air as the credits roll, thus rejecting the idea that the masculinist violence of the state will win. It recalls Toni Morrison's *Song of Solomon*, and Yoruban folktales of Africans that could fly away home. This image, along with its companion, *Coral Hairstreak*, invokes a futurity associated with space, with the literalization of other worlds, and with Afrofuturism. In *Sleepy Orange Sulphur*, Tourmaline kneels and bends over a field of late summer September pumpkins, one arm wraps around her back to raise her skirt and show us her ass. *Swallowtail*, an equally sultry photo, features the artist sitting back in a dried wheat field, bodice undone. A pearl necklace drapes over her while she pulls her skirt up to her waist to reveal the lower half of her body.

In my reading, these images differ from the ecstasy of Warhol's image in that they imagine a really beautiful portrait not for us, but for the self. These images challenge Manet's art historical nude in that they do not give over the naked body to judgment or as a gesture of sexual availability. The question that Crimp asks—"How do you produce a really beautiful portrait?"—is the question Tourmaline seems to take up and refigure into the landscape and butterflies that connect each flower to the next. *Pleasure Garden* presents us with a way to rethink sites of pleasure apart from fantasies of enclosure, the sovereign subject, and possession. The photographic lens becomes not a site of capture, but a play on feeling oneself. This is a pleasure that appears in line with Amber Musser's theorization of sensuality distinct from "discourses of sexuality and desire."[65] For Musser, sensuality emphasizes opacity, the interior, and the affective sense of the flesh. She describes her theory of "brown jouissance" as an "embodied hunger that takes joy and pain in this gesture of radical openness toward otherness."[66] Thinking with Hortense Spillers's understanding of the pornotrope, Musser imagines a "yes, and" with Afropessimist conceptions of Blackness as the site of violent un/gendering and relational refusal. Instead of separating Blackness from other minoritar-

4.5　Tourmaline, *Coral Hairstreak*, 2020.

ian epistemologies, Musser ties them more thoroughly together in her theorization of Brownness. She argues for an inhabitation of the violence and joy of enfleshment, and proposes a "dwelling in the selfhoods, intimacies, and knowledge systems that emerge from thinking with the flesh."[67] If theorizations of sexuality and ecstasy are always caught up in the language of the subject surpassing itself, of the "Thing, Other, and object," then epistemologies of sensuality and Brown jouissance create space in which to revel "in fleshiness, its sensuous materiality that brings together pleasure and pain."[68] Grounded in Black thought, I understand this theory of Brown jouissance and sensuality as a going deeper into the fleshiness of self and its affective sensuous contours through hunger, vulnerability, citation, and ingestion. Tourmaline emphasizes the pleasure in *Pleasure Garden* as a kind of rescaffolding of the ways in which it can be thought apart from the dominant paradigms in philosophy and psychoanalysis. Such images pressure a reckoning with the history of enfleshment, of Blackened life and pleasure amid constant threats to being. There is a rewriting of public sex beyond the architectures of enclosure that I read in Tourmaline's work, where, when the right to property and ecstatic self-annihilation is denied, an opening into pleasure becomes available outdoors. *Pleasure Garden*, and the pollinator self-portraits that populate it, give us a version of feeling and excess found in nature, ingestion, and dress. If Lacanian jouissance is understood as "excess sensation" for the individual, Musser theorizes Brown jouissance in relation to the social.

The title of the show references not only the lush visual world of Tourmaline's photographs, but also that of the historical pleasure garden. Initially conceived of as private spaces, the "dressed" pleasure garden was kept separate from the more practical kitchen garden, the grazing farmlands, and the prying eyes of passersby.[69] However, in the seventeenth century, pleasure gardens also began to refer to the public lands and urban parks meant for outdoor enjoyment and walking, such as the Boston Commons.[70] In contrast to lands meant for recreational use or husbandry, these were gardens created with an eye toward their aesthetic composition. Tourmaline's pleasure garden, with its proximity to her film *Salacia*, is explicitly connected to the space of Seneca Village, a Black and Irish autonomous community in the nineteenth century that was later torn down to make what is now Central Park. When New York City was very active in the commerce of the slave trade, Seneca Village became a space apart where Black people could own property and have relief from the constant threat of violence in lower Manhattan. As historian Cynthia Copeland explains,

> Once upon a time, the people who lived in Seneca Village and in the pre-park expanse were considered tramps, squatters, and thieves that didn't have a right to the land. There was this smear campaign in the newspapers to say that these people lived in shanties and shacks.... Seneca Village was a self-determining community, with loving families and loving relationships. It was a response and a reaction to living life in isolation, living life as de-humanized, living life as, you're just not supposed to be here. Well, these people found a way to be here and these people found a way to make a way out of no way.[71]

To call the inhabitants of this land "tramps, squatters, and thieves" was an attempt to undermine their legibility as landowners and rights-deserving citizens. It was meant to justify the decision to destroy the community and to avoid compensating members of a Black community under the law of eminent domain.

Tourmaline's film, *Salacia*, follows the story of Mary Jones, a Black trans woman who lived in the 1930s. Jones appears in the violent historical archive not through access to her own journals or photographs, but through her arrest for stealing a white john's wallet.[72] In a newspaper article from 1836, her elegance and fine dress are immediately noted, but it isn't until she is searched by the constable that she is "discovered" and her gender is called into question. *Salacia* reimagines Jones's life and criminalization, refusing the archive as the end of the story. Instead, Jones, who was told she "looked so much better in Women's clothes" and "always attended parties among the people of [her] own Colour dressed in this way," is given a space of pleasure and sensuality in Seneca Village. It becomes Jones's own pleasure garden, a speculative sensual landscape.

In an August 2020 piece for *T Magazine*, Tourmaline proposed the creation of the Nanny Goat Hill Pleasure Gardens in the space of the violent monumentality of Rikers Island prison. Referencing Seneca Village, which featured "a rocky outcrop" known as Nanny Goat Hill, this countermonument would "amplif[y] the historic existence of Black space beyond ownership."[73] The pleasure garden emerges here as a reference to historically Black-owned pleasure gardens, "havens on the periphery of Lower Manhattan," emphasizing the pleasures of fresh air and safety, of being left alone to live among people you love. Nanny Goat Hill would be part mutual aid resource, part space of ecstasy, reminding us that enjoyment and sensuality are not disconnected from well-being. Pleasure and the self are conceived of here in relation to the collective dreams. Tourmaline explains, "The pleasure gardens may become many things: a sauna for queer and trans people to be naked in nature; a shelter for homeless survivors of intimate violence; a polycultural food source available for sustainable foraging; a bar. We won't know until we assemble ourselves (with ramps, toilets and free food) and decide what we want by asking questions in the tradition of the freedom dreaming of the civil rights movement."[74] In this vision of the Nanny Goat Hill Pleasure Gardens, I also hear the proposal and wish for a proliferation of such sites that emphasize food security, safety, play, and mutual aid—what Mariame Kaba calls "survival work."[75] In the "pleasure gardening" audio tour, conceived of with Thomas (T.) Jean Lax, the listener is taken to different key sites for freedom dreaming. Here, Tourmaline continues to emphasize the historical abolitionist projects, as well as the aesthetic and sensual elements of space-making. In the sound walk, Robin D.G. Kelly emphasizes the importance of Black spaces built from community action against the logics of enclosure and eradication. Kelly explains, "When you're talking about the embrace of another in a world where that embrace is rendered illegal or immoral, you know, you're basically seizing freedom."[76] This is an understanding of freedom not as geographic, but as built into "small everyday moments of intimacy and pleasure."[77] Standing in front of 330 Pearl Street, just south of the Brooklyn Bridge, at what used to be a boarding house for Black sailors, Tourmaline explains, "What feels most compelling is thinking about those moments of lightness and fun and pleasure in the gaps that surround our historical archive of Black life in New York city, thinking about all the delicious sex that was happening at the boarding house between Black sailors as an extension of the pleasure ground."[78] Where Nanny Goat Hill Pleasure Gardens "provides flint to imagine a blueprint for possibility," the tour of historic sites reminds us of pleasures passed. Like Musser's desire to dwell in the flesh and the pornotrope in order to articulate the sensual, the many iterations of pleasure gardens that Tourmaline conjures embrace a "yes, and" approach that allows for moments of lightness, fun, and pleasure to emerge while simultaneously refusing the logics of private property and enclosure. Instead, such grounds imagine pleasure as a momentary reprieve, an escape toward the embrace of kin, where freedom's whole dream is to be insatiably ingesting among loved ones. Kelly continues, "Liberation is not necessarily something that we achieve by getting to the mountaintop. But it's a constant process of cultivation." Like gardening, weeding, tending to the earth and its small pleasures, Kelly suggests that liberation is something to be cultivated, that it is an ongoing process. And part of this work in *Pleasure Garden* would seem to be about being a nobody in a world of somebodies. Tourmaline explains, "Capitalism cares about the somebody, it cares about the individual. It wants individual figures separated from one another and from the ground that has produced them. It wants the stage."[79] The individual, the figure that "is easily captured, easily tweeted about," is also easily consumed, derailed, scapegoated, or recorded. Instead of being a somebody, she suggests "small personal acts of nobody-ness of resistance and refusal [that] create space for us to come together and support one another." Being a nobody is theorized apart from anonymity, where being anonymous means being neither named nor identified. Tourmaline's understanding of nobody-ness, however, has more to do with being unimportant, unnoticeable by the state or the institution. "As nobodies we run roots underground like rhizomes like crab grass, only to pop up above ground to do our thing, to bring our thing to the world, or to bring our thing back home. Because sometimes when you're a nobody you still gotta be a somebody for a moment." Being a nobody and being a somebody are not opposing ways of working, being, or moving in the world. They are strategies of opacity and visibility, of staying on the ground, in community, and part of an entangled collective. Being a nobody means naming thought and practice as never coming from just one place, but as coming out of long conversations; nobodiness is about coming together in pleasure, on pleasure grounds, or organizing consensus is "escape subsistence." This is the practice that Hartman names, "How can I live? I want to be free. Hold on."[80]

> There's a new world coming, everything's gonna be turnin' over, everything gon' be turnin' over, where you gon' be standin' when it comes.
>
> —**Toshi Reagon**

CODA

Less of a Theater Audience

The *Parable of the Sower* opera opens with benches in a wide yawn facing out to the audience. The cast wanders onto the stage from the lit house amid the audience, like folks showing up for church. Toshi Reagon walks onstage and the audience roars. As she sits down in her spot at the center of the band, which takes up a large portion of the middle of the big Emerson Cutler Theater stage in Boston, she explains: "We come here to sing this story." Reagon talks for a while, talks like we're sitting there around a campfire, talks like we are in a community gathering house. She tells us that this story is about "letting go of what is not serving us so we can get down to the relationships we need to have with each other." She narrates, "This is a story is about Lauren Olamina, a girl with hyperempathy." It is the musical adaptation of Octavia Butler's 1993 science fiction novel, *Parable of the Sower*.

Reagon, along with adrienne maree brown, with whom she cohosts the podcast *Octavia's Parables*, has taken up Butler's many theories of relationality in an effort to apply them to the present. Her *Parable of the Sower* opera premiered in concert form as part of The Public's *Under the Radar Festival* in January of 2015. It was later staged as a full production at NYU Abu Dhabi in

2017, directed by Eric Ting. While Butler's writing has inspired many authors and thinkers, what is unique to Reagon's project is the way she puts Butler's story into song. With its rich history in social movements, music's breathy collectivity braids voices together into a being in concert. The sonic is simultextual in the way it communicates opaque strategies through song and engages the sensual inside the political. *Parable of the Sower* is a performance with the musicians on the stage, providing the audience with a sense of collaborative devising which figures Reagon as the reluctant song leader. Co-written and composed with her mother, the famed Bernice Johnson Reagon of *Sweet Honey in the Rock*, the opera follows the tradition of a capella movement music inspired by both African folk songs and gospel. The texture of these songs are meant to be familiar, even as their content connect reflects the specifics of Butler's story. Reagon and Johnson Reagon's music pulls from the rich history of folk choral responses, repetitions, and rhythms. They use the infrastructure of the Black church to dub in a social commentary on coalition and movement building. Pushing against the conventions of theater, Toshi Reagon explains that she wants everyone in attendance to "be a little less of a theater audience and more of a community." Reagon's folk, funk, and disco sounds are deeply invested in gathering and the queer and Black stories that have always been there. But as we know, theater communities are temporary and do not depend upon each other for survival. In contrast, the folk singer is a figure of the people; she is embedded in community relationships and, as such, asks her audience to consider themselves as responsible social actors.

In *The Only Way Out* I have traced the white uptake of generic escape and the pale fantasies of change that can often only be imagined through an evacuating sentimental understanding of Black experience. I have variously attempted to show artwork by Black and non-Black queer artists that engage escape as an episodic subsistence inside a hypervigilant white supremacist landscape. This is at times a linguistic strategy, and at other times, an aesthetic intervention where the telling of the story is always attuned to the form in which it is told. The American fascination with escape shows the stories that accrue around freedom and confinement—both the white framing desires for escape and the ways in which Blackened life is tied to enclosure. I have traced stories of escape that are attuned to comingling, care, and cohabitation not predicated on movement from A to B. In these stories, the capacity for change is reoriented from episodes of individual progress to alternate imaginings of escape where the individual's journey is tangled with the narrative of the collective. This is a change which prioritizes the freedom of being among loved ones. Furthermore, I have argued that stories of escape are not private property, but generational and collaborative. In this conclusion, I focus on escape and entanglement in Toshi Reagon's opera adaptation of Octavia Butler's novel. Stories emerge here as coauthored, not as private property, but credited, generational, and collaborative. I continue to ask how do narratives of change emerge outside the terms of a specific cosmogeny? How might escape produce futures not already predetermined by common sense? What sorts of affects and practices collect around stories of escape? Can escape be a generative site for reimaging the force of narrative itself as a vehicle for freedom, collectivity, and entanglement?

Octavia Butler's *Parables* series, *Kindred* (1979), and *Wildseed* (1980) have each been discussed as both science fiction and as neo-slave narrative. Ashraf Rushdy describes the neo-slave narrative as originating out of racial and social consciousness of the late '60s, where "contemporary novels . . . assume the form, adopt the conventions, and take on the first-person voice of the antebellum slave narrative."[1] In *Parable of the Sower*, Butler has many references to slavery, not as a distant past, but as a contemporary practice, from the debt slavery experiences by Zahara and Tori to the sex trafficking of children. The story itself is one of movement, as the characters escape from the ashes of Robledo, the gated community where Lauren Olamina, our main character, grows up. It is an escape to the dream of an elsewhere where life is livable among continuing environmental degradation and the resurgence of a conservative Christian nationalist movement. That livable life arrives in glimpses and in community, but a place to build never quite appears.

Butler's important and timely novel, set in the year 2024, imagines a space of collective survival at the intersection of climate and financial collapse. In the Los Angeles suburb of Robledo, a walled community tries to keep out the thieves and the unhoused; inside their walls they try to make do with the meager resources each household has managed to hold onto, whether that be a few chickens, a small garden, or a working television. Reagon stages these scenes of coming together not exactly in friendship, but in survival and trust. Her song "There's a New World Comin'," both a warning and an anthem, repeats the inevitable: that change is coming and "everything gon' be turnin over." Just as Lauren asks her family to start planning for a future of wildfires, indentured servitude, and conservative religious violence, Reagon asks her audience: "Where you gon' be standing when it comes?" Here, change is not just an inevitability, but something that must be seen and acknowledged. Butler and Reagon warn that if we cling to the past instead of tracking the change that has already begun, we will be left vulnerable and unprepared.

In the opera, we are slowly introduced to the characters on the stage, not by name, but by the way each person moves in the world. An elderly woman makes her way into the church circle, as does a stern-looking man and his meek wife, and finally a preacher and his family come in through the audience. The daughter in the family is tall and wearing overalls. She is our lead. The characters spread out around the benches on the stage; some are clearly eager to be there, and others, like Lauren's younger brother, Keith, are resentful for being trapped inside their small neighborhood community. Inside the gates of Robledo, the old ways of the church still stand. The staged benches hold the church together as a space for discussion, and in the grounding belief that God will save them. But as Lauren explains through journal entries in the novel, the walls of the community are slowly breaking apart. And the people outside of the walls are desperate and hungry, with no infrastructure to support them and nowhere to turn for help. Keith is a brooding teenager in the pews and in a rhythmic low grumble he sings, "I wanna go outside, I don't like living locked up like I'm a child or a prisoner even. There's got to be something more than this." Alongside her brother's teenage masculine angst and rage, Lauren is starting to realize that this is, as the band later plays loudly and in full chorus, "a dying world." Eventually the walls fall, Lauren's family is killed, and those who are still alive after the looters and arsonists are finished do their best to survive.

From her position in the early '90s, Butler describes a United States of 2024 that is still engaged in the murder and subjugation of poor people of color across Southern California. Themes of escape, enslavement, and forced migration emerge in the eventual trip Lauren takes north with two others from Robledo. Along the way, the group hears stories of sex trafficking, of wage slavery being "offered" to folks as a way out of the debt they accrue from simply being poor. As Butler describes in in the book, the sleepy middle-class town of Olivar is bought by a private company intent on establishing water, power, and agribusiness. Olivar is searching for "skilled professionals who would be willing to . . . work for room and board."[2] A different kind of walled community, the company town is reminiscent of early mining towns of the nineteenth century which provided "quality of life" in exchange for increasing amounts of debt owed back to the company. Later in the book, Butler describes another agribusinnes conglomerate where wages are paid "in company scrip, not in cash." Having to pay for rent, food, and clothing at the company store (with their company money), workers realize that they don't have enough to make ends meet and quickly become increasingly indebted to the company store just to scrape by. Butler writes:

According to new laws that might or might not exist, people were not permitted to leave an employer to whom they owed money. They were obligated to work off the debt either as quasi-indentured people or convicts. That is, if they refused to work, they could be arrested, jailed, and in the end, handed over to their employers. Either way, such debt slaves could be forced to work longer hours for less pay, could be "disciplined" if they failed to meet their quotas, could be traded and sold with or without their consent, with or without their families, to distant employers who had temporary or permanent need of them. Worse, children could be forced to work off the debt of their parents if their parents died, became disabled, or escaped.[3]

The punishment for failing to pay back one's debt, which definitionally could never be paid back due to the cost of living, was the indenture of oneself and one's children. This, as we know, would often result in the splitting up of families. While Olivar provided fresh drinking water, food, and safety, the cost was participation in a system of bonded labor. Butler traces the criminalization of the poor, referencing the violent kinship-destroying history of racial slavery in the United States, as well as forms of debt bondage that continue to affect over forty million people worldwide today.[4]

While Olivar is discussed in passing in the book, shown as a warning of the corporate greed being offered as salvation, Reagon takes this plot point as inspiration for one of her key songs. "Don't let your baby go, don't let your baby go to Olivar," she sings as though she were a folk singer on a local porch in Robledo. Olivar is a company town that cannot provide the freedom and sustainability it seems to promise; but what is more, it represents a contemporary refusal to look at the rise of conservatism and the focus on private property and goods as symbolic of the good life. Reagon asks the audience in the large theater to sing along with the chorus, "don't let your baby go," so that they might keep the words in their mouths and bring them home to their families. She sings, "You put your Amazon purchase groceries in your fridge and you listened to Pandora or Spotify. . . . Wait, the good good days, how did they turn so soon? We thought we had escaped, we thought we had the room." From Amazon Whole Foods grocery delivery to music streaming services that pay record labels but not artists, Reagon critiques the instant gratification which keeps the middle class quiet and disengaged inside our own boxes. As a response, Reagon chants, "Fight, fight, fight, stra-te-gize, stay together. Equal rights." Then she gets very quiet, almost whisper-singing in the same style of the chant,

Cuz it's all about race, it's all about race, no matter what they tell you about race. At Olivar, we're all here, they don't care if you're white, they don't care if you're queer, they don't care if you're trans, they don't care if you're Black. Just pick up those boxes put 'em on your back. And we work and we work for a few dollars a day, cuz the government don't care what they pay. In the interest of the economy they say it's only fair to give them more slaves and make more billionaires.

The song ends with the chorus again, sung soft and low, almost a plea: "Don't let your baby go, don't let your baby go to Oooo-lee-var." This song holds Butler's own ominous warning, developed through an attention to news reports on global sex trafficking, anti-Black violence, climate collapse, and late stage capitalism. Written in Reagon's words, the story of Olivar becomes a warning that we can carry in song as a reminder to ourselves and others. As she names it, the company town is both "all about race" and simultaneously deeply "inclusive." The people who need the company town are forced there in their desperation caused by systemic inequality, and yet when they get there, everyone is seen as mutually interchangeable. Put differently, the profit margin of late capitalism has all the room in the world for "diversity and inclusion" as long as you continue to increase the company's profit margin.

As the three main characters who survived the attack on Robledo—Lauren, Harry, and Zahra—travel up California's Interstate 5, we see more poverty, the privatization of natural resources like water, and the ongoing destruction of fires. Reagon's shared narrators, who sit with her centerstage, give us statistics of the number of refugees in 1993 (the year that Butler wrote the book), and tell us how that number had jumped from the previous year by over a million. According to the United Nations High Commissioner for Refugees (UNHCR), "21.5 million people were forcibly displaced each year by sudden onset weather-related hazards between 2008 and 2016."[5] Discussing her novel with filmmaker Julie Dash in 1995, Butler explained, "I wanted to look at the possibilities of global warming, global warming is a kind of character in the book." From rising sea levels and the increase in "weather events," to drought and the scarcity of drinking water, Butler predicts what is to come because she is paying attention to the behavior of power-hungry humans. She continues, "We've got a lot of things that we would be expecting if global warming were a fact and not just something still very questionable, but I think it's going to stay questionable until we can't ignore or deny it any longer."[6] Climate change as a character provides much of the impetus to keep moving, to travel further north, and then eventually to get off the planet. Both Butler and Reagon reluctantly warn their readers and listeners about what is to come. Change, they say, must be shaped by those of us who are here right now, otherwise we will eventually be chased into the embers of this "dying world."

In order to survive as a refugee, amid people who are not her kin, Lauren must also learn how to be a witness to devastation, pain, abuse, suffering, and murder without letting herself be undone by it. This is only further compounded by the fact that Lauren, who has at this point begun to go by her surname Olamina, is what they call a "sharer." Early on in the book she explains: "I can take a lot of pain without falling apart. I've had to learn to do that. But it was hard to do that today, to keep [pedaling] and keep up with the others when just about everyone I saw made me feel worse and worse."[7] Sharing, "what the doctors call 'organic delusional syndrome,'" is the result of a drug dependency Olamina's mother had while she was pregnant. As a result, when she is in the outside world she feels "shadows and ghosts, twists and jabs of unexpected pain."[8] Olamina feels the pain that she sees, but she can also share much more fleeting feelings of pleasure. Much of Olamina's journey north is spent with her trying to hide her hyperempathy in order to prevent strangers from using it to torture her and make her bleed along with others. Sharers make good slaves, she reminds us, because they are easy to hurt.[9] As Reagon explains in the opera, hyperempathy syndrome is "an overwhelming situation for her but she still wants to go." The actor who plays Olamina sings, "If I feel all you feel would I know you better? If I share all your pain would I know you better? if I fly within your joy would I know you better?" Asking questions about both the fictional hyperempathy syndrome and empathy as a strategy for accessing the affective interior lives of others, she questions as an avenue toward ethical relations. Hyperempathy would seem to be a nod to Butler's own attunement to the social world, to the environmental destruction she was watching occur around the globe and feared would come to pass. Butler and Reagon seem to ask: What is the effect of feeling "all you feel," of experiencing all an other feels based on a perception or projection? Different from what Saidiya Hartman names as the "precariousness of empathy" for the white progressive imagining of Black pain, hyperempathy emerges as something that, through its permeability, encourages connection or death.[10] It is a feeling that cannot be turned off and runs the risk of doing great harm to the person in tune to the pain of others. As a literary strategy introduced by Butler, it tasks the reader not with sentimental identification from a distance, but instead with the demand to watch what it means to share pain.

Writing a confessional story out of journal entries, Olamina also writes poetic scripture. "All that you touch / You Change. / All that you Change / Changes you. / The only lasting truth / Is Change / God is Change."[11] (Her verses become *Earthseed: The Books of the Living*.) These poetic observations are compiled into a new belief system to account for the ways that change itself is the only consistent force in her world. Kara Keeling argues that it is through the poetic that Butler is able to release "the subterranean energies of past freedoms" and radically break from the here and now. Poeisis, as Tavia Nyong'o explains, is the act of doing; it is "work in the world" as opposed to "work on the self." Poesis creates new futures. Olamina moves through the world learning how to survive it. She writes, "Out here you adapt to your surroundings or you get killed."[12] Attunement with one's surroundings is not a choice one can make in Butler's 2024. In *Emergent Strategy*, adrienne maree brown applies Butler's "adaptive and relational leadership model" to the worlds of facilitation and organizational development.[13] "We are brilliant at survival," brown writes, "but brutal at it. We tend to slip out of togetherness the way we slip out of the womb, bloody and messy and surprised to be alone. And clever—able to learn with our whole bodies the ways of this world."[14] In survival mode the self emerges as though it must survive despite those around it, instead of with their help. This is a narrative of escape that demands entanglement in order to sustain itself. Here, escape has something to do with sociality, a theory of being together not in a space time of arrival, but in the embrace of what Denise Ferreira da Silva calls nonlocality or nonseparability. As da Silva writes, "The principle of nonlocality supports a kind of thinking that does not reproduce the methodological and ontological grounds of the modern subject, namely linear temporality and spatial separation."[15] She continues, "Without separability, difference among human groups and between human and nonhuman entities, has very limited explanatory purchase and ethical significance."[16] Entanglement describes the phenomenon wherein particles share spatial proximity and one cannot distinguish the independence or separability of each particle. Da Silva is naming a sociality that does not rely on the modern framings of time and space. She asks: "What if, instead of The Ordered World, we could imagine The World as a Plenum[?]"[17] Imagining the world as plenum is to imagine the world as completely filled with matter, matter touching matter, nonlocal and nonseparable. How might this change the way we think about human difference and the terms we use to describe such purportedly fundamental descriptors? Escape, imagined alongside entanglement, shifts from the sense of escape as ever a solitary act. Where a generic escape is articulated as individual, we know that Black and minoritarian escape is never done alone, but always in concert with others.

Imaging space as the final frontier, in her sequel, *Parable of the Talents*, Butler propels *Earthseed* into the other worlds of the sky. This Afrofuturist vision is often taken up by others in their engagement with Butler. In 2021, NASA even named its touchdown site on Mars's Jezero Crater the "Octavia E. Butler Landing." While both her *Imago* and her *Patternist* series rethink being in excess of the human species, in the *Parable* books, Butler gets trapped imagining the future in a couple-oriented heteronormativity. Jayna Brown argues that Olamina is humanist in her focus on species survival. She asks, instead, "What would it mean to let go of the assumption of human superiority and open up to new forms of sociality and modes of being?"[18] Butler's third book in the series, *Parable of the Trickster*, was never written but we know from her archive that it was meant to follow Olamina's daughter to the gray and bleak planet Bow, short for rainbow, and outline the emergence of a new world. *Parable of the Trickster* was a story where, according to Butler, the intergalactic settlers' real problem was "dealing with themselves, surviving their promised land."[19] Instead of being able to enact a geographic relocation in order to escape humanity's problems, on Bow, the problems remain the same until humanity learns to deal with them.

The 2019 space opera *Star Choir* by Malik Gaines and Xandro Segade—which takes inspiration from Butler's archival notes in which the planetary colonists of Rainbow are infected with mind-altering microbes—shows us the perspective of life from the microbes already on the planet. *Star Choir* shifts from the perpetuation of the human, toward an understanding that, as Jayna Brown writes, "we may have to let go of the very idea of single-species existence, of the idea of species itself."[20] While in *Parable of the Sower*, Butler envisions a coming together in survival against forces that wish all but the white, Christian, and wealthy to be either subservient or dead, Gaines and Segade use *Parable of the Trickster* to imagine a coming together that exceeds the species survival of the human. Even as Butler was never able to finish *Parable of the Trickster*, the ideas she presents in the first two books, and seeds in her archive, continue to be engaged in ways that contrast the structures of ownership and dispossession. This is "a dying world," but one that, in its detritus, illuminates the ways in which we come to know and reproduce questions of genre, species, and the individual.

How does looking toward the "collective experience" of change as it is manifest in the aesthetic and literary illustrate the next right actions for unmaking the current world? Can escape retain the histories of freedom that are associated with it, even as it presents a genre of change that shifts the discourses of freedom away from ideas of the individual and the human? Speculative and visionary fiction promotes ideas and ways of being which, as Kara Keeling notes, "are not recuperated into the familiar ones undergirding property, ownership, dispossession, white supremacy, and misogyny, as well as their attendant modes of propriety."[21] Imagining the way out of an economic, social, and climate collapse of the near future, Butler writes her version of escape in the necessarily serial episode of science fiction. Indeed, Butler meant to create a whole new trilogy out of the *Parable of the Trickster* plot. Like an episode, a series is an ordered progression, a story told in an ongoing fashion. A series might give way to three episodes, making a trilogy, or in science fiction and fantasy standards, it might be productive of a yet undetermined number of installments. *Trickster* (and its potential subtrilogy, which was meant to include *Parable of the Teacher*, *Parable of Chaos*, and *Parable of Clay*) invites participation in the story as we painfully watch the slow-motion coming-to-pass of the events that Butler narrated some thirty years ago.[22] The episode of escape traces humanity's capacity for change. Yet, as we can see from her archive, Butler struggled with precisely this question: How does one script visionary change? How does one tell a story about moving away from humanity when their life and language is so shaped by the vestiges and enclosures inaugurated by the human? These are episodes that are not paradigms of success or failure, but open-ended questions.

In the opera, Reagon invites the theater audience in to shape change with her, suggesting, as adrienne maree brown has, that "there is a conversation in the room that only these people at this moment can have." Reagon asks that the spectator be not separate, but known to the performer, and connected to the others in the room. This, however, is not an easy coming together in coalition or change. The audience is not meant to leave the room feeling good. In a 1981 speech, Bernice Johnson Reagon described coalition as uneasy and painful. "I feel as if im gonna keel over any minute and die. That is often what it feels like if you're really doing coalition work. Most of the time you feel threatened to the core and if you don't, you're not really doing no coalescing. . . . You don't go into coalition because you just like it. The only reason you would consider trying to team up with somebody who could possibly kill you, is because that's the only way you can figure you can stay alive."[23] Johnson Reagon's understanding of relationality is born out of a desire to stay alive, all the while knowing that the people you are teaming up with could likely bring about your demise. This is the kind of survival imagined in *Parable of the Sower*. This teaming-up is not in friendship and love, but a painful coalescing in the name of continued existence.[24] Johnson Reagon reminds me of the ways that escape is also coalitional work. That is, visionary work that imagines entangled and collective ways out from dominant structures that orient thought and embodiment. It is work that requires more than one.

Toshi Reagon's opera ends with all the characters sitting in a semicircle on the stage, feet planted on the ground, singing in full harmonic chorus. The performers sing the parable of the sower, an old story in which Jesus spreads the word of God. Adapting Luke 8:5 from the King James version of the Bible, the cast sings "the sower went out to sow her seed" in tight multipart rounds. They sing through the parable, describing the seed that falls by the wayside, and that which falls on the rock and the thorn. In the final verse, some seed falls on the "good ground, and spr[i]ng up, and bear fruit a hundredfold."[25] The Bible verse, for Reagon as for Butler, becomes a placeholder. It is a familiar story, a genre to rework. Reagon takes the parable from the Bible and hands it back to the theater audience as an oral tradition, a transmittable story for how to change this dying world.

NOTES

ESCAPE IS SUCH A THANKFUL WORD. AN INTRODUCTION

Epigraph 1: Dickinson, We like a Hairbreadth 'scape," *Complete Poems of Emily Dickinson*, 522.
Epigraph 2: Jefferson, "The difference is fixed in nature," 178.
1. Shakespeare, *Othello*, act 1, scene 3.
2. Finnerty, *Emily Dickinson's Shakespeare*, 132.
3. Friedlander, "Auctions of the Mind," 2. See also the Emily Dickinson poems "I never heard the word 'Escape'" and "Escape is such a thankful Word."
4. Brand, *Map to the Door of No Return*, 5.
5. Hartman, *Wayward Lives, Beautiful Experiments*, 24.
6. Tourmaline, "Making a Way Out of No Way."
7. Spillers, *Black, White, and in Color*, 14.
8. Muñoz, *Cruising Utopia*, 1.
9. Crawley, *Blackpentecostal Breath*, 2.
10. *Oxford English Dictionary*, s.v. "escape (v.)," accessed May 28, 2022.
11. Barnhart, *Barnhart Concise Dictionary of Etymology*.
12. Strong, *Captive Selves, Captivating Others*, 1.
13. Crawley, *Blackpentecostal Breath*, 36.
14. My thinking here greatly benefits from Shana Redmond's observation that "In the U.S., blackness knows no haven. In the U.S., whiteness knows no enclosure." Shana Redmond, Twitter, June 1, 2021.
15. Berlant, "Austerity, Precarity, Awkwardness," 2.

16 Berlant and Luciano, "Lauren Berlant with Dana Luciano."
17 In *The Female Complaint*, Lauren Berlant continues to explain the ways in which the genre of social identity is simultaneously an affective and aesthetic one, explaining that "for femininity to be a genre like an aesthetic one means that it is a structure of conventional expectation that people rely on to provide certain types of affective intensities and assurances" (192).
18 McKittrick, *Sylvia Wynter*, 9.
19 McKittrick, *Sylvia Wynter*, 34.
20 McKittrick, *Sylvia Wynter*, 7.
21 Marriott "Inventions of Existence," 48.
22 Weheliye, *Habeas Viscus*, 24.
23 McKittrick, *Sylvia Wynter*, 2. Emphasis mine.
24 "Commonsense is not only intellectual, as it is generally understood, but also the whole ensemble of how the senses experience the world. Especially how ideas and experiences of pleasure and unpleasure, beauty and ugliness, good and bad, are framed. Commonsense as aesthetic experience is marked by the fractures created by colonial modernity." Macharia, *Frottage*, 37.
25 Hobbes, "Leviathan."
26 Bergman, *Joyful Militancy*, 38.
27 Bogues, *Empire of Liberty*, 15.
28 Bogues, *Empire of Liberty*, 24.
29 "There is a dialectic of freedom that emerges not from the liberal tradition and its double structure but out of the interstices of domination. This practice of freedom disrupts normalized imperial liberty. It is a form of freedom in which there is a poiesis of life with no foreclosures. Such a practice of freedom requires invention and is predicated upon the radical imagination." Bogues, *Empire of Liberty*, 37.
30 Bogues, *Empire of Liberty*, 101–2.
31 Jefferson, "The difference is fixed in nature," 1781. Emphasis mine.
32 Cervenak, *Wandering*, 80.
33 *Oxford English Dictionary*, "escape."
34 *Oxford English Dictionary*, "escape."
35 McKittrick, *Demonic Grounds*, 35.
36 Brooks, *Bodies in Dissent*, 66.
37 Morrison, *Playing in the Dark*, 51.
38 Morrison, *Playing in the Dark*, 51–52.
39 Hartman, *Scenes of Subjection*, 19.
40 Morrison, *Playing in the Dark*, 38.
41 Goyal, *Runaway Genres*, 18.
42 Olney, "I Was Born," 50–51.
43 Kawash, "New Directions in Motherhood Stories," 28.
44 Hesse, "Escaping Liberty," 301.
45 Foreman, *Activist Sentiments*, 7.

46 Mullen, *Cracks Between What We Are*, 149.
47 Moten, *Black and Blur*, 68.
48 Mackey, *Splay Anthem*, 68.
49 Mackey, *Splay Anthem*, 55; Moten, "Blackness and Nothingness," 778.
50 Best and Hartman, "Fugitive Justice," 5.
51 Crawley, *Blackpentecostal Breath*, 5.
52 Weheliye, *Habeas Viscus*, 2.
53 Eve Tuck, "What Is Your Theory of Change These Days," https://reworlding.creativetime.org/TUCK.
54 Papadopoulos, Stephenson, and Tsianos, *Escape Routes*.
55 Derrida, "Signature, Event, Context," 18.
56 Foucault, "Ethics of the Concern," 282.
57 Sedgwick, *Tendencies*, 8.
58 Sedgwick, *Tendencies*, 3.
59 Weheliye, *Habeas Viscus*, 97.
60 Spillers, *Black, White, and in Color*, 206.
61 Scott, *Extravagant Abjection*, 8.
62 Weheliye, *Habeas Viscus*, 97.
63 Rohy, *Chances Are*, 139.
64 Rohy, *Chances Are*, 13.
65 Love, *Feeling Backward*, 13.
66 Such writing includes Sianne Ngai's attention to "negative affects" and their relationship to "obstructed agency" in *Ugly Feelings*, Elizabeth Freeman's articulation of "deep lez" aesthetics in *Time Binds*, and José Esteban Muñoz's animation of "negative sentiments" as a form of political refusal against the mandates of work and productivity in *Cruising Utopia*.
67 Eshun, "Motion Capture (Interview)," 175.
68 Eshun, "Further Considerations on Afrofuturism," 297. Emphasis mine.
69 Keeling, *Queer Times, Black Futures*, 62.
70 Jefferson, "The difference is fixed in nature," 100.
71 Wilderson, *Red, White & Black*, 139.
72 Wilderson, *Red, White & Black*, 27–28.
73 Wilderson, *Red, White & Black*, 27.
74 Wilderson, *Red, White & Black*, 27.
75 Olney, "I Was Born," 48.
76 Olney, "I Was Born," 49.
77 Olney, "I Was Born," 49.
78 Garrett, *Episodic Poetics*, 13.
79 Garrett, *Episodic Poetics*, 4.
80 Wilderson, *Red, White & Black*, 9.
81 Garrett, *Episodic Poetics*, 5.
82 McKittrick, *Demonic Grounds*, 3.
83 Crawley, *Blackpentecostal Breath*, 32.

84 Moten, "Knowledge of Freedom," 219.
85 "That there is an irreducible relationship between blackness, criminality and the aesthetic; that escape-in-confinement is a fundamental audio-visual motif for black expressive culture; that this motif is essential to modernity and to modernism in their broadest conceptions insofar as it instantiates a relationship between the history of race and the history of cinema. This complex of assertions revolves around the stilled, fugitive performance of a little girl." Moten, "Knowledge of Freedom," 217.
86 Moten, "Knowledge of Freedom," 217.
87 Moten, "Knowledge of Freedom," 242.
88 Moten, "Knowledge of Freedom," 243.
89 Keeling, *Queer Times, Black Futures*, xv.
90 Sedgwick, *Touching Feeling*, 68.

CHAPTER 1. THE REPETITIONS OF HENRY "BOX" BROWN

1 Lee, "Borrowed Speech," 679–706.
2 Ruggles, *Unboxing of Henry Brown*, 29.
3 Ruggles, *Unboxing of Henry Brown*, 125.
4 Brooks, *Bodies in Dissent*, 125.
5 Brooks, *Bodies in Dissent*, 121.
6 Brooks, *Bodies in Dissent*, 121.
7 Brooks, *Bodies in Dissent*, 103.
8 Wolff, "Passing beyond the Middle Passage," 27.
9 Douglass, *My Bondage and My Freedom*, 234. Emphasis mine.
10 Abbot, *Cambridge Introduction to Narrative*, 18.
11 Healy, "For N.Y.U., Tony Kushner Pulls Script from Drawer."
12 NYU's production of *The Henry Box Brown Play* premiered in the fall of 2010 and was revived for one show in the spring as part of a star-studded fundraiser for graduate acting scholarships. It is unclear if Kushner will revive his interest in Henry "Box" Brown either for a full production of the play or as an adaptation for a cable television series. In an interview with the *New York Times*, Kushner confessed that he was not done with the play: "I'll figure out what to do with it sometime soon. I do think I'll be working on it again." Healy, "For N.Y.U., Tony Kushner Pulls Script from Drawer."
13 Post-performance Q&A with Tony Kushner, Mark Wing-Davey, and Mary Schmidt-Campbell at the Graduate Acting Program at New York University Tisch School of the Arts, May 15, 2011.
14 Fielden, *Autobiography of Samuel Fielden*, 142.
15 Ruggles, *Unboxing of Henry Brown*, 151.
16 Brown, *Narrative of the Life of Henry Box Brown*, 98.
17 Brown, *Narrative of the Life of Henry Box Brown*, 99.
18 Gilbert, *American Vaudeville*, 4.

19 Brown, *Narrative of the Life of Henry Box Brown*, 123.
20 Kushner, *Henry Box Brown Play*, 1.
21 Kushner, *Henry Box Brown Play*, 1.
22 Kushner, *Henry Box Brown Play*, 1.
23 As Daphne Brooks explains, "critics often allude to Brown's 1849 narrative as a casebook study of the erasure of black subjectivity in the fugitive slave narrative genre. It is a text in which the slave's body is, in effect, buried and displaced by the voice of a white editor." It was not until 1851 in Manchester, England, that Brown was able to publish his own version of the story, *Narrative of the Life of Henry Box Brown, Written by Himself*. Brooks, *Bodies in Dissent*, 73.
24 Bond-Stockton, *Beautiful Bottom, Beautiful Shame*, 180.
25 Nyong'o, *Amalgamation Waltz*, 136.
26 Kushner, *Henry Box Brown Play*, 1.
27 Perry, *Radical Abolitionism*, 25.
28 Thoreau, *Civil Disobedience*, 275.
29 Perry, *Radical Abolitionism*, 24.
30 Kushner, *Henry Box Brown Play*, 14–15.
31 Kushner, *Henry Box Brown Play*, 10.
32 Kushner, *Henry Box Brown Play*, 82–83.
33 Kushner, *Angels in America*, 39.
34 Moten, *Black and Blur*, 243.
35 Hartman, *Scenes of Subjection*, 120.
36 Kushner, *Angels in America*, 237.
37 Moten, *In the Break*, 3.
38 Steindler, "Tony Kushner, the Art of Theater."
39 Brecht, "Alienation Effects in Chinese Acting," 98.
40 Brecht, "Alienation Effects in Chinese Acting," 98.
41 Brecht, "Alienation Effects in Chinese Acting," 98.
42 Benjamin, *Correspondence of Walter Benjamin*, 236.
43 Brooks, *Bodies in Dissent*, 5.
44 Brooks, *Bodies in Dissent*, 5.
45 Hartman, *Scenes of Subjection*, 19.
46 Hartman, *Scenes of Subjection*, 34.
47 Copeland, *Bound to Appear*, 113.
48 Copeland, *Bound to Appear*, 132.
49 Meyer, "Borrowed Voices: Glenn Ligon and the Force of Language."
50 Copeland, *Bound to Appear*, 138.
51 Copeland, *Bound to Appear*, 122.
52 Copeland, *Bound to Appear*, 9.
53 Hurston, *Mules and Men*, 3.
54 Browne, *Dark Matters*, 21.
55 Browne, *Dark Matters*, 21.

56 Hartman, *Scenes of Subjection*, 110–11.
57 Lepecki, *Exhausting Dance*, 13.
58 Cervenak, *Wandering*, 10.
59 Moten, *Black and Blur*, 58.
60 Freedman, "Disembarking."
61 Browne, *Dark Matters*, 68.
62 Brewer Ball, "Katherine Brewer Ball in Conversation with Wilmer Wilson IV."
63 A. Will Brown, "Wilmer Wilson IV: 'Moving between mediums is my way of remaining nimble.'" https://www.studiointernational.com/index.php/wilmer-wilson-iv-interview-keef-wulf-my-paper-bag-colored-heart.
64 Brown, "Wilmer Wilson IV: 'Moving between mediums is my way of remaining nimble.'"
65 Brewer Ball, "Katherine Brewer Ball in Conversation with Wilmer Wilson IV."
66 Brewer Ball, "Katherine Brewer Ball in Conversation with Wilmer Wilson IV."
67 Cervenak, *Wandering*, 14.
68 Brewer Ball, "Katherine Brewer Ball in Conversation with Wilmer Wilson IV."
69 Brewer Ball, "Katherine Brewer Ball in Conversation with Wilmer Wilson IV."
70 Howard, "(Afro) Future of Henry Box Brown."
71 Piepzna-Samarasinha, *Care Work*, 33.

CHAPTER 2. FEELING OUT OF THIS WORLD: THAT'S WHAT I GUESS THESE STORIES ARE ALL ABOUT

Epigraph 1: Díaz, *Brief Wondrous Life of Oscar Wao*, 81.
Epigraph 2: Derrida and Ronell, "Law of Genre," 57.
1 Imarisha, *Octavia's Brood*, 4.
2 Díaz, *Brief Wondrous Life of Oscar Wao*, 81.
3 Díaz, *Brief Wondrous Life of Oscar Wao*, 80.
4 Díaz, *Brief Wondrous Life of Oscar Wao*, 81.
5 Díaz, *Brief Wondrous Life of Oscar Wao*, 81.
6 Moten, "Taste Dissonance Flavor Escape," 242–43.
7 Radway, *Reading the Romance*, 95–96.
8 Radway, *Reading the Romance*, 97.
9 Adorno, "Culture Industry Reconsidered."
10 Marcuse, *Eros and Civilization*, 149.
11 Marcuse's student, Angela Davis, explains his work, saying, "Art criticizes and negates the existing social order by the power of its form, which in truth creates another universe, thus hinting at the possibility of building a new social order." Davis, "Marcuse's Legacies," 46.

12 Marcuse, "Some Remarks on Aragon Art," 214.
13 Díaz, *Brief Wondrous Life of Oscar Wao*, 79.
14 Díaz, *Brief Wondrous Life of Oscar Wao*, 173.
15 Díaz, *Brief Wondrous Life of Oscar Wao*, 268
16 Díaz, *Brief Wondrous Life of Oscar Wao*, 11.
17 Díaz, *Brief Wondrous Life of Oscar Wao*, 11.
18 Díaz, *Brief Wondrous Life of Oscar Wao*, 22.
19 Díaz, *Brief Wondrous Life of Oscar Wao*, 22.
20 Díaz, *Brief Wondrous Life of Oscar Wao*, 22.
21 Marquez, "Solitude of Latin America."
22 To be clear, when I say speculative fiction, I am talking about what Díaz calls "the more speculative genres." For Díaz, "genre" becomes shorthand for such speculative works that fall into and exceed the genre of science fiction and fantasy. These are works by authors such as J. R. R. Tolkien, Philip Pullman, Marion Zimmer Bradley, Phillip K. Dick, and George R. R. Martin. The category of speculative fiction also expands from traditional science fiction to include works by authors such as Haruki Murakami, Jonathan Lethem, Gabriel García Márquez, Toni Morrison, and William Shakespeare.
23 *Oxford English Dictionary*, s.v. "escapism (n.)."
24 *Oxford English Dictionary*, "escapism."
25 Halberstam. *The Queer Art of Failure*, 1.
26 Phillips, *Houdini's Bo*, 8.
27 Miller, "Preternatural Narration," 96.
28 Díaz. "Q&A: Junot Díaz."
29 Díaz, *Brief Wondrous Life of Oscar Wao*, 32.
30 Díaz, *Brief Wondrous Life of Oscar Wao*, 224.
31 In J. R. R. Tolkien's *The Lord of the Rings* (1954), Sauron is the evil ruler of the realm of Mordor. Sauron wants to take over all of Middle Earth and consolidate all the power into his own hands.
32 Díaz, *Brief Wondrous Life of Oscar Wao*, 1.
33 Díaz, *Brief Wondrous Life of Oscar Wao*, 224–25.
34 Díaz, *Brief Wondrous Life of Oscar Wao*, 7.
35 Díaz, *Brief Wondrous Life of Oscar Wao*, 7.
36 Díaz, *Brief Wondrous Life of Oscar Wao*, 185.
37 Díaz, *Brief Wondrous Life of Oscar Wao*, 6.
38 Williams, "Structure of Feelings," 132.
39 Díaz, *Brief Wondrous Life of Oscar Wao*, 1.
40 Díaz, *Brief Wondrous Life of Oscar Wao*, 2.
41 Parker and Sedgwick, "Performance and Performativity," 10.
42 Díaz, *Brief Wondrous Life of Oscar Wao*, 79–80.
43 Díaz, *Brief Wondrous Life of Oscar Wao*, 251.
44 In the footnotes, Díaz/Yunior writes: "I lived in Santo Domingo only until I

was nine, and even I knew criadas. Two of them lived in the callejéon behind our house, and these girls were the most demolished, overworked human beings I'd known at the time. One girl, Sobeida, did all the cooking, all the cleaning, fetched all the water, and took care of two infants for a family of *eight*—and chickie was only seven years old!" Díaz, *Brief Wondrous Life of Oscar Wao*, 253.

45 Díaz, *Brief Wondrous Life of Oscar Wao*, 78, 260.
46 Díaz, *Brief Wondrous Life of Oscar Wao*, 80.
47 Díaz, *Brief Wondrous Life of Oscar Wao*, 80.
48 Casid, *Sowing Empire*, xvii. Casid writes, "In her essay, hooks uses the term diaspora to refer historically to the Middle Passage, slavery, and forced transplantation from Africa to the Americas but also to connect diaspora to a particular notion of exile, exile as a contemporary critical process of crossing borders. While diaspora and exile suggest a displacement from home, here longing is at once the action of a long journey and a feeling of desire never extinguished by a destination object that takes the place of a homeland. Longing puts the engulfing distance back into 'diasporic' to reorient it from nostalgia to an active future making that hooks finds in the phototext work with the genre of landscape photography by the African American artist Carrie Mae Weems."
49 Casid, *Sowing Empire*, xvii.
50 Díaz, *Brief Wondrous Life of Oscar Wao*, 160.
51 Díaz, *Brief Wondrous Life of Oscar Wao*, 55.
52 Díaz, *Brief Wondrous Life of Oscar Wao*, 57.
53 Díaz, *Brief Wondrous Life of Oscar Wao*, 61.
54 Díaz, *Brief Wondrous Life of Oscar Wao*, 77.
55 Díaz, *Brief Wondrous Life of Oscar Wao*, 209.
56 Díaz, *Brief Wondrous Life of Oscar Wao*, 209.
57 Grossman, "Literary Revolution in the Supermarket Aisle."
58 Rieder, *Colonialism and the Emergence of Science Fiction*, 2.
59 Danticat, "Junot Díaz," 92.
60 Danticat, "Junot Díaz," 92.
61 Díaz, *Brief Wondrous Life of Oscar Wao*, 23.
62 "This performance of whiteness primarily transpires on an affective register. Acting white has everything to do with the performance of a particular affect, the specific performance of which grounds the subject performing white affect in a normative life world. Latinas and Latinos, and other people of color, are unable to achieve this affective performativity on a regular basis." Muñoz "Feeling Brown: Ethnicity and Affect," 61.
63 Muñoz, "Feeling Brown, Feeling Down," 677.
64 Winnicott, *Playing and Reality*, 129.
65 Díaz, *Brief Wondrous Life of Oscar Wao*, 21.

66 Díaz, *Brief Wondrous Life of Oscar Wao*, 49.
67 Díaz, *Brief Wondrous Life of Oscar Wao*, 49.
68 Díaz, *Brief Wondrous Life of Oscar Wao*, 170.
69 Díaz, *Brief Wondrous Life of Oscar Wao*, 185.
70 Díaz, *Brief Wondrous Life of Oscar Wao*, 180.
71 Reyes, *Embodied Economies*, 88.
72 Warner, *Trouble with Normal*, 35–36.
73 "Social Life? . . . Once a week he drove out to Woodbridge Mall and checked the RPGs at the Game Room, the comic books at Hero's World, the fantasy novels at Waldenbooks. The nerd circuit. Stared at the toothpick-thin blackgirl who worked at the Friendly's, whom he was in love with but with whom he would never speak." Díaz, *Brief Wondrous Life of Oscar Wao*, 266.
74 Muñoz, *Cruising Utopia*, 111.
75 Flatley, *Affective Mapping*, 13.
76 Stewart, *Ordinary Affects*, 3.
77 Williams, "Structures of Feeling," 134.
78 Williams, "Structures of Feeling," 134.
79 Flatley, *Affective Mapping*, 17.
80 Flatley, *Affective Mapping*, 17.
81 We might also make this argument for other forms of genre including, but not limited to, romance, detective stories, tales of the Wild West, and so on. The only difference would be that in each of these particular genres, the attendant feelings and their political import would vary according to attendant content, themes, and conventions that they bring with them.
82 Muñoz "Feeling Brown: Ethnicity and Affect," 72.
83 Muñoz "Feeling Brown: Ethnicity and Affect," 72.
84 Díaz, *Brief Wondrous Life of Oscar Wao*, 264–65.
85 Díaz, *Brief Wondrous Life of Oscar Wao*, 23.
86 Díaz, *Brief Wondrous Life of Oscar Wao*, 191.
87 Díaz, *Brief Wondrous Life of Oscar Wao*, 201.
88 Díaz, *Brief Wondrous Life of Oscar Wao*, 279.
89 Díaz, *Brief Wondrous Life of Oscar Wao*, 319.
90 Díaz, *Brief Wondrous Life of Oscar Wao*, 333.
91 Freud. "Creative Writers and Day-Dreaming," 422.
92 Freud, "Creative Writers and Day-Dreaming," 428.
93 Warmelink, Harteveld, and Mayer, "Press Enter or Escape to Play."
94 Díaz, "The Silence: The Legacy of Childhood Trauma," 72.
95 Díaz, "The Silence: The Legacy of Childhood Trauma," 72.
96 Leon, "Reconciling Rage and Compassion: The Unfolding #MeToo Moment for Junot Diaz."
97 Reyes, *Embodied Economies*, 88.
98 Smillie, "Radical Imagination," 11.

99 Smillie. "Radical Imagination," 24.
100 Muñoz, *Cruising Utopia*, 111.
101 Grossman, "Literary Revolution in the Supermarket Aisle."

CHAPTER 3. THE OPTICS OF ESCAPE:
PATTY HEARST THROUGH THE MOUTH OF SHARON HAYES

1 Mielke, "Transforming Captivity Narratives," 14.
2 Bercovitch, *Puritan Origins of the American Self*.
3 Slotkin, *Gunfighter Nation*, 649, 14.
4 Slotkin, *Gunfighter Nation*, 14–15.
5 Pearsall writes that SLA members would adopt markedly Black vocal inflections and language, which he claims were indicative of the SLA's "play-school tactic of 'let's pretend.'" Pearsall, *Symbionese Liberation Army*, 123. Elsewhere he calls these vocal performances by members such as Teko and Gelina "conscious projection[s] of emotional tones [through] counterfeited Black accents" (94).
6 Pearsall, *Symbionese Liberation Army*, 117.
7 Hearst, *Every Secret Thing*, 39, 100.
8 Hearst, *Every Secret Thing*, 97.
9 Pearsall, *Symbionese Liberation Army*, 106.
10 That Hearst was the only one prosecuted for the bank robbery and that she was tried before her kidnappers, Bill and Emily Harris, were tried for their witness-verified crime of abduction, indicated the priorities of the US government in prosecuting Hearst not just for the bank robbery—which the Harrises participated in as well—but more nearly for everything Hearst's abduction and defection to the SLA meant for the nation. In a 1997 interview with *Dateline*, Hearst said, "It's really shocking the way the case was presented. I mean no other people were prosecuted for that bank robbery except me, none of my kidnappers were charged or prosecuted. That is another thing that America has just accepted, like that's normal." Mankiewicz, "Kidnapped Heiress."
11 Moten, *In the Break*, 13–14.
12 After serving twenty-two months in prison, Hearst was released and eventually married her bodyguard and settled in the affluent suburbs of Connecticut. She has since appeared in five John Waters films: *Crybaby* (1990), *Serial Mom* (1994), *Pecker* (1998), *Cecil B. DeMented* (2000), and *A Dirty Shame* (2004). As Christopher Castiglia notes, "Waters chose Hearst to appear in his films, she reports, because he knew she could play a role without being any trouble. In treating Hearst like an obedient participant in any script he put before her, Waters used Hearst as much as the SLA or the FBI did, even while his deployment of the figure of Patty Hearst continues the subversive work of her autobiography." (*Bound and Determined*, 105). *The Radical Story of Patty Hearst* is

the title of the 2018 CNN miniseries based on Jeffrey Toobin's book, *American Heiress* (2016).
13 Sedgwick, *Touching Feeling*, 15.
14 US Government, *Symbionese Liberation*. Each member would adopt a new name for the revolution in an effort to relinquish times with their white "bourgeois" backgrounds; Hearst calls them their "reborn Swahili African names." The SLA drew from the rhetoric of the recently defunct East Bay Venceremos Organization, which the US government committee on internal security named "the most violent of the Maoist communist groups operating in the U.S. from 1971 until...1973"; Hearst, *Every Secret Thing*, 50.
15 Cumming and Sayles, *Symbionese Liberation Army and Patricia Hearst*, 491.
16 Hearst, *Every Secret Thing*, 77.
17 In "Did Anyone Ever Truly Decide?," Laura Tannenbaum discusses these two novels—*American Woman* by Susan Choi and *Trance* by Christopher Sorrentino—arguing that they extend the conversation on Hearst's kidnapping in complicated and insightful ways that haven't been seen in other postmodern academic analyses.
18 Pearsall, *Symbionese Liberation Army*, 58.
19 Chakrabarty, *Provincializing Europe*, 35.
20 Graebner, *Patty's Got a Gun*, 119.
21 Castiglia, *Bound and Determined*, 88.
22 Pearsall, *Symbionese Liberation Army*, 60.
23 Cumming and Sayles, *Symbionese Liberation Army and Patricia Hearst*, 492.
24 Pearsall, *Symbionese Liberation Army*, 123.
25 Pearsall, *Symbionese Liberation Army*, 94.
26 Toobin, *American Heiress*, 63.
27 Toobin, *American Heiress*, 37.
28 Stoever-Ackerman, "Splicing the Sonic Color-Line," 65.
29 Stoever-Ackerman, "Splicing the Sonic Color-Line," 66.
30 Rogin, "Blackface, White Noise," 419.
31 Lott, *Love and Theft*, 6.
32 Lott, *Love and Theft*, 7.
33 Hartman, *Scenes of Subjection*, 19.
34 Hartman, *Scenes of Subjection*, 20.
35 Pearsall, *Symbionese Liberation Army*, 16.
36 Castiglia, *Bound and Determined*, 4.
37 Mullen, *Cracks Between What We Are*, 244.
38 Donald DeFreeze's, aka Cinque's, voice explained, "The Symbionese Liberation Army is a federated union of military/political elements of many different liberation struggles, and of many different races. Our unified purpose is to liberate the oppressed people around the world in their struggle against fascist imperialism and the robbery of their freedom and homeland." Pearsall, *Symbionese Liberation Army*, 55.

39 Isenberg, "Not 'Anyone's Daughter,'" 649.
40 Pearsall, *Symbionese Liberation Army*, 59.
41 Dolar, *Voice and Nothing More*, 14.
42 Dolar, *Voice and Nothing More*, 17.
43 Dolar, *Voice and Nothing More*, 17.
44 Dolar, *Voice and Nothing More*, 20.
45 Pearsall writes, "Her voice was thin and strained, and it was immediately conjectured that she spoke under the influence of medical sedation or street drugs. Her discourse was also chopped into short sections by starting and stopping of the tape recorder." *Symbionese Liberation Army*, 58. In his effort to contextualize Hearst's message, we can see the confusion that he imagines she must have felt, the projection of chemical interference in Hearst's person that he finds evidenced in the sound of her voice. This interpretation of her voice brings our attention to the need to project the role of victim onto Hearst. Pearsall's interpretation marks her as both unable to fight back (through the infliction of force, drugs, etc.) and as unable to access her true self—a self that should automatically and intrinsically try to resist the captors and escape. For more on the various tape experts employed by the FBI, see "FBI Statement on Recording by Kidnapped Hearst"; and US Government, *Symbionese Liberation Army: A Study*.
46 Pearsall, *Symbionese Liberation Army*, 66. Emphasis added to illustrate Hearst's vocal inflections.
47 Pearsall, *Symbionese Liberation Army*, 66.
48 Hearst, *Every Secret Thing*, 58.
49 Hearst, *Every Secret Thing*, 58.
50 Pearsall, *Symbionese Liberation Army*, 67.
51 Hearst, *Every Secret Thing*, 100.
52 Hearst, *Every Secret Thing*, 99.
53 Pearsall, *Symbionese Liberation Army*, 90.
54 Pearsall, *Symbionese Liberation Army*, 97; Hearst, *Every Secret Thing*, 172.
55 Hearst, *Every Secret Thing*, 173.
56 In a 1997 interview, *Dateline*'s Dennis Murphy asked Hearst, "Patricia, the world is still divided into two camps of what happened to you. There is the one camp that says that the men became her lovers; what is your version about Willie Wolf (Cujo)? . . . It wasn't rape at first that then became a seduction and romance?" Hearst replies, "I think it's insulting to anyone whose [sic] ever been raped to suggest that that could turn into a seduction and a love affair afterward; it's outrageous." Castiglia, *Bound and Determined*, 97.
57 Pearsall, *Symbionese Liberation Army*, 116.
58 Pearsall, *Symbionese Liberation Army*, 115.
59 Pearsall, *Symbionese Liberation Army*, 117.
60 Pearsall, *Symbionese Liberation Army*, 117.

61 Graebner, *Patty's Got a Gun*, 7.
62 Graebner, *Patty's Got a Gun*, 161.
63 Graebner, *Patty's Got a Gun*, 41–43.
64 As William Graebner writes, "In contrast [to the weight of the Hearst name and the family home at San Simeon], the SLA offered Patty a variety of new, intense forms of identity." Graebner, *Patty's Got a Gun*, 128–29.
65 Young, "Missing Action," 55.
66 Young, "Missing Action," 52.
67 Young, "Missing Action," 55.
68 Haag, "Putting Your Body on the Line," 59.
69 Haag, "Putting Your Body on the Line," 60.
70 Frankel, "Exploring Ferenczi's Concept of Identification," 102.
71 Frankel, "Exploring Ferenczi's Concept of Identification," 61.
72 Chow, *Protestant Ethnic and the Spirit of Capitalism*, 107.
73 Sharon Hayes, interview with the author, Queens, NY, February 20, 2012.
74 Hayes, "Morning Session Keynote Address."
75 Hayes, "Morning Session Keynote Address."
76 Speaking in an interview about another project, Hayes asks, "What if queer studies didn't steer itself so intensely toward visibility but instead steered itself toward questions of speech? What if, following Gayatri Chakravorty Spivak, we were focused as much on hearing and speaking as on seeing?" Bryan-Wilson, *Sharon Hayes*, 90.
77 Austin, *How to Do Things with Words*, 16.
78 Felman, *Scandal of the Speaking Body*, 57.
79 Muñoz, *Cruising Utopia*, 154.
80 Sedgwick and Parker, *Performativity and Performance*, 5.
81 Isenberg, "Not 'Anyone's Daughter,'" 641.
82 Spivak, *A Critique of Postcolonial Reason*.
83 Sharon Hayes, interview with the author.
84 Dolar, *Voice and Nothing More*, 71.
85 "Full body quotation is a performance technique I've been working on, but the name could change as it evolves. The performer has a hidden audio source and she re-speaks voices mimetically—not just the text but tone, breath, accent, idiom, etc. The idea is to question authenticity and intention of the speaker, and understand content differently, out of its original context.... The full body quotation technique is a way to perform our ambivalences." Wyma, "I Dislike the Word Visibility."
86 Bryan-Wilson, *Sharon Hayes*, 28.
87 Lee, "Borrowed Speech," 702.
88 Bryan-Wilson, *Sharon Hayes*, 28.
89 Grant, "Peculiar Attunements," 569.
90 Willse, "Protest Event during Republican National Convention," 23.
91 Kessler, "Puppet Love," 71.

92 Bryan-Wilson, "We Have a Future," 35.
93 Hayes, "Certain Resemblances," 90.
94 As William Graebner speculates, "Had Patty been tried in 1965, she would surely have been acquitted, judged to be nothing more, nothing less than the unfortunate victim of kidnapping, rape and physical and mental torture. Had she been tried in 1985, she would surely have been convicted, steamrolled by the Reagan revolution, judged to be just another person who had failed to take personal responsibility for her acts. The moment of her conviction, in March 1976, was somewhere between, participating at once in a culture of the victim, grounded in experience and deeply felt, and an incipient culture of personal responsibility." Graebner, *Patty's Got a Gun*, 8.
95 Here, I am thinking about "survivance," a term articulated by Gerald Vizenor to mark both the survival and resistance of Native American narrative presence that happens against Native genocide and settler colonialism and continues to mark the representational erasure of Native American lives. See Vizenor, *Manifest Manners*, 15.

CHAPTER 4. "THIS FACE IS NOT FOR US": GROUNDING PLEASURE

1 Humphreys, *Tearoom Trade*, 68.
2 Delph, *Silent Community*, 90.
3 Delph, *Silent Community*, 91.
4 Scott, *Extravagant Abjection*, 8.
5 Musser, "Queering Sugar," 6.
6 *Oxford English Dictionary*, s.v. "glory hole (n.)," May 28, 2022.
7 *Oxford English Dictionary*, "glory hole."
8 Bapst, "Glory Holes and the Men Who Use Them," 90.
9 See George Chauncey's "Christian Brotherhood or Sexual Perversion? Homosexual Identities and the Construction of Sexual Boundaries in the World War One Era," in which Chauncey outlines the 1919 Naval investigation of homosexual activity in the "cottages" along Bellevue Avenue at the Newport (Rhode Island) Naval Training Station.
10 Humphreys, *Tearoom Trade*, 6.
11 As Michael Warner, Samuel R. Delany, Douglas Crimp, and others have articulated, gay male public sex culture is productive of a myriad of social and sexual values that cannot fully be named or traced or displayed in their fleeting interactions. See Bersani, *Homos*; Crimp, "Mourning and Militancy"; Delany, *Times Square Red*; Warner, *Trouble with Normal*.
12 Franke, "Public Sex, Same-Sex Marriage," 157.
13 Stranack, "Glory-Holes," 42.
14 With the prevalence of mobile phone applications such as Grindr and Manhunt, and internet "dating" sites from Match.com to OKCupid, it would seem that the nature, the virtual and physical space of "anonymous" sex,

has changed significantly from the heyday of the glory hole. Rogers, "Pines' Summer of Discontent."
15 Holmes, O'Byrne, and Murray, "Faceless Sex," 253.
16 Dean, *Beyond Sexuality*, 274.
17 Love, *Feeling Backwards*, 142.
18 Sedgwick, *Epistemology of the Closet*, 3.
19 Sedgwick, *Epistemology of the Closet*, 8.
20 Brown, *Closet Space*, 8.
21 Snorton, *Nobody Is Supposed to Know*, 17.
22 Snorton, *Nobody Is Supposed to Know*, 18.
23 Snorton, *Nobody Is Supposed to Know*, 22.
24 Pérez, *Taste for Brown Bodies*, 5.
25 Pérez, *Taste for Brown Bodies*, 106.
26 As Scott Lauria Morgensen writes: "Modern sexuality arose in the United States as crucial to a colonial society of normalization. The violent sexual regulation of Native peoples became a proving ground for forming settler subjects as agents and beneficiaries of modern sexuality." Morgensen, "Settler Homonationalism," 117.
27 Manalansan, "In the Shadows of Stonewall," 432.
28 Manalansan, "In the Shadows of Stonewall," 435.
29 Musser, "Queering Sugar," 7.
30 Musser, "Queering Sugar," 7.
31 Bersani, *Is the Rectum a Grave?*, 222.
32 Weiss, *Techniques of Pleasure*, 7.
33 Amin, *Disturbing Attachments*, 94.
34 Amin, *Disturbing Attachments*, 94–95.
35 Amin, *Disturbing Attachments*, 98.
36 Amin, *Disturbing Attachments*, 98.
37 Musser, "Queering Sugar," 97.
38 Crimp, *Our Kind of Movie*, 7.
39 Ligon, "A Feast if Scraps," 37.
40 Warren, "Onticide," 8.
41 Warren, "Onticide," 20.
42 Warren, "Onticide," 6.
43 Warren, "Onticide," 20.
44 bergman and Montgomery, *Joyful Militancy*, 49.
45 Coulthard and Simpson, "Grounded Normativity," 254.
46 Virno, *Multitude*, 114
47 Amin, *Disturbing Attachments*, 47.
48 Vaccaro, "Come to My Window."
49 Ross, "Beyond the Closet as Raceless Paradigm," 162.
50 Moten, *Black and Blur*, 73.
51 Moten, *Black and Blur*, 75.

52 Moten, *Black and Blur*, 69.
53 Zola, "Une nouvelle maniere en peinture, Edouard Manet."
54 Hartman, *Wayward Lives*, 27.
55 Moten, *Black and Blur*, 85.
56 Hartman, *Wayward Lives*, 27.
57 Hartman, *Wayward Lives*, 16–17.
58 Hartman, *Wayward Lives*, 17.
59 Hartman, *Wayward Lives*, 17.
60 Hartman, *Wayward Lives*, 349.
61 Hartman, "Venus in Two Acts," 4.
62 Burton, Stanley, and Tourmaline, *Trapdoor*, xiv.
63 Burton, Stanley, and Tourmaline, *Trapdoor*, xvii.
64 Burton, Stanley, and Tourmaline, *Trapdoor*, xxiii.
65 Musser, *Sensual Excess*, 11.
66 Musser, *Sensual Excess*, 15.
67 Musser, *Sensual Excess*, 9.
68 Musser, *Sensual Excess*, 3.
69 Repton, *Observations on the Theory and Practice of Landscape Gardening*, 180.
70 National Gallery of Art, "Pleasure Ground/Pleasure Garden."
71 Tourmaline, Hernandez, and Lax, "Pleasure Gardening with Tourmaline."
72 Katz, *Love Stories*.
73 Tourmaline, "American's Monuments Reimagined for a More Just Future."
74 Tourmaline, "American's Monuments Reimagined for a More Just Future."
75 Kaba quoted in Tourmaline, Hernandez, and Lax, "Pleasure Gardening with Tourmaline."
76 Tourmaline, Hernandez, and Lax, "Pleasure Gardening with Tourmaline."
77 Tourmaline, Hernandez, and Lax, "Pleasure Gardening with Tourmaline."
78 Tourmaline, Hernandez, and Lax, "Pleasure Gardening with Tourmaline."
79 Tourmaline, Hampshire College commencement keynote speech.
80 Hartman, *Wayward Lives*, 349.

CODA. LESS OF A THEATER AUDIENCE

Epigraph: Toshi Reagon, *Parable of the Sower*. New York Lincoln Center, 2017.
1 Rushdy, *Neo-Slave Narratives*, 3.
2 Butler, *Parable of the Sower*, 120.
3 Butler, *Parable of the Sower*, 287–88.
4 Guterres, "Debt Bondage."
5 The White House, "Report on the Impact of Climate Change Migration."
6 Segal, "Decades ago, Octavia Butler saw a "grim future" of climate denial and income inequality."
7 Butler, *Parable of the Sower*, 11.
8 Butler, *Parable of the Sower*, 12, 13.

9 Butler, *Parable of the Sower*, 300.
10 Hartman, *Scenes of Subjection*, 19.
11 Butler, *Parable of the Sower*, 3.
12 Butler, *Parable of the Sower*, 182.
13 Brown, *Emergent Strategy*, 23.
14 Brown, *Emergent Strategy*, 6.
15 Da Silva, "On Difference Without Separability," 64.
16 Da Silva, "On Difference Without Separability," 65.
17 Da Silva, "On Difference Without Separability," 63.
18 Brown, *Black Utopias*, 133.
19 Canavan, *Octavia E. Butler*, 145–56.
20 Brown, *Black Utopias*, 110.
21 Keeling, *Queer Times, Black Futures*, 68–69.
22 Canavan, *Octavia E. Butler*, 147.
23 Reagon, "Coalition Politics," 357.
24 Walsh, "Afro-pessimism and Friendship in South Africa," 76.
25 Luke 8:5 (King James Standard Version).

BIBLIOGRAPHY

Abbott, H. Porter. *The Cambridge Introduction to Narrative*. Cambridge: Cambridge University Press, 2002.
Adorno, Theodor. "Culture Industry Reconsidered." In *The Culture Industry: Selected Essays on Mass Culture*, edited by J. M. Bernstein. London: Routledge, 1991.
Alexander, Shana. *Anyone's Daughter: The Times and Trials of Patty Hearst*. New York: Viking Press, 1979.
American's Monuments Reimagined for a More Just Future." *T: New York Times Style Magazine*, August 24, 2020. https://www.nytimes.com/2020/08/2/t-magazine/confederate-monuments-reimagined-racism.html.
Amin, Kadji. *Disturbing Attachments: Genet, Modern Pederasty, and Queer History*. Durham, NC: Duke University Press, 2017.
Arthur, Marc. "Wu Tsang: Full Body Quotation." Review of *Full Body Quotation* performance, created by Wu Tsang, at the New Museum. Performa 11: Staging Ideas, 2011.
Austin, J. L. *How to Do Things with Words*. Cambridge, MA: Harvard University Press, 1975.
Bapst, Don. "Glory Holes and the Men Who Use Them." *Journal of Homosexuality* 41, no. 1 (October 12, 2008).
Barnhart, Robert. *Barnhart Concise Dictionary of Etymology*. New York: HarperCollins, 1995.
Barthes, Roland. *Camera Lucida: Reflections on Photography*. New York: Hill and Wang, 1981.

Benjamin, Walter. *The Correspondence of Walter Benjamin 1910–1940*. Edited and annotated by Gershom Scholem and Theodor W. Adorno. Chicago: University of Chicago Press, 1994.

Benjamin, Walter. *Illuminations: Essays, Aphorisms, Autobiographical Writing*. Translated by Harry Zohn. Edited by Hannah Arendt. New York: Harcourt Brace Jovanovich, 1978.

Bercovitch, Sacvan. *The Puritan Origins of the American Self*. New Haven, CT: Yale University Press, 1975.

bergman, carla, and Nick Montgomery. *Joyful Militancy: Building Thriving Resistance in Toxic Times*. Chico, CA: AK Press, 2017.

Berlant, Lauren. "Austerity, Precarity, Awkwardness." *Supervalent Thought* (blog), November 2011. https://supervalentthought.files.wordpress.com/2011/12/berlant-aaa-2011final.pdf.

Berlant, Lauren. *The Female Complaint: The Unfinished Business of Sentimentality in American Culture*. Durham, NC: Duke University Press, 2008.

Berlant, Lauren. "Intuitionists: History and the Affective Event." *American Literary History* 20, no. 4 (Winter 2008): 845–60.

Berlant, Lauren, and Dana Luciano. "Conversation: Lauren Berlant with Dana Luciano." *Social Text*, January 13, 2013. https://socialtextjournal.org/periscope_article/conversation-lauren-berlant-with-dana-luciano/.

Bersani, Leo. *Is the Rectum a Grave? and Other Essays*. Chicago: University of Chicago Press, 2009.

Best, Stephen. "Neither Lost nor Found: Slavery and the Visual Archive." *Representations* 113, no. 1 (Winter 2011): 150–63.

Best, Stephen, and Saidiya Hartman. "Fugitive Justice." *Representations* 92, no. 1 (2005): 1–15.

Bogues, Anthony. *Empire of Liberty: Power, Desire, and Freedom*. Lebanon, NH: Dartmouth College Press, 2010.

Bond-Stockton, Kathryn. *Beautiful Bottom, Beautiful Shame: Where "Black" Meets "Queer."* Durham, NC: Duke University Press, 2006.

Bradbury, Ray. "All Summer in a Day." *Magazine of Fantasy and Science Fiction* (March 1954): 1–4.

Brand, Dionne. *A Map to the Door of No Return: Notes to Belonging*. New York: Vintage Canada, 2012.

Brecht, Bertolt. "Alienation Effects in Chinese Acting." In *Brecht on Theatre: The Development of an Aesthetic*. 13th ed. New York: Hill and Wang, 1977.

Brewer Ball, Katherine. "Katherine Brewer Ball in Conversation with Wilmer Wilson IV." *Critical Correspondence*, February 18, 2019.

Brooks, Daphne. *Bodies in Dissent: Spectacular Performances of Race and Freedom*. Durham, NC: Duke University Press, 2006.

Brooks, Daphne. *The Great Escapes: Four Slave Narratives*. New York: Barnes & Noble Books, 2007.

Brooks, Gwendolyn. *Blacks*. Chicago: Third World Press, 2001.
brown, adrienne maree. *Emergent Strategy: Shaping Change, Changing Worlds*. Chico, CA: AK Press, 2017.
Brown, Henry Box. *Narrative of the Life of Henry Box Brown, Written by Himself*. Manchester: Lee and Glynn, 1851.
Brown, Jayna. *Black Utopias: Speculative Life and the Music of Other Worlds*. Durham, NC: Duke University Press, 2021.
Brown, Michael P. *Closet Space: Geographies of Metaphor from the Body to the Globe*. London: Routledge, 2000.
Browne, Simone. *Dark Matters: On the Surveillance of Blackness*. Durham, NC: Duke University Press, 2015.
Bryan-Wilson, Julia. *Sharon Hayes*. Edited by Julia Bryan Wilson, Lanka Tattersall, and Jeannine Tang. New York: Phaidon, 2018.
Bryan-Wilson, Julia. "We Have a Future: An Interview with Sharon Hayes." *Grey Room* 37 (Fall 2009): 78–93.
Bryant, Tisa. *Unexplained Presence*. Boston: Leon Works Press, 2007.
Burton, Johanna, Eric Stanley, and Tourmaline. *Trapdoor: Trans Cultural Production and the Politics of Visibility*. Cambridge, MA: MIT Press, 2017.
Butler, Octavia. *Parable of the Sower*. New York: Grand Central Publishing, 2019.
Canavan, Gerry. *Octavia E. Butler*. Urbana: University of Illinois Press, 2016.
Casid, Jill H. *Sowing Empire: Landscape and Colonization*. Minneapolis: University of Minnesota Press, 2004.
Castiglia, Christopher. *Bound and Determined: Captivity, Culture-Crossing, and White Womanhood from Mary Rowland to Patty Hearst*. Chicago: University of Chicago Press, 1996.
Cervenak, Sarah Jane. *Wandering: Philosophical Performances of Racial and Sexual Freedom*. Durham, NC: Duke University Press, 2014.
Chakrabarty, Dipesh. *Provincializing Europe: Postcolonial Thought and Historical Difference*. Princeton, NJ: Princeton University Press, 2007.
Choi, Susan, and Emily Woo Zeller. *American Woman: A Novel*. Ashland, OR: Blackstone Audio, 2019.
Chow, Rey. *The Protestant Ethnic and the Spirit of Capitalism*. New York: Columbia University Press, 2002.
Cooper, Thomas. "Purgatory of Suicides." In *The Poetical Works of Thomas Cooper*. London: Hodder and Stoughton, 1877.
Copeland, Huey. *Bound to Appear: Art, Slavery, and the Site of Blackness in Multicultural America*. Chicago: University of Chicago Press, 2013.
Copeland, Huey. "Glenn Ligon and Other Runaway Subjects." *Representations* 113, no. 1 (Winter 2011): 73–110.
Coulthard, Glen, and Leanne Betasamosake Simpson. "Grounded Normativity/Place-Based Solidarity." *American Quarterly* 68, no. 2 (June 2016): 249–55.
Crawley, Ashon. *Blackpentecostal Breath: The Aesthetics of Possibility (Commonalities)*. New York: American Literatures Initiative, 2016.

Crimp, Douglas. "Mourning and Militancy." *October* 51 (Winter 1989): 3–18.
Crimp, Douglas. *"Our Kind of Movie": The Films of Andy Warhol*. Cambridge, MA: MIT Press, 2014.
Cummings, Gregory, and Stephen Sayles. *The Symbionese Liberation Army and Patricia Hearst, Queen of the Revolution*. Temecula, CA: Great Oak Press, 2019.
Danticat, Edwidge. "Junot Díaz." *Bomb*. October 1, 2007.
da Silva, Denise Ferreira. "On Difference Without Separability." Exhibition catalogue of the 32nd São Paulo Art Biennial, "Incerteza viva" (Living Uncertainty), September 7–December 11, 2016.
Davis, Angela. *Freedom Is a Constant Struggle*. Chicago: Haymarket, 2016.
Davis, Angela Y. "Marcuse's Legacies." In *Herbert Marcuse: A Critical Reader*. London: Routledge, 2004.
Dean, Tim. *Beyond Sexuality*. Chicago: University of Chicago Press, 2000.
Delany, Samuel R. *Times Square Red, Times Square Blue*. New York: NYU Press, 2001.
de Leon, Aya. "Reconciling Rage and Compassion: The Unfolding #MeToo Moment for Junot Díaz." Aya de Leon (blog), May 5, 2018. https://ayadeleon.wordpress.com/2018/05/05/reconciling-rage-and-compassion-the-unfolding-metoo-moment-for-junot-diaz/.
Delph, Edward. *The Silent Community: Public Homosexual Encounters*. Newbury Park, CA: Sage Publications, 1978.
Dennis, Kelly. "Performance Art: History." Expanded and updated in *The Encyclopedia of Aesthetics*, edited by Michael Kelly. London: Oxford University Press, 2014.
Derrida, Jacques. "Signature, Event, Context." In *Limited Inc*. Evanston, IL: Northwestern University Press, 1977.
Derrida, Jacques, and Avital Ronell. "The Law of Genre." *Critical Inquiry* 7, no. 1 (1980): 55–81.
Díaz, Junot. *The Brief Wondrous Life of Oscar Wao*. London: Faber and Faber, 2008.
Díaz, Junot. "Q&A: Junot Díaz." *Nylon*, August 2021, n.p.
Díaz, Junot. "The Silence: The Legacy of Childhood Trauma." *New Yorker*, April 9, 2018. https://www.newyorker.com/magazine/2018/04/16/the-silence-the-legacy-of-childhood-trauma.
Dickinson, Emily. *The Complete Poems of Emily Dickinson*. Edited by Thomas H Johnson. Boston: Back Bay Books, 1976.
Dolar, Mladen. *A Voice and Nothing More*. Cambridge, MA: MIT Press, 2006.
Douglass, Frederick. *My Bondage and My Freedom*. New York: Miller, Orton and Mulligan, 1885.
Edelman, Lee. *No Future: Queer Theory and the Death Drive*. Durham, NC: Duke University Press, 2004.
Ellis, Havelock. "Sexual Inversion." In *Studies in the Psychology of Sex, Volume I*. Philadelphia: F. A. Davis, 1915.
Emad, Parvis, and Thomas Kalary. Translator's foreword to *Mindfulness* by Martin Heidegger. New York: Continuum International Publishing Group, 2006.

Eng, David. *The Feeling of Kinship: Queer Liberalism and the Racialization of Intimacy.* Durham, NC: Duke University Press, 2010.
Eshun, Kodwo. "Further Considerations on Afrofuturism." *New Centennial Review* 3, no. 2 (Summer 2003): 287–302.
Eshun, Kodwo. "Motion Capture (Interview)." In *More Brilliant Than the Sun: Adventures in Sonic Fiction*, 175–93. London: Quartet, 1998.
"FBI Statement on Recording by Kidnapped Hearst." Associated Press. AP Archive, February 16, 1974. http://www.aparchive.com/metadata/youtube/d1e8de38090d709c75ece72afdff5372.
Felman, Shoshana. *The Scandal of the Speaking Body: Don Juan with J. L. Austin, or Seduction in Two Languages.* Palo Alto, CA: Stanford University Press, 2002.
Fielden, Samuel. *Autobiography of Samuel Fielden.* Online Anarchist Archives of Pitzer College. Accessed September 2011. http://dwardmac.pitzer.edu/Anarchist_Archives/haymarket/Fielden.html.
Finnerty, Páraic. *Emily Dickinson's Shakespeare.* Amherst: University of Massachusetts Press, 2006.
Flatley, Jonathan. *Affective Mapping: Melancholia and the Politics of Modernism.* Cambridge, MA: Harvard University Press, 2008.
Foreman, P. Gabrielle. *Activist Sentiments: Reading Black Women in the Nineteenth Century.* Urbana: University of Illinois Press, 2009.
Foucault, Michael. "Ethics of the Concern for Self as a Practice of Freedom." *Ethics: Subjectivity and Truth.* New York: The New Press, 1997.
Franke, Katherine. "Public Sex, Same-Sex Marriage and the Afterlife of Homophobia." In *Petite Mort: Recollections of a Queer Public.* New York: Forever and Today, 2011.
Frankel, Jay. "Exploring Ferenczi's Concept of Identification with the Aggressor: Its Role in Trauma, Everyday Life, and the Therapeutic Relationship." *Psychoanalytic Dialogues* 12, no. 1 (2002): 101–39.
Freedman, Alex. "Disembarking: Christina Knight on 'Glenn Ligon: America.'" *Art:21* (blog), April 14, 2011. http://blog.art21.org/2011/04/14/disembarking-christina-knight-on-glenn-ligon-america/.
Freeman, Elizabeth. *Time Binds: Queer Temporalities, Queer Histories.* Durham, NC: Duke University Press, 2010.
Freud, Sigmund. "Creative Writers and Day-Dreaming." In *Criticism: The Major Statements.* Edited by Charles Kaplan, 419–28. New York: St. Martins, 1991.
Friedlander, Benjamin. "Auctions of the Mind: Emily Dickinson and Abolition." *Arizona Quarterly: A Journal of American Literature, Culture, and Theory* 54, no. 1 (Spring 1998): 1–26.
Garrett, Matthew. *Episodic Poetics.* Oxford: Oxford University Press, 2014.
Gates, Henry Louis, Jr.. Foreword to *Narrative of the Life of Henry Box Brown Written by Himself.* Oxford: Oxford University Press, 2002.
Gilbert, Douglas. *American Vaudeville: Its Life and Times.* New York: Dover Publications, 1963.

Goyal, Yogita. *Runaway Genres: The Global Afterlives of Slavery*. New York: NYU Press, 2019.

Graebner, William. *Patty's Got a Gun: Patricia Hearst in 1970s America*. Chicago: University of Chicago Press, 2015.

Grant, Roger Mathew. "Peculiar Attunements: Comic Opera and Enlightenment Mimesis." *Critical Inquiry* 43, no. 2 (Winter 2017): 550–69.

Grossman, Lev. "Literary Revolution in the Supermarket Aisle: Genre Fiction Is Disruptive Technology." *Time Magazine*, May 23, 2012. https://entertainment.time.com/2012/05/23/genre-fiction-is-disruptive-technology/.

Guterres, António. "Debt Bondage, Forced Labour, Sex Trafficking Continue Worldwide, Secretary-General Warns, Urging Stronger Action to End Modern Slavery, in International Day Message." Press release from UN Secretary General António Guterres, November 24, 2021. https://www.un.org/press/en/2021/sgsm21039.doc.htm.

Haag, Pamela. "Putting Your Body on the Line: The Question of Violence, Victims, and the Legacies of Second-Wave Feminism." *differences* 8, no. 2 (1996): 23–67.

Halberstam, Jack. *The Queer Art of Failure*. Durham, NC: Duke University Press, 2011.

Hartman, Saidiya. *Scenes of Subjection: Terror, Slavery, and Self-Making in Nineteenth Century America*. Oxford: Oxford University Press, 1997.

Hartman, Saidiya. "Venus in Two Acts." *Small Axe: A Caribbean Journal of Criticism* 12, no. 2 (2008): 1–14.

Hartman, Saidiya. *Wayward Lives, Beautiful Experiments: Intimate Histories of Social Upheaval*. New York: W. W. Norton, 2019.

Hartman, Saidiya. "Will Answer to the Name Glenn." In *Glenn Ligon: America*, edited by Scott Rothkopf, 35–45. New York: Whitney Museum of Art, 2011.

Hartnell, Anna. *Rewriting Exodus: American Futures from Du Bois to Obama*. London: Pluto Press, 2011.

Harvey, David. *A Brief History of Neoliberalism*. Oxford: Oxford University Press, 2007.

Hayes, Sharon. "Certain Resemblances: Notes on Performance, Event, and Political Images." In *On Horizons: a Critical Reader in Contemporary Art*, edited by Maria Hlavajova, Simon Sheikh, and Jill Winder, 84–99. Utrecht: BAK, basis voor actuele kunst, 2011.

Hayes, Sharon. "Morning Session Keynote Address." The Creative Time Summit: Revolutions in Public Practice. New York City, October 9, 2009.

Hayes, Sharon. *Symbionese Liberation Army (SLA) Screeds #13, 16, 20 & 29*. 2003. https://whitney.org/collection/works/39044.

Healy, Patrick. "For N.Y.U., Tony Kushner Pulls Script from Drawer." *New York Times*, October 6, 2010.

Hearst, Patricia Campbell, and Alvin Moscow. *Every Secret Thing*. New York: Doubleday, 1982.

Heidegger, Martin. *The Fundamental Concept of Metaphysics: World, Finitude, Solitude.* Bloomington: Indiana University Press, 1996.

Hesse, Barnor. "Escaping Liberty: Western Hegemony, Black Futility." *Political Theory* 42, no. 3 (2014) 288–313.

Hobbes, Thomas. "Leviathan." *Project Gutenberg,* accessed 1651. March 27, 2021. https://www.gutenberg.org/files/3207/3207-h/3207-h.htm.

Holland, Sharon Patricia. *The Erotic Life of Racism.* Durham, NC: Duke University Press, 2012.

Holmes, Dave, Patrick O'Byrne, and Stuart J. Murray. "Faceless Sex: Glory Holes and Sexual Assemblages." *Nursing Philosophy* 11, no. 4 (October 2010): 250–59.

Howard, Danielle A. D. "The (Afro) Future of Henry Box Brown." *TDR* 65, no. 3 (2021): 125–42. https://www.cambridge.org/core/journals/the-drama-review/article/abs/afro-future-of-henry-box-brown/A4838E69EBF4F44C9D492CF4AA7A3626.

Humphreys, Laud. *Tearoom Trade: Impersonal Sex in Public Places.* London: Routledge, 1975.

Hurston, Zora Neal. *Mules and Men.* New Dehli: Grapevine India, 2022.

Iles, Chrissie. "Document from FBI Files of Patty Hearst Kidnapping Case, 1974." In *Sharon Hayes: There's So Much I Want to Say to You.* Whitney Museum American Art. New Haven, CT: Yale University Press, 2012.

Imarisha, Walidah. Introduction to *Octavia's Brood.* Edited by adrienne maree brown, Walidah Imarisha, and Sheree Renee Thomas. Chico, CA: AK Press, 2015.

Isenberg, Nancy. "Not 'Anyone's Daughter': Patty Hearst and the Postmodern Legal Subject." *American Quarterly* 52, no. 4 (2000): 639–81.

Jefferson, Thomas. "The difference is fixed in nature." In *Race and the Enlightenment: A Reader,* edited by Emmanuel Chukwudi Eze. Hoboken, NJ: Wiley/Blackwell, [1781] 1997.

"Junot Díaz Wins MacArthur 'Genius Grant.'" *MIT News,* October 2, 2012. https://news.mit.edu/2012/macarthur-genius-winners-1002.

Kakutani, Michiko. "Travails of an Outcast." Review of *The Brief Wondrous Life of Oscar Wao* by Junot Díaz. *New York Times Book Review,* September 4, 2007.

Katz, Jonathan Ned. *Love Stories: Sex Between Men Before Homosexuality.* Chicago: University of Chicago Press, 2003.

Kawash, Samira. "New Directions in Motherhood Stories." *Signs: Journal of Women in Culture and Society* 36, no. 4 (2011): 969–1003.

Keeling, Kara. *Queer Times, Black Futures.* New York: NYU Press, 2019.

Kelly, Robin D.G. *Freedom Dreams: The Black Radical Imagination.* Boston: Beacon Press, 2002.

Kessler, Sarah. "Puppet Love: Documenting Ventriloquism in Nina Conti's Her Master's Voice." *Camera Obscura* 31, no. 2 (92): 61–91.

Kester, Grant. "The Sound of Breaking Glass, Part I: Spontaneity and Consciousness in Revolutionary Theory." *E-flux Journal*, no. 30 (December 2011). http://www.e-flux.com/journal/the-sound-of-breaking-glass-part-i-spontaneity-and-consciousness-in-revolutionary-theory/.

King James Bible. King James Bible Online. https://www.kingjamesbibleonline.org.

Konner, Jeremy, dir. *Drunk History*. 2013. Season 1, Episode 5, "San Francisco." Aired August 6, 2013, on Comedy Central. https://www.youtube.com/watch?v=N17n8yleZKY.

Kushner, Tony. *Angels in America: A Gay Fantasia on National Themes: Part One: Millennium Approaches, Part Two: Perestroika*. New York: Theater Communications Group, 1995.

Kushner, Tony. *The Henry Box Brown Play*. 1992. NYU draft, courtesy of Tony Kushner and Joyce Ketay at the Gersh Agency, 2010.

Lee, Summer Kim. "Borrowed Speech: Giving an Account of Another with Wu Tsang's Full Body Quotation." *ASAP/Journal* 6, no. 3 (September 2021): 679–706.

Lepecki, Andre. *Exhausting Dance: Performance and the Politics of Movement*. London: Routledge, 2006.

Levinas, Emmanuel. *On Escape: De l'evasion*. Palo Alto, CA: Stanford University Press, 2003.

Locke, John. *Two Treatises on Government*. North Clarendon, VT: Everyman Books, 1993.

Lott, Eric. *Love and Theft: Blackface Minstrelsy and the American Working Class*. Oxford: Oxford University Press, 2013.

Love, Heather. *Feeling Backward: Loss and the Politics of Queer History*. Cambridge, MA: Harvard University Press, 2009.

Macharia, Keguro. *Frottage: Frictions of Intimacy Across the Black Diaspora*. New York: NYU Press, 2019.

Mackey, Nathaniel. *Splay Anthem*. New York: New Directions, 2006.

Manalansan, Martin F. "In the Shadows of Stonewall: Examining Gay Transnational Politics and the Diasporic Dilemma." *GLQ: A Journal of Lesbian and Gay Studies* 2, no. 4 (1995): 425–38.

Mankiewicz, Josh. "Interview with Patricia Hearst." *NBC News*, July 25, 2009. http://www.msnbc.msn.com/id/32089504/ns/dateline_nbc-newsmakers/t/kidnapped-heiress-patty-hearst-story/#.T8dXR5lYv68.

Mankiewicz, Josh. *Dateline NBC*. Season 17, episode 62, "Kidnapped Heiress: The Patty Hearst Story." July 24, 2009.

Marcuse, Herbert. "The Affirmative Character of Culture." *Collected Papers of Herbert Marcuse*. Vol. 4, *Art and Liberation*, edited by Douglas Kellner. London: Routledge, 2007.

Marcuse, Herbert. *Eros and Civilization: A Philosophical Inquiry into Freud*. Boston: Beacon, 1974.

Marcuse, Herbert. "Some Remarks on Aragon Art and Politics in the Totalitar-

ian Era." In *Technology, War and Fascism*, edited by Douglas Kellner. London: Routledge, 1998.
Márquez, Gabriel García. "The Solitude of Latin America." Nobel Lecture, December 8, 1982. http://www.nobelprize.org/nobel_prizes/literature/laureates/1982/marquez-lecture.html.
Marriott, David. "Inventions of Existence: Sylvia Wynter, Frantz Fanon, Sociogeny, and 'the Damned.'" *CR: The New Centennial Review* 11, no. 3 (Winter 2011): 45–89.
McKittrick, Katherine. *Demonic Grounds: Black Women and the Cartographies of Struggle*. Minneapolis: University of Minnesota Press, 2006.
McKittrick, Katherine. *Sylvia Wynter: On Being Human as Praxis*. Durham, NC: Duke University Press, 2015.
Meyer, Richard. "Borrowed Voices: Glenn Ligon and the Force of Language." Accessed September 2011. https://queerculturalcenter.org/glen-ligon/.
Mielke, Laura. "Transforming Captivity Narratives in Kevin Willmott's 'The Only Good Indian' (2009)." *American Studies* 55, no. 1 (2016): 5–30.
Miller, D. A. *The Novel and the Police*. Berkeley: University of California Press, 1988.
Miller, T. S. "Preternatural Narration and the Lens of Genre Fiction in Junot Díaz's *The Brief Wondrous Life of Oscar Wao*." *Science Fiction Studies* 38, no. 1 (March 2012): 92–114.
Morgensen, Scott Lauria. "Settler Homonationalism: Theorizing Colonialism with Queer Modernities." *GLQ: A Journal of Lesbian and Gay Studies* 16, nos. 1–2 (2010): 105–31.
Morrison, Toni. *Playing in the Dark: Whiteness and the Literary Imagination*. New York: Vintage, 1993.
Moten, Fred. *Black and Blur*. Durham, NC: Duke University Press, 2017.
Moten, Fred. "Blackness and Nothingness (Mysticism in the Flesh)." *South Atlantic Quarterly* 112, no. 4 (2013): 737–80.
Moten, Fred. *In the Break: The Aesthetics of the Black Radical Tradition*. Minneapolis: University of Minnesota Press, 2003.
Moten, Fred. "Knowledge of Freedom." *CR: The New Centennial Review* 4, no. 2 (Fall 2004): 269–310.
Mullen, Harryette. *The Cracks Between What We Are and What We Are Supposed to Be: Essays and Interviews*. Tuscaloosa: University of Alabama Press, 2012.
Muñoz, José Esteban. *Cruising Utopia: The Then and There Culture of Queer Futurity*. New York: NYU Press, 2009.
Muñoz, José Esteban. "Feeling Brown: Ethnicity and Affect in Ricado Bracho's *The Sweetest Hangover (and Other STDs)*." *Theatre Journal* 52, no. 1 (March 2000): 67–79.
Muñoz, José Esteban. "Feeling Brown, Feeling Down: Latina Affect, the Performativity of Race, and the Depressive Position." *Signs: Journal of Women in Culture and Society* 31, no. 3 (Spring 2006): 675–88.

Muñoz, José Esteban. "Sharing Public Sex." In *Petite Mort: Recollections of a Queer Public*. New York: Forever and Today, 2011.

Muñoz, José Esteban. "2013 Feminist Theory Workshop Keynote Speaker José Esteban Muñoz." *Duke Women's Studies Channel*, May 8, 2013. https://www.youtube.com/watch?v=huGN866GnZE.

Musser, Amber. "Queering Sugar: Kara Walker's Sugar Sphinx and the Intractability of Black Female Sexuality." *Signs: Journal of Women in Culture and Society* 42, no. 1 (2016): 153–74.

Musser, Amber. *Sensual Excess: Queer Femininity and Brown Jouissance*. New York: NYU Press, 2018.

Nash, Jennifer Christine. "Black Anality." *GLQ* 20, no. 4 (2014): 439–60.

National Gallery of Art. "Pleasure Ground/Pleasure Garden." *The History of Early American Landscape Design*, accessed May 5, 2022. https://heald.nga.gov/mediawiki/index.php/Pleasure_ground/Pleasure_garden.

Newman, Richard. Introduction to *Narrative in the Life of Henry "Box" Brown*. New York: Oxford University Press, 2002.

Nyong'o, Tavia. *Afro-fabulations: The Queer Drama of Black Life*. New York: NYU Press, 2018.

Nyong'o, Tavia. *The Amalgamation Waltz: Race, Performance, and the Ruses of Memory*. Minneapolis: University of Minnesota Press, 2009.

O'Dell, Kathy. *Contract with the Skin: Masochism, Performance Art, and the 1970s*. Minneapolis: University of Minnesota Press, 1998.

Olney, James. "'I Was Born' Slave Narratives, Their Status as Autobiography and as Literature." *Callaloo*, no. 20 (Winter 1984): 43–73.

Papadopoulos, Dimitris, Niamh Stephenson, and Vassilis Tsianos. *Escape Routes: Control and Subversion in the 21st Century*. London: Pluto Press, 2008.

Patterson, Orlando, and David Scott. "The Paradox of Freedom." *Small Axe: A Caribbean Journal of Criticism* 17, no. 1 (2013): 96–242.

Pearsall, Robert Brainard. *The Symbionese Liberation Army: Documents and Communications*. Amsterdam: Rodopi, 1974.

Pérez, Hiram. *A Taste for Brown Bodies: Gay Modernity and Cosmopolitan Desire*. New York: NYU Press, 2015.

Perry, Lewis. *Radical Abolitionism*. Knoxville: University of Tennessee Press, 1995.

Phillips, Adam. *Houdini's Box: The Art of Escape*. New York: Pantheon Books, 2001.

Piepzna-Samarasinha, Leah Lakshmi. *Care Work: Dreaming Disability Justice*. Vancouver: Arsenal Pulp Press, 2018.

Post-performance Q&A with Tony Kushner, Mark Wing-Davey, and Mary Schmidt-Campbell at the Graduate Acting Program at New York University Tisch School of the Arts, May 15, 2011.

Proudhon, Pierre-Joseph. *What Is Property?: An Inquiry into the Principle of Right and of Government*. Accessed November 2011. http://archive.org/details/whatisproperty00360gut.

Puar, Jasbir. Terrorist *Assemblages: Homonationalism in Queer Times*. Durham, NC: Duke University Press, 2007.

Quijano, Anibal, and Immanuel Wallerstein. "Americanity as a Concept, or the Americas in the Modern World-System." *International Journal of Social Sciences* 134 (1992): 549–57.

"The Radical Story of Patty Hearst." *CNN*, February 11, 2018. https://www.cnn.com/shows/radical-story-patty-hearst.

Radway, Janice. *Reading the Romance: Women, Patriarchy, and Popular Literature*. Chapel Hill: University of North Carolina Press, 2009.

Reagon, Bernice Johnson. "Coalition Politics: Turning the Century." In *Home Girl: A Black Feminist Anthology*, edited by Barbara Smith, 355–68. New York: Kitchen Table: Women of Color Press, 1983.

Repton, Humphry. *Observations on the Theory and Practice of Landscape Gardening*. London: T. Bensley, 1803.

Reyes, Israel. *Embodied Economies: Diaspora and Transcultural Capital in Latinx Caribbean Fiction and Literature*. New Brunswick, NJ: Rutgers University Press, 2022.

Rieder, John. *Colonialism and the Emergence of Science Fiction*. Middletown, CT: Wesleyan University Press, 2013.

Rogin, Michael. "Blackface, White Noise: The Jewish Jazz Singer Finds His Voice." *Critical Inquiry* 18, no. 3 (Spring 1992): 417–53.

Rohy, Valerie. *Chances Are: Contingency, Queer Theory and American Literature*. London: Routledge, 2019.

Ross, Marlon B. "Beyond the Closet as Raceless Paradigm." In *Black Queer Studies: A Critical Anthology*. Edited by Patrick Johnson and Mae Henderson, 161–89. Durham, NC: Duke University Press, 2005.

Ruggles, Jeffrey. *The Unboxing of Henry Brown*. Richmond: Library of Virginia, 2003.

Rushdy, Ashraf. *Neo-Slave Narratives: Studies in the Social Logic of a Literary Form*. Oxford: Oxford University Press, 1999.

Schrader, Paul, dir. *Patty Hearst*. Artistic Entertainment Group. September 23, 1988. 108 minutes.

Scott, Darieck B. *Extravagant Abjection: Blackness, Power, and Sexuality in the African American Literary Imagination*. New York: NYU Press, 2010.

Sedgwick, Eve Kosofsky. *Epistemology of the Closet*. Oakland: University of California Press, 1990.

Sedgwick, Eve Kosofsky. *Tendencies*. Durham, NC: Duke University Press, 1993.

Sedgwick, Eve Kosofsky. *Touching Feeling: Affect, Pedagogy, Performativity*. Durham, NC: Duke University Press, 2003.

Sedgwick, Eve Kosofsky, and Andrew Parker. *Performativity and Performance*. Abingdon: Routledge, 1996.

Segal, Corrine. "Decades Ago, Octavia Butler Saw a "Grim Future" of Climate Denial and Income Inequality." *Literary Hub*, June 23, 2020. https://lithub.com/decades-ago-octavia-butler-saw-a-grim-future-of-climate-denial-and-income-inequality/.

Shakespeare, William. *Othello*. Arden Shakespeare. 3rd ed. Edited by E. A. J. Honigmann. London: Bloomsbury, 1996.
Slotkin, Richard. *Gunfighter Nation: Myth of the Frontier in Twentieth-Century America*. Norman: University of Oklahoma Press, 1998.
Smillie, Tuesday. "Radical Imagination, Autocritique, and Accountability: Ursula K. Le Guin's Construction of Gethen and the Modelling of Creative Practice as a Radical Tool." In *Seized by the Left Hand*. Dundee: Dundee Contemporary Arts, 2020.
Smith, Valerie. "'Loopholes of Retreat': Architecture and Ideology in Harriet Jacobs' *Incidents in the Life of a Slave Girl*." In *Reading Black, Reading Feminist: A Critical Anthology*, edited by Henry Louis Gates Jr., 128–37. New York: Penguin Books, 1990.
Snorton, C. Riley. *Nobody Is Supposed to Know: Black Sexuality on the Down Low*. Minneapolis: University of Minnesota Press, 2014.
Spillers, Hortense. *Black, White, and in Color: Essays on American Literature and Culture*. Chicago: University of Chicago Press, 2003.
Spivak, Gayatri Chakravorty. "Can the Subaltern Speak?" In *Marxism and the Interpretation of Culture*. Edited by Cary Nelson and Lawrence Grossberg, 271–313. Urbana: University of Illinois Press, 1988.
Steindler, Catherine. "Tony Kushner, the Art of Theater." *Paris Review*, no. 201 (Summer 2012).
Stewart, Kathleen. *Ordinary Affects*. Durham, NC: Duke University Press, 2007.
Stoever-Ackerman, Jennifer. "Splicing the Sonic Color-Line: Tony Schwartz Remixes Postwar Nueva York." *Social Text* 28, no. 1 (102) (Spring 2010): 59–85.
Stranack, John. "Glory-Holes." *Christopher Street* 2, no. 1 (1977): 41–44.
Strong, Pauline Turner. *Captive Selves, Captivating Others: The Politics and Poetics of Colonical American Captivity Narratives*. London: Routledge, 2000.
Tannenbaum, Laura. "'Did Anyone Ever Truly Decide?': Rereading Cultural Feminism through the Patty Hearst Case." *The Sixties: A Journal of History, Politics, and Culture* 3, no. 2 (2010): 207–23.
Thoreau, Henry David. *Civil Disobedience and Other Essays*. New York: Dover Publications, 1849.
Tolkien, J. R. R. *The Lord of the Rings*. New York: HarperCollins, 1991.
Toobin, Jeffrey. *American Heiress: The Wild Saga of the Kidnapping, Crimes and Trial of Patty Hearst*. New York: Anchor, 2016.
Tourmaline. "American's Monuments Reimagined for a More Just Future." *T: The New York Times Style Magazine*, August 24, 2020. https://www.nytimes.com/2020/08/24/t-magazine/confederate-monuments-reimagined-racism.html.
Tourmaline. Hampshire College commencement keynote speech, Hampshire College, May 2016. https://www.youtube.com/watch?v=6fwrJjkxEec.
Tourmaline. "Making a Way Out of No Way." Keynote address at the Scholar and

Feminist Conference 41: Sustainabilities, February 27, 2016. https://vimeo.com/157653800.

Tourmaline, Arlette Hernandez, and Tomas Jean Lax. "Pleasure Gardening with Tourmaline." *Museum of Modern Art*, accessed May 5, 2022. https://www.moma.org/magazine/articles/576.

United Nations High Commissioner for Refugees (UNHCR). "The State of the World's Refugees 1993: The Challenge of Protection." Accessed May 18, 2022. https://www.unhcr.org/en-us/publications/sowr/4a4c6da96/state-worlds-refugees-1993-challenge-protection.html#:~:text=By%201993%2C%2018.2%20million%20men,displaced%20within%20their%20own%20countries..

Vaccaro, Jeanne. "Come to My Window." *Bomb*, June 24, 2021. https://bombmagazine.org/articles/come-to-my-window/.

Virno, Paolo. *Multitude: Between Innovation and Negation*. Los Angeles: Semiotext(e), 2008.

Vizenor, Gerald Robert. *Manifest Manners: Postindian Warriors of Survivance*. Middletown, CT: Wesleyan University Press, 1994.

Walsh, Shannon. "Afro-pessimism and Friendship in South Africa." In *Ties That Bind: Race and the Politics of Friendship in South Africa*, edited by Shannon Walsh and Jon Soske, 70–99. Johannesburg: Wits University Press, 2016.

Warmelink, Harald, Casper Harteveld, and Igor Mayer. "Press Enter or Escape to Play: Deconstructing Escapism in Multiplayer Gaming." In *Breaking New Ground: Innovation in Games, Play, Practice and Theory: Proceedings of DiGRA 2009*, 1–9. Digital Games Research Association conference, Brunel University, London, September 1–4, 2009.

Warner, Michael. *The Trouble with Normal: Sex, Politics, and the Ethics of Queer Life*. Cambridge, MA: Harvard University Press, 1999.

Warren, Calvin. "Onticide: Afropessimism, Queer Theory, & Ethics." *Ill Will*, November 18, 2014. https://illwill.com/onticide-afropessimism-queer-theory-and-ethics.

Waters, John, dir. 1977. *Desperate Living*. Dreamland Production. 90 minutes.

Weheliye, Alexander. *Habeas Viscus: Racializing Assemblages, Biopolitics, and Black Feminist Theories of the Human*. Durham, NC: Duke University Press, 2014.

Weiss, Margot. *Techniques of Pleasure: BDSM and the Circuits of Sexuality*. Durham, NC: Duke University Press, 2011.

Wilderson, Frank. *Red, White & Black: Cinema and the Structure of U.S. Antagonisms*. Durham, NC: Duke University Press, 2010.

Williams, Raymond. "Structure of Feelings." In *Marxism and Literature*. Oxford: Oxford University Press, 1977.

Willse, Craig. "Protest Event during Republican National Convention, New York, August 30, 2004." In *Sharon Hayes: There's So Much I Want to Say to You*, edited by Sharon Hayes, 14. New Haven, CT: Yale University Press, 2012.

Wilson, Robert Anton. Preface to *Semiotext(e)* SF. Edited by Rudy Rucker, Peter Lamborn Wilson, and Robert Anton Wilson. Los Angeles: Semiotext(e), 1989.

Winnicott, D. W. *Playing and Reality*. London: Routledge, 2005.

Wolff, Cynthia Griffin. "Passing beyond the Middle Passage: Henry 'Box' Brown's Translations of Slavery." *Massachusetts Review* 37, no. 1 (Spring 1996): 23–44.

Wyma, Chloe. "'I Dislike the Word Visibility': Wu Tsang on Sexuality, Creativity, and Conquering New York's Museums." Blouin Artinfo, March 2, 2012.

Wynter, Sylvia. "Unsettling the Coloniality of Being/Power/Truth/Freedom: Towards the Human, After Man, Its Overrepresentation—An Argument." *CR: The New Centennial Review* 3, no. 3 (2003): 257–337.

Young, Charles. "Missing Action: POW Films, Brainwashing and the Korean War, 1954–1968." *Historical Journal of Film, Radio and Television* 18, no. 1 (1998): 49–74.

INDEX

Page numbers in italics refer to illunstrations.

Abbott, H. Porter, 36
abjection, 21, 75, 87–88, 118
abolition, 2–6, 13–15, 107, 154; and anarchy, 40–41, 44, 46, 64; "black abolitionist escape art," 34; Black suffering as focus of, 107; Brown's performances on lecture circuit, 27, 32–38. *See also* (anti)slave narratives
Adorno, Theodor, 71
aesthesis, 64
aesthetic, the, 172n85; alienating function of, 71–72; and politics, 11–12, 36, 69; radical potential of, 25
affect, 171n66; and emotion, 88–89; impoverished white as norm, 84, 89, 90; racially marked, 84–85; reader expectations for genre categories, 85, 94, 130; as relational and transformative, 88–89; in speculative fiction, 69. *See also* genre affect/feeling of escape
affirmative culture, 71–72
African American Girl Nude, Reclining on a Couch (Eakins), 147–48

Afrofuturism, 21–22, 64, 165. *See also* speculative genres
Afropessimism, 22–23, 151
Aiken, George, 39
Alcatraz Prison, 80
Alexander, Shana, 104
alienation, 44–45, 56, 71–72, 88; afro-alienation, 45
All Summer in a Day (Bradbury), 90
amanuensis, white, 15, 27, 39–40, 52–53
Amin, Kadji, 140
anarchy, 36, 37, 65; and abolition, 40–41, 44, 46, 64; ideals of, 40–41, 45–46; proto-anarchists, 40, 45
angel of history, 43
Angels in America (Kushner), 37, 43–44
anonymity, 131–33; as liberating, 135–36; "faceless sex," 135, 136
(anti)slave narratives, 5, 7; amanuensis and narrator dyad, 15–16, 27, 39–40, 52–53; as abolitionist master narrative, 13–14; autobiographical form of, 6, 13–14, 17, 23–24, 27, 109;

(anti)slave narratives (*continued*)
centrality of literacy to, 13–14; complicity of white reader in, 93; erasure of Black subject in, 53, 173n23; exposition as escape in, 14–15; framing devices, 23–25, 50, 53–54; frontispieces, 52–53, *54*; lack of memory in, 23–24; pleas for acceptance and authenticity on title page, 54–55; and plot, 55–56; sentimental novel grafted onto, 108–9

anti-Blackness, 3, 26; Afropessimist framework, 22–23; and Brown's story, 41, 43, 46, 49, 55; in closet metaphors, 138; demand for life beyond, 19; escape from, 3–4; global, 3, 7, 23; woven into narrative possibilities, 24

antiportraiture, 51, 61, 63

Antwon Fisher (film), 22

archive, 147–48, 154–55; Butler's, 165–66; in Díaz's work, 92; in Ligon's work, 53, 55; in Wilson's work, 61–64, 142–43

arrival, 6, 7, 81, 137, 159, 164

art institutions, racialized genre demands of, 49, 55, 56

Atwood, Angela "Gelina" (SLA member), 101, 105, 112–13

audience: and alienation effect, 44–45; bourgeois private self, 103–4; choice of genre, 70–71; complicity in violence, 93; coproduction of storytelling by, 29; on DC streets, 56–57; deferred, 103–4; of *To Disembark*, 48; durational performance, responses to, 58–59; expectations and brainwashing explanation, 115; expectations for genre categories, 85, 94; expectations for private self's disclosures, 103–4; female, of captivity narratives, 108; female romance readers, 71; and *Henry Box Brown Play*, 38, 39, 42; onstage and "real," 39; and *Parable of the Sower*, 159, 166; participation in corrections of Hayes, 98, 121; responsibility of, 44–45, 47, 65, 126; for speculative genres, 68; subaltern or minoritarian, 58; white, recentering of, 46–47, 55, 64

Austin, J. L., 18, 78, 120

autobiography: as form of (anti)slave narrative, 6, 13–14, 17, 23–24, 27, 109; Hearst's, 102, 107, 111–12; and historical conditions, 120

Bass, Math, 131
Bassichis, Morgan, 3
Benjamin, Walter, 43, 45, 71
bergman, carla, 10, 11, 144
Berlant, Lauren, 8, 169–70n17
Bersani, Leo, 139
Best, Stephen, 16
Beyond Sexuality (Dean), 136
Black aesthetic tradition, 2, 15–16, 75
Black Cultural Association, 101
blackface minstrel shows, 38–39, 46, 106
Blackness: co-constitutive with queerness, 20; as criminality, 14, 19, 100, 105, 113, 147, 172n85; evacuation of sentience, 14, 46, 107; as illicit alternative capacity to desire, 16; as "impossible possibility," 22; as inappropriate, 10–11; as ontological impossibility, 22–23, 143; paradigmatic understanding of, 22–24; produced as sexual history, 133; proximal, 100; as a thing of the past, 68; transatlantic cultural constructions of, 45

Black studies, 2, 7, 9, 16, 26, 133–34
Bloch, Ernst, 4, 71
Blowjob (Warhol), 141–42, *142*
body: absence of, 48, 51, 111; asymmetry of voice with, 100, 122; care as interdependence, 65; film of, 57; "full body quotation," 31, 119, 123, 181n85; individual bodily perseverance, 111; opaque, 62–63

body, Black: theatrical mastery of, 34; as tool of defiance, 34; white appropriation of in blackface minstrelsy, 106; white investiture in, 106

Bogues, Anthony, 10–11, 170n29
Bond-Stockton, Kathryn, 40
Boucicault, Dion, 39
Bound & Determined (Castiglia), 107
bourgeois private self, 103–4
Boyarin, Jonathan, 107
Bradbury, Ray, 90

Bradford, William, 5
brainwashing, 101, 115–17; aggressor, identification with, 118, 126; national fear of, 116–17; Stockholm syndrome, 115, 118, 126
Brand, Dionne, 2
Brecht, Bertolt, 44–45, 72, 123
The Brief Wondrous Life of Oscar Wao (Díaz), 16, 27–28, 72–95; footnotes, 76; fukú curse in, 77–79; genre affect and racialization in, 83–95; historical narration in, 69–70; history of the Americas in, 72–83; multiplicity of perspectives in, 76; outsider status in, 73, 85; queer sensibility in, 69, 73, 87–88, 91; as realist fiction, 73; zafa counterspell in, 78–79
Brody, Nancy Brooks, 146
Brooks, Daphne, 13, 34, 45, 173n23
Brooks, Gwendolyn, 36
brown, adrienne marie, 68, 157, 164
Brown, Henry "Box," 13, 31–66, 74; box, focus on by artists and writers, 49–50; children's books and animations, 33; Douglass's criticism of, 35; escape narrative connected to white supremacy and systemic inequality, 43, 46; escape of as anarchy, 41; as escapologist, 33–34; frame of escape, 64–66; Fugitive Slave Act of 1850 forces exile, 32; in Great Blacks in Wax Museum, 64; as magician, 34, 44–45, 50; *Mirror of Slavery* touring show, 32, 37; performances on abolitionist lecture circuit, 27, 32–38; as protoanarchist, 45; as spiritualist performer, 45, 50; transcribed by white amanuensis, 27, 39–40. *See also To Disembark* (Ligon); *The Henry Box Brown Play: Political-Historical-Doggerel-Vaudeville* (Kushner)
Brown, Jayna, 38, 165
Brown, Michael P., 137–38
Brown, William Wells, 13
Browne, Simone, 52, 61, 64
"brown jouissance," 151–52
Bryan-Wilson, Julia, 123
burlesque, 38
Burton, Johanna, 149
Butler, Octavia E., 17, 29; Works: Earthseed: *The Books of the Living*, 164, 165; *Imago*, 165; *Kindred*, 159; *Parable of the Talents*, 165; *Parable of the Trickster*, 165–66; *Parables* series, 159, 166; *Patternist* series, 165; *Wildseed*, 159. *See also Parable of the Sower* (Butler)

camera obscura, 131
"Can the Subaltern Speak?" (Spivak), 121
cape metaphor, 5, 139, 145, 147, 150–51; dark sousveillance of, 63
capital: critique of, 41, 44, 49, 71–72; history of in Americas, 28, 69, 73; racial, horrors of, 38
capitalism: affective tonalities of, 84; breakdown between person and property, 49–50; individualist logics of, 155
capital-oriented performance principle, 71–72
captivity narratives, 5; altered script in Hearst's story, 99; founding myth of, 97; Hearst's infidelity to, 100, 107, 126; as justification for Indigenous extermination, 107–8; Rowlandson's, 5, 97, 99; whiteness shocked by, 97. *See also* Hearst, Patty
capture: Afrofuturism as counter to, 68; grammar of, 3; as inner trial, 117; white traditions of, 46
care: escape as turn inward and away, 34; as interdependence, 65; protection from visibility, 61–63, 65–66; reader's experience of, 71; theories of, 36; white framing replaced with, 64–65
care-filled surfaces, 34
Casid, Jill, 81, 176n48
Castiglia, Christopher, 104, 107, 113, 178n12
Cervenak, Sarah Jane, 11, 55, 63
Chakrabarty, Dipesh, 103
change: collective experience of, 165–66; desire for, 65, 70; escape as genre of, 3, 4, 7–8, 10, 16–18, 29, 65, 67, 69, 72, 128, 166; in *Parable of the Sower*, 164; progressive theories of, 17
Chaucer, 5
Chow, Rey, 119
Christopher Street Magazine, 134
Citron, Matt, 37

civil rights movement, 98, 101, 154
"claustrophillia," 147
closet, theorizations of, 137–39, 146–47
code switching, 77
coercive mimeticism, 119
collective, 8–9, 34, 127–28; experience of change, 165–66; and genre, 65, 88–90; and music, 158; state, escape from, 57–58, 65–66
Colón, Cristóbal, 73, 77
colonialism, 183n26; fukú curse born in Dominican colonization, 77–78; identitarian categories of, 9; imagination shaped by logics of, 68; libidinal economies of, 93; moment of, 73; "nigh unbearable historical experiences" of, 28, 69, 83–84; queer modernity shaped by, 134, 138–39; science fiction influenced by, 83; sexuality and histories of white supremacy, 133–34
color line, permeability of, 106
commonsense logics, 2, 7, 10–12, 22, 29, 100, 170n24
confession, 111, 116–17, 125, 164; homosexual, 135, 137; theater of, 103–4
configurational, the, 23
Confusion of Tongues Between Adults and the Child (Ferenczi), 118
"consciousness-raising" rhetoric, 114
conservatism, rise of, 161
containment, 51, 56, 131, 134, 139
containment logics, 51, 56–57, 134, 139
Cooper, T., 134
Copeland, Cynthia, 154
Copeland, Huey, 47, 51, 63
Coulthard, Glen, 144
Craft, Ellen, 35
Craven, Wes, 145
Crawley, Ashon T., 4, 5, 25
criminality, Blackness as, 14, 19, 147, 172n85; in Hearst's screeds, 100, 105, 113
Crimp, Douglas, 141–42, 151

dark sousveillance, 52, 61–62
Dash, Julie, 162
Davis, Angela, 174n11
debt bondage, 160–61

decolonization, 2, 68
Defreeze, Donald "Cinque Mtume" (SLA member), 101, 105, 106
Delph, Edward, 132
Derrida, Jacques, 18, 67
desire: for change, 65, 70; for escape, 3–4, 74–76, 80–81, 134; queer, 21, 139
Desperate Living (film), 144–45
Diamond, Elin, 45
diaspora, 69, 73–76, 176n48; abjection of, 75; as futurist project, 81; and performative utterances, 79
Díaz, Junot, 16, 27–28; "more speculative genres, 27, 175n22; pressure on to adopt one discourse, 76–77; queer sensibility in writing of, 87–88; sexual violence, accusations and experience of, 68, 92–93; *This is How You Lose Her*, 90
Dickinson, Emily, 1–3, 5, 15, 100
distancing effect, 72
doggerel genre, 38–39, 42
Dolar, Mladen, 109, 122
Dominican Republic, 69; Antihaitianismo, 77; Trujillo dictatorship, 69, 73, 77–79
Douglass, Frederick, 2, 5, 13; criticism of "Box" Brown's narrative, 35, 56; *My Bondage, My Freedom*, 35

Eakins, Thomas, 147–48
Earthseed: The Books of the Living (Butler), 164, 165
Edelman, Lee, 140
El Paso Wrecking Corp (film), 131
Emergent Strategy (brown), 164
empathy: as evacuation of Black sentience, 107; hyperempathy, 157, 163; in *Parable of the Sower*, 163; precariousness of, 46, 163; second-wave feminism emphasis on, 117
Empire of Liberty (Bogues), 10–11
enclosure, 4, 5, 158; affective textures of, 69; anti-Black fantasy of, 25; and Enlightenment thought, 7, 11; ontological, 26; queer architectures of, 131; and structure of closet, 138, 139; whiteness as not limited by, 143, 147

engagement, 13, 26–27, 49, 52–53, 63, 65, 70, 72
Enlightenment logics, 5, 7, 10–12, 19; Afrofuturist refusal of, 21–22; deconstruction of, 26
entanglement, 4, 18, 26, 64, 143–44, 149, 156, 159, 167; survival dependent on, 164–65
"enthnocultural code," 9
episodic, the, 22–25, 55, 69, 94, 158; structure of escape narratives, 13–14, 23–24
Epistemology of the Closet (Sedgwick), 137, 138
Epps, Omar, 145
Eros and Civilization (Marcuse), 72
escape: adolescent desires for, 81–82; agential narrative quality of, 14–15; as birthing white creative possibility, 1–2, 15, 46; constant, 25, 148, 149; contradictions within term, 6–7; as critical project, 26; cultural imaginary of, 5, 18, 25, 104; desire for, 3–4, 14, 74–76, 80–81, 80–82; directionality of, 3, 8, 11, 15, 25, 29, 63, 82, 92, 115; in Enlightenment thought, 10–12; etymology of, 5, 82; as event within larger structure, 24; facelessness of, 58; as fantasy for white people, 1–2; feeling of, 69, 70, 80, 92; into fiction, 82–83; freedom and humanity as starting point for, 3, 8; as fugitive practice, 8, 13; generic, 4, 6–8, 11, 15, 17–19, 21, 55, 70, 136, 158, 164; as genre of change, 3, 4, 7–8, 10, 16–18, 29, 65, 67, 69, 72, 128, 166; impossibility of, 81–82, 94; interiority of, 63; as iterative act, 6, 7; literal and figurative elements of intertwined, 33; as magic act, 34, 45, 135; as movement, 8, 15–16, 29; as otherwise strategy, 6, 16, 25; possibility of, 61; queer pleasure of, 132–33; recitation of, 18–19; sensorial register of, 15, 25; sexualized structures of, 131–32, 134; as social activism, 21, 26; as solitary act, 5; from subjectivity, 133, 135–36; temporality of, 3, 6, 13, 15, 19; tension between political acts and aesthetic retreats, 11–12; tethered to racial slavery in the United States, 2–3; of thin things, 57–58, 62, 65; as transgressive, 12; visual language of, 47, 63; white fantasy of black redemption, 35–36

escape-in-confinement, 148
escape narratives: always already racialized and sexualized, 2, 4; American, 2, 5–6; crafted for multiple audiences and ends, 27; ecstasy and pleasure of, 28–29; episodic structure of, 13.14, 23–24; escapism within, 74; feelings of, 69; multitude of meanings in, 27; otherwise possibilities of, 16, 25; past, present, and future of, 19. *See also* (anti)slave narratives; captivity narratives
escapism, 6–7; affective and social potential of, 70–71; cause-based and effect-based, 92; compensatory function, 71; as daily desire for escape, 74; defined, 12; dismissal of, 12, 69, 75; distraction, seeking of, 74; failure and passivity as strategies, 75–76; felt experience of, 84, 85, 94–95; and genre fiction/literature, 27, 70, 71, 77, 79, 82, 87, 90, 94; literature's relationship to, 70–71; as opposite of engagement, 75–76; as synonym for the ineffectual, 69
Eshun, Kodwo, 21–22
Ethics of the Concern for Self (Foucault), 19
Every Secret Thing (Hearst), 102, 107, 111–12
excappare, 5

fabulation, 149
faciality, refusal of, 141–42
failure, 75–76, 79; of Hearst to perform in the courtroom, 111, 118–19; of performative utterance, 120
failure to escape, 28, 99, 100
fantasies: white, of Black emotions, 106
"fantastical" writing, 11–12
fantasy: queer, 20, 136, 141
fantasy, white: of black escape, 35–36; and overdetermined Black body, 42
FBI, 113–14
Feeling Backward (Love), 21, 137
feeling of escape. *See* genre affect/feeling of escape
Felman, Shoshana, 120, 126
feminist movement, 113; trap of sexual subjectivity in, 118
Ferenczi, Sándor, 118

Index 205

Ferreria da Silva, Denise, 29, 164
Fielden, Samuel, 36, 37, 39, 46; opening monologue in *Henry Box Brown Play*, 40–41
film, of body, 57
filmic form, as anti-black, 22–23, 172n85
Finnerty, Páraic, 1
Flatley, Jonathan, 88–89
Foreman, P. Gabrielle, 15, 56
form, 18
Foster, Marcus, 105
Foucault, Michel, 19, 137
Fowler, Eve, 131, 146
framing, white, 2, 3, 6, 19, 23–25, 53–55, 158; replaced with care and interiority, 64–65
Frankel, Jay, 118
Frankfurt School thinkers, 71
freedom: "absolute," anarchist ideal of, 4041; active pursuit of, 54, 55; acts of reading and writing, 13–14; of anonymity, 135–36; to be among loved ones, 10, 11, 65, 144, 147, 155, 158–59; competing definitions of, 114; critique of, 75; deformations of, 17; drive for, 70; in Enlightenment thought, 5, 10; escape as movement toward, 15; escape as one strategy toward, 26; in fugitivity narratives, 36; Hearst's use of word, 114; of imagination, 68; liberal imperial tradition, 10–11; limitations of definitions of, 63; as performative, 10; (im)possibility of, 2; practices of, 19, 52, 63, 170n29; remembrance of through art, 72; sensory work of, 65; as starting point for escape, 3, 8; as telos of escape, 3, 6, 21; unfreedom tied to, 25
Freud, Sigmund, 5, 92
Fried, Michael, 26–27
Friedlander, Benjamin, 2
friend, as term, 10, 144
Front homosexuel d'action révolutionnnaire (FHAR), 140
frontispieces, in (anti)slave narratives, 52–54, *54*
Fugitive Slave Act of 1850, 32; "wanted" posters, 50
Fugitive Slave Acts of 1793 and 1850, 16

fugitivity, 8, 13, 35, 51, 101, 148; in Black aesthetic tradition, 15–16. *See also* escape
fukú curse (Dominican), 77–79
"full body quotation," 31, 119, 123, 181n85

Gaines, Malik, 165
Galton, Francis, 147
García Márquez, Gabriel, 75
Garrett, Matthew, 24
Garrison, William Lloyd, 2
Gates, Henry Louis, Jr., 33
generic escape, 4, 6–8, 11, 15, 17–19, 21, 55, 70, 136, 158, 164
Genet, Jean, 87, 140, 146
genre, 8–9, 67, 177n81; (anti)slave narratives as, 14; audience's choice of, 70–71; history as, 76; of the human, 9, 15, 23, 25; literature's relationship to escapism, 70–71; mixed, 130–31; monstrous, 130; politics of, 70–83; reader expectations for affect in, 85, 94, 130; social identity, genre of, 169–70n17. *See also* (anti)slave narratives; novel; speculative genres
genre affect/feeling of escape, 28, 69, 70, 80; and collective feelings, 88–90; as identity, 85–86; and racialization, 83–95; subaltern and antinormative feelings, 89. *See also* affect
genre literature, 27, 70, 71, 77, 79, 82, 87, 90, 94; dismissal of, 85–86. *See also* speculative genres
genre scenes, 79, 88
Gilbert, Douglas, 38
global warming, 162
Gloria Hole (Fowler), 131, 146
glory hole, 28; etymology of, 134; facelessness of, 135, 136, 141; locations of, 131–32; in nonbinary and lesbian imaginings, 146; popular representation of, 144–46; sexuality, enclosure, and freedom connected by, 147; as sexual-spatial formation, 134, 146. *See also* pleasure; queer escape narrative
Glory Hole Series (Fowler, Wright, and Brody), 146
Goyal, Yogita, 14
Graebner, William, 104, 116, 182n94

206   Index

Grant, Roger, 123
"The Great Refusal," 72
Grossman, Lev, 82–83, 95
"grounded normativity," 144
Guevara, Che, 114

Haag, Pamela, 117, 118
Habermas, Jürgen, 103
Harris, Bill "Teko," 101, 102, 115
Harris, Emily "Yolanda," 101, 115
Harteveld, Casper, 92
Hartman, Saidiya, 3, 14, 16, 23, 46, 53, 107, 147, 156; "escape subsistence," 148–49; "precariousness of empathy," 46, 163
Hayes, Sharon, 16, 28, 97; Hearst audio tapes spoken by, 98, 100–101, 102, 104; queer reading of Hearst, 126–28; respeaking, 98, 100, 102, 119–20, 123, 124; respeaking of documents, 119; Works: *Combatant Status Review Tribunals, pp. 002954-003064: A Public Reading*, 119; *In the Near Future*, 109, 119; *My Fellow Americans: 1981-1988*, 119. See also *Symbionese Liberation Army (SLA) Screeds #13, 16, 20 & 29* (Hayes)
Haymarket riots (Chicago, 1886), 36, 37
Hearst, Patty, 180n56; audio communiqués, 97–99, 100.28, 102, 112–15, 120–21; brainwashing defense, 115–16; as "cipher," 121; cloaked as media heiress, 100; *Every Secret Thing*, 102, 107, 111–12; failed performance in the courtroom, 111, 118–19; failure to escape, 28, 99, 100; Hibernia Bank robbery, 99, 111, 115; historical context of sentencing, 125–26, 182n94; hypervisible erasure of, 127; kidnapping as racialized, 104–5; projections of audience onto, 103–4; queer reading of, 126–28; as race traitor, 108; and rescue, 28, 113–14, 127; rhetoric of choice employed by, 114; *Screed #13*, 103, 120–21; *Screed #16*, 110; *Screed #20*, 112–13; *Screed #28*, 114–15; sexualization of captivity of, 113; as Tania, 99, 114, 115, 126; *The Tania Interview*, 102; vocal analysis of, 103, 180n45, 180n47; in Waters films, 100, 103, 113, 178n12; whitewashed as "normal," 104
Henry Box Brown: Forever (Wilson), 27, 31, 56–63; escape of thin things, 57–58, 62, 65; as performance and installation, 33, 57; photographed by gallery and curator, *32, 33, 57, 58, 62*; "skin works," 57
The Henry Box Brown Play: Political-Historical-Doggerel-Vaudeville (Kushner), 32, 36, 37–47; audience, 38, 39, 42; Brechtian style in, 36, 38, 42, 44, 45; opening monologue, 40–41; premiere of at New York University, 37, 172n12. See also Kushner, Tony
Hesse, Barnor, 14–15
History of Sexuality (Foucault), 137
Hobbes, Thomas, 10
Holiday, Billie, 36, 48–49
Holland, Sharon P., 133
Holmes, Dave, 135, 136
Homosexual Desire (Hocquenghem), 140
homosexuality, criminalization of, 134–35, 138. See also glory hole; queer escape narrative; queer theory and logics
Hong, Cathy Park, 21
hooks, bell, 176n48
Houdini, Harry, 33, 80, 81
Howard, Danielle A. D., 64
"How It Felt to Be Colored Me" (Hurston), 51–52
human, the, 61, 139, 147, 165–66; genres of, 9, 15, 23, 25
humanity, 132, 165–66; Black critiques of white models, 12–13; denied to nonwhite subjects, 12, 14, 44, 107; as relational practice and praxis, 9–10; as starting point for escape, 3, 8
Humphreys, Laud, 132, 135
Hurston, Zora Neale, 51–52
hyperempathy, 163
hypervisibility, 26, 42, 56, 147; and afro-alienation, 45; Black and Black queer life as marked, 51; erasure of Hearst, 127

identity, 169–70n17; genre affect as, 85–86; queer, 136, 139; as relationally constituted, 127; white American, 6
imagination, 1, 14, 22, 63–64, 68, 94; radical, 10, 94, 170n29

Imarisha, Walidah, 68
improvisation, 5, 7, 13, 17–18, 29, 63, 148–49; and fugitivity, 15–16
Incidents in the Life of a Slave Girl (Jacobs), 15, 25
individualist logics, 8, 11, 136, 138, 155
The Interesting Narrative of the Life of Oloudah Equiano, or Gustavs Vasso, the African, Written by Himself, 5–6
interiority, Black, 15, 18, 36, 46, 55, 109–10; of Brown, 45, 57; resistance to fetishization, 58
In the Near Future (Hayes), 109, 119
invention, 10, 34, 64–65, 170n29
Isenberg, Nancy, 104
"Is the Rectum a Grave?" (Bersani), 139

Jackson, George, 101, 102, 105, 106, 126
Jacobs, Harriet, 13, 15, 148; "scrawl space" of, 25148
The Jazz Singer, 106
Jefferson, Thomas, 1, 2, 6, 11–12, 22
Jeffery Toobin, 105
Jolson, Al, 106
Jones, Mary, 154

Kaba, Mariame, 154
Kawash, Samira, 14
Keeling, Kara, 22, 26, 164, 166
Kelly, Robin D.G., 154–55
Kessler, Sarah, 125
King, Martin Luther, Jr., 101
Klein, Melanie, 4
Korean War, 116–17
krs-One, 36, 48, 49, 51
Kushner, Tony, 27, 32, 34; alienation effect used by, 44–45; Brechtian leanings, 36, 38, 42, 44, 45; reboxing of Brown, 46; white anarchist goals of, 37, 45–46. See also *The Henry Box Brown Play: Political-Historical-Doggerel-Vaudeville* (Kushner)

Lacan, Jacques, 136
lantern laws, 52
Laure (in Manet painting), 148

Lax, Thomas (T.) Jean, 154
Lee, Summer Kim, 123
Le Guin, Ursula K., 94
Leon, Aya de, 93
Lepecki, Andre, 55
liberal imperial tradition, 10–11
"liberationist negativity," 140
Ligon, Glenn, 27, 32, 34, 36, 47–56; antiportraiture, 51, 61, 63; on Black queer photographic archives, 142–43; inside archive of escape narratives, 53; light and dark in visual representation, 56; *Narratives*, 47, 49, 52–55, *54*; *Runaways*, 47, 49–52, 55; "wanted" posters of, 50. See also *To Disembark* (Ligon)
Ling, Nancy "Fahizah" (SLA member), 101, 105
literature: escapism, relationship to, 70–71; genre literature, 27, 70, 71; white American middle-class experience as norm, 74–75. See also genre literature
Little, Russ, 101, 105, 106
Lott, Eric, 38, 106
Love, Heather, 21, 137
Luciano, Dana, 8

Mackey, Nathaniel, 15–16, 25
magic, 78–79, 84, 135
magical realism, 68, 75
"Mama's Baby, Papa's Maybe" (Spillers), 20
"Man," 9, 12, 25, 61
Manalansan, Martin, 139
Manet, Édouard, 147–48, 151
Marcuse, Herbert, 71–72, 174n11
Marley, Bob, 49
Marriot, David, 9
Marx, Karl, 44
Massumi, Brian, 86
Mayer, Igor, 92
McKittrick, Katherine, 9–10, 25
memory: function of in present, 49; lack of in (anti)slave narrative, 23–24; "viral," 40
Meurent, Victorine, 148
microphone, 124
Middle Passage, 34, 81, 176n48

Mielke, Laura, 97
Miller, T. S., 76
mimesis, 123, 181n85
Minh-ha, Trinh, 125
"minor" or "weak" feelings, 21
"miscegenated texts," 15
modernity, 4, 20, 55, 170n24, 172n85; queer, shaped by settler colonialism, 134, 138–39
monstrous genres, 130
Montgomery, Nick, 10, 11, 144
Morgensen, Scott Lauria, 138, 183n26
Morrison, Toni, 13–14, 151
Moten, Fred, 15, 16, 55–56, 158, 172n85; "constant escape," 25, 148, 149; "disappointing under achievement/s of emancipation," 70; "escape-in-confinement," 25; on fugitive movement, 147–48; "irruption of phonic substance," 100
movement: across plot, 55–56; in Butler's *Parables* series, 159; escape as, 8, 15–16, 29; in excess of white captive frames, 56; inextricable from feeling and fantasy, 70; in Reagon's *Parable of the Sower*, 160; without appearing to move, 45
Mules and Men (Hurston), 52
Mullen, Haryette, 15, 56, 108
Muñoz, José Esteban, 4, 8, 84, 88, 89, 94, 120, 126, 176n62
Murray, Stuart, 135, 136
Musser, Amber, 29, 139, 141, 151–52
My Bondage, My Freedom (Douglass), 35

Nanny Goat Hill Pleasure Gardens, 154–55
A Narrative of the Life of Frederick Douglass (Douglass), 5, 14
Narrative of the Life of Henry Box Brown Written by Himself, 32, 48, 173n23
Narratives (Ligon), 47, 49, 52–55, 54
Nash, Jennifer, 134
National Great Blacks in Wax Museum (Baltimore), 64
negativity, practice of, 71–72
"New Left" movement, 101–3
"new social order," 72, 174n11
New York City, 46; lantern laws, 52; performance scene in early 1990s, 119–20; Seneca Village, 154–55; "Stop and Frisk" program, 51
nobody, theorization of, 155–56
No Future (Edelman), 140
nonlocality/nonseparability, 29, 164
novel: as "easy reading," 70–71; as meta scene of escape, 70; sentimental, 108–9
Nyong'o, Tavia, 164

object, 85, 89; and anonymous sex, 136; love object, 86, 89; *object petite a*, 136
O'Byrne, Patrick, 135, 136
Octavia's Brood (Imarisha and brown), 68
Octavia's Parables (podcast), 157
The Octoroon (Boucicault), 39
Of Plymouth Plantation (Bradford), 5
Old Post Office pavilion (Washington, DC), 58
Olney, James, 14, 23
opacity, 4, 24, 26, 55, 63; of collective textures, 34; as portraiture technique, 51; racist optics of Black suffering, 107; and refusal, 51–52; and reprieve, 62–63; sensuality as, 151–52; in the spectacular, 63; and structure of closet, 138
optics, racist, 107
optics of escape, 28, 100
Othello (Shakespeare), 1, 39
"otherwise possibility," 5
Olympia (Manet), 147, 148

Paisley Massacre, 77
Parable of the Sower (Butler), 29, 157, 159–65; global warming as character in, 162; hyperempathy in, 163
Parable of the Sower (Reagon's adaptation), 29, 157–60, 166–67
Parable of the Trickster (Butler), 165–66
paradigmatic, the, 22–24, 94
Parker, Andrew, 79, 121
passivity, 75–76
Patty Hearst (Schrader), 105
Pearsall, Robert, 103, 105, 106, 178n5, 180n45
Pérez, Hiram, 138

Index 209

performance: as critical analytic of experience and perception, 27; demanded of Blackness, 66; of freedom, 10; "misfire," 120, 126; performative utterances, 78–79, 120–22; periperformativity, 27, 79, 100; raced and sexed, 16–17, 38; riskiness of to artist, 58–59; social doing of artwork, 18; of whiteness, 176n62

Performance and Performativity (Parker and Sedgwick), 79

Perry, Lincoln Theodore Monroe Andrew (aka Stepin Fechit), 42

Piepzna-Samarashina, Leah Lakshmi, 65

Playing in the Dark (Morrison), 13–14

pleasure: Black and non-Black strategies, 132; and *object petite a*, 136; queer, of escape, 132–33; spatialization and architectures of, 131; white queer, 131. *See also* glory hole; sexuality

Pleasure Garden (Tourmaline), 29, 129–30, 133, 149–53; *Coral Hairstreak*, 151, *152*; *Morning Cloak*, *150*, 150–51; self-portraiture, 149–51; *Sleepy Orange Sulphur*, 151; *Summer Azure*, 151; *Swallowtail*, 151; *Violet Copper*, 129, *130*

pleasure gardens, 153–55

pleasure principle, 72

plot, 55–56

Plymouth, Massachusetts, 5

poeisis, 10–11, 164

pornotrope, 134, 139, 151, 155

portraiture: antiportraiture, 51, 61; opacity and refusal as techniques of, 51; self-portraiture, 149–51

practices of freedom, 19, 52, 63, 170n29

progressive logics, 8, 13, 15, 17–18, 28, 163

Proudhon, Pierre-Joseph, 40–41

Purgatory of Suicides (Cooper), 134

queer escape narrative: closet, theorizations of, 137–39, 146–47; coming out story, 136–37; coming out as "unfurling the cape," 139; white self-shattering fantasy, 140–41

queerness: Black queer photographic archives, 142–43; co-constitutive with Blackness, 20; queer identity, 136, 139; queer modernity shaped by settler colonialism, 134, 138–39; queer narrative structures, 4, 21, 137; queer scenes, 87–88; radical negativity/antirelational thesis, 139–40; refusal of gender norms, 20–21; shaped by histories of settler colonialism and white supremacy, 134; as shared feeling of social abjection, 87–88; as utopian mode, 4; whiteness, analogy with, 136

queer theory and logics, 3, 16, 20–21, 26, 143, 181n76; in *The Brief Wondrous Life of Oscar Wao*, 69, 73, 87–88, 91; fantasy of escape, 133–34; in Ligon's work, 53; queer of color critique, 2–3, 21; queer reading of Hearst, 126–28; sex positivity, examination of, 144

queer visual culture, 130, 132–33; film depictions of glory hole, 144–46

Ra, Sun, 21, 64, 75

racialization: of closet, 137–38; as genre, 9; and genre affect, 83–95; of Hearst's kidnapping, 104–5; in queer fantasy of escape from subjectivity, 136, 140; of sexuality, 140–41; of voice, 98–99, 105–6, 125

Radio Peking broadcasts, 116–17

Radway, Janice, 71

Rankin, John, 46, 107

Reading the Romance (Radway), 71

Reagan, Ronald, 119

Reagon, Bernice Johnson, 158, 166

Reagon, Toshi, 29, 157–59; *Songs:* "Don't let your baby go, don't let your baby go to Olivar," 161; "There's a New World Comin,'" 159

realist fiction, 73

recitation, 18; citationality, 18–19, 123

redemption, 1, 6–8, 21, 24, 36, 49, 55, 61, 63, 68, 93, 118

Redemption Song (Marley), 49

Redmond, Shana, 169n14

referent-we, 9

refugees, 162

refusal, and opacity, 51–52

Reider, John, 83

relationship: and affect, 88–89; Butler's theories of, 157; coalition work as painful, 166–67; humanity as relational practice,

210 Index

9–10; identity as relationally constituted, 127; queer reading as relational move, 20

Remiro (SLA member), 105, 106

repetition, 6, 18, 145, 148–49, 158; in *The Brief Wondrous Life of Oscar Wao*, 93–94; of captivity narratives, 107; in *To Disembark*, 50; and Hearst's narrative, 28, 102, 111, 120, 122, 127; of Henry Box Brown's escape story, 31, 33–34, 48, 63–64, 66; and interiority of escape, 63; of trauma, 94

reprieve, 34, 46, 58; and opacity, 62–63; from visibility, 61–62, 66; white imagining of, 46

respeaking, 98, 100, 102, 119–20, 123, 124

Reyes, Israel, 87, 93

Rogin, Michael, 106

Rohy, Valerie, 21

romance literature, 71

Rosenberg, Julius and Ethel, 116

Ross, Marlon, 147

Roulet, Laura, 58–59

Rousseau, Jean Jacques, 10

Rowlandson, Mary, 5, 97, 99

Runaways (Ligon), 47, 49–52, 55

"Runaway Tongues" (Mullen), 108

safety, white American notions of, 51, 98

Sancho, Ignatius, 1, 11, 22

Sartre, Jean-Paul, 89

Sauron *(The Lord of the Rings)*, 77, 175n31

Scary Movie (film), 145

Scenes of Subjection (Hartman), 46

Schrader, Paul, 105

science fiction, 28; colonialism's influence on, 83; fukú compared with, 78; "new wave," 83; as performative genre, 79; visionary fiction, 68. *See also* Afrofuturism; *The Brief Wondrous Life of Oscar Wao* (Diaz); *Parable of the Sower* (Butler)

Scott, Darieck B., 20, 133

Scream 2 (film), 145–46

Sedgwick, Eve Kosofsky, 4, 20, 121, 138; "periperformative vicinity," 27, 79, 100; on structure of closet, 137

Segade, Xandro, 165

self-narratives, 103–4

Seneca Village (New York), 154–55

sentimental fiction, 6, 13–15, 23, 34, 117–18

sentimental novel, 108–9

sexuality: "anonymous" sex, space of, 182n14; freedom to be among loved ones, 144, 147; Indigenous relegated to the past, 138; pornotrope, 134, 139, 151, 155; production of through speech act, 137; public sex, 29, 132–35, 140, 146–47, 153, 182n11; racialization of, 140–41; regulation of Black and Indigenous, 4; sensuality distinct from discourses of, 151–52; sexual-spatial formations, 134, 146; tearoom, 135, 142–43; violence in theorizations of, 139; white as de facto, 133–34. *See also* glory hole; pleasure

Shakespeare, William, 1, 39

The Silent Community (Delph), 132

Simpson, Leanne, 144

simultexts, 15, 20, 52, 56, 158

Sinker, Mark, 21

slavery, 1–2, 41, 51; panoptic culture of, 34; parallels to in *Parable of the Sower*, 160–61; sexual history of, 20, 133–34; as social death, 53; white imagination enriched by, 14

Slotkin, Richard, 97

Smillie, Tuesday, 94

Smith, James C. A., 32

Snorton, C. Riley, 137–38

Soltysik, Patricia "Mizmoon" (SLA member), 101, 105

Song of Solomon (Morrison), 151

sonic, the, 28; in *To Disembark*, 48; listening ear, dominant, 106; as multitextual, 158

sonic blackface, 105

sonic texture, 100, 105–6, 124–25

Sound of da Police (KRS-One), 48

sousveillance, 52

Space is The Place (Sun Ra), 22

speculative genres, 27–28, 68–70, 84, 86, 92, 95, 175n22; affective tonalities of, 69; and decolonization, 68; as episodic genres of change, 69; excess of, 80; magical realism, 68, 75; opacity in, 63; themes of difference and unbelonging in, 89–90; visionary work of, 68, 70, 166–67. *See also* Afrofuturism; *The Brief Wondrous Life of Oscar Wao* (Diaz)

Spillers, Hortense, 3, 4, 20, 134, 151
Spivak, Gayatri Chakravorty, 121, 181n76
Stanley, Eric, 149
Star Blazers (anime television show), 92
Star Choir (Gaines and Segade), 165
state: collective escape from, 57–58, 65–66; critique of, 41; masculinist violence of, 151; SLA opposition to, 114
Stearns, Charles, 39–40
Stewart, Kathleen, 88
Stockholm syndrome, 115, 118, 126
Stoever-Ackerman, Jennifer, 105–6
Stowe, Harriet Beecher, 108
Stranack, John, 134–35
Strange Fruit (Holiday), 48–49
Students for a Democratic Society (SDS), 101
subjectivity, 127–28; and affect, 86; Black, in (anti)slave narratives, 14, 34, 36, 53, 55, 173n23; in Enlightenment thought, 5; escape from, 133, 135–36; liberal, 8, 10, 13; literacy required for entry into realm of, 14–15; post-Enlightenment, 55; private self and production of, 103–4; racialization in queer fantasy of escape from, 136, 140; victim required to remake self, 118; white logics of, 136
surveillance, dark sousveillance as counter to, 52, 61–62
survival, 164
survivance, 127, 182n95
swardspeak, 139
Sweet Honey in the Rock, 158
Symbionese Liberation Army (SLA), 101–9, 178n5, 179n14, 179n38; *Communiqué #12*, 109; counterfeited Black accents, 105–6, 125; focus on white radical desires, 106–7; freedom, concept of, 114; Hibernia Bank robbery, 99, 111, 115; Mel's Sporting Goods confrontation, 115; members, 101–2; racial drag worn by, 105; as racialized voices of radicalism, 98–99; ransom demands, 102, 106; *Screed #16*, 110; *Screed #20*, 112–13; *Screed #28*, 114–15; *The Tania Interview*, 102; theatrics of, 104, 112–13; written communiqués, 109
Symbionese Liberation Army (SLA) Screeds #13,
16, 20 & 29 (Hayes), 16, 28, 96, 119–28; citation process, 98, 121; *Screed #13*, 103, 120–21; sounds of, 109–19; VHS format tapes, 121–22, *122*, 127

Tannenbaum, Laura, 179n17
Taste Dissonance Flavor Escape (Moten), 25, 158
Tate, Greg, 21
Taxi Zum Klo (film), 131–32, *133*
Techniques of Pleasure (Weiss), 140
temporality, 21–25; and Afrofuturism, 21–22; of escape, 3, 6, 13, 15, 19; queer time, 21
texture, 100–101; of acapella movement music, 158; racialized sonic, 100, 105–6, 124–25
theater, as negation of art, 26–27
theatricality, 19, 26–27, 33–34; in "Box" Brown's narrative, 35–36
Thelma and Louise (film), 151
thin things, 57–58, 61–62, 65
Thoreau, Henry David, 41
Ting, Eric, 158
To Disembark (Ligon), 27, 32, 36, 47–56, *48*; box as framing mechanism in, 49–50; disappearance in, 47–48, 55; episodic in, 55; sonic aspect of, 48
Toobin, Jeffrey, 126
Tourmaline, 3, 29, 133; films of, 149; Nanny Goat Hill Pleasure Gardens proposal, 154–55; nobody, theorization of, 155–56; Works: *The Atlantic is a Sea of Bones*, 149; *Happy Birthday, Marsha!*, 149; *Salacia*, 149, 154; *Trapdoor: Trans Cultural Production and the Politics of Visibility*, 149. See also *Pleasure Garden* (Tourmaline)
trans activists, 149
Trapdoor: Trans Cultural Production and the Politics of Visibility (Tourmaline, Stanley, and Burton), 149
trespass, white, 45, 52, 55–56
Trujillo Molina, Rafael Leonidas, 69, 73, 77–79
Truth, Sojourner, 2
"truth," production of, 112
Tsang, Wu, 31, 109, 119, 123

Tuck, Eve, 17
Tupamaros (Uruguay), 101, 105

unbelonging, 69, 89
Un Chant D'amour (film), 146
Uncle Tom's Cabin (Stowe), 39, 108
Under the Radar Festival, 157
unfreedom, 25, 143, 148
United Nations High Commissioner for Refugees (UNHCR), 162
utopian modes, 4, 8, 17, 19, 23, 27, 71, 83, 88, 143–44
utterances, 120–23, 127–28, 180n46; initial escape as, 19; performative, 78–79, 120; textures of, 100, 120, 128

Vaccaro, Jeanne, 146
vaudeville genre, 38–39, 42
ventriloquism, 125
Venus in Two Acts (Hartman), 23
"viral memory," 40
Virno, Paolo, 145
visibility, care and protection from, 61–63, 65–66
visual register, 39, 42; glory hole, in queer visual narratives, 28; in language of escape, 47, 63; light and dark in representation, 56
voice: analysis of Hearst's audio tapes, 103, 180n45, 180n47; asymmetry of body with, 100, 122; counterfeited Black accents, 105–6, 125; extralinguistic elements of, 110; and inner psychological truths, 117; racialization of, 98–99, 105–6, 125; respeaking, 98, 100, 102, 119–20, 123, 124; as separate from other sounds, 109–10; technologically mediated, 123–24; ventriloquism, 125

Warhol, Andy, 141–42, *142*, 151
Warmelink, Harald, 92
Warner, Michael, 87–88
Warren, Calvin, 143
Waters, John, 100, 103, 113, 144, 178n12
Wayans, Marlon, 145
Wayans, Shawn, 145

Weed, Steven, 113
Weheliye, Alexander, 17, 20, 139
Weiss, Margot, 140
West London Observer, 37
What Is Property? (Proudhon), 41
Wheeler, Thero, 105
white logics: imagination shaped by, 68; of individualism and self-possession, 136; progressive, 13, 15, 17–18, 28, 163; reason and clarity as, 28
whiteness: escape as fantasy for white people, 1–2; instability of, 108; performativity of, 19, 176n62; queerness, analogy with, 136; sexuality of as de facto, 133–34; shocked by captivity, 97
white supremacy, 3, 39, 41, 43–46, 65, 69, 134; looking, politics of, 143
Wiig, Kristen, 126
Wilde, Oscar, 87
wilderness, 5
Wilderson, Frank, 22–24, 55, 143
Williams, Pat Ward, 43
Williams, Raymond, 88
Willse, Craig, 123–24
Wilson, Wilmer IV, 27, 31, 34, 36, 56–63; postage stamps in work of, *32*, *33*, 57, 57–58; staple series, 59–63, *60*; thin things, theorization of, 57–58, 61–62, 65
Wing-Davey, Mark, 37
Winnicott, D. W., 85
witness, act of, 79
Woff, Cynthia Griffin, 34
Wolfe, George C., 37
Wolfe, William, 101
Woodard, Alfre, 33
Works Progress Administration (WPA), 131, 135
Wright, Suzanne, 146
Wynter, Sylvia, 9–10, 12

X-Men allusion, 74–75

Young, Charles, 116–17

zafa (counterspell for fukú curse), 78–79
Zola, Emile, 148

www.ingramcontent.com/pod-product-compliance
Lightning Source LLC
Chambersburg PA
CBHW020838160426
43192CB00007B/698